SLAPSTICK MODERNISM

SLAPSTICK MODERNISM

Chaplin to Kerouac to Iggy Pop

WILLIAM SOLOMON

UNIVERSITY OF ILLINOIS PRESS
Urbana, Chicago, and Springfield

First Illinos paperback, 2018

1 2 3 4 5 C P 5 4 3 2 1
∞ This book is printed on acid-free paper.

The Library of Congress cataloged the cloth edition as follows:
Names: Solomon, William, author.
Title: Slapstick modernism : Chaplin to Kerouac to Iggy Pop / William Solomon.
Description: Urbana : University of Illinois Press, 2016. | Includes bibliographical references and index.
Identifiers: LCCN 2015046962 (print) | LCCN 2016008362 (ebook) | ISBN 9780252040245 (hardcover : alk. paper) | ISBN 9780252098468 (e-book)
Subjects: LCSH: American literature—20th century—History and criticism. | Modernism (Literature)—United States—History. | Literature, Experimental—United States—History and criticism. | Silent films—United States—History and criticism. | Motion pictures and literature—United States.
Classification: LCC PS310.M57 S55 2016 (print) | LCC PS310.M57 (ebook) | DDC 810.9/005—dc23
LC record available at http://lccn.loc.gov/2015046962

Paperback ISBN 978-0-252-08394-5

For Molly, Eliot, and my parents

For us to appreciate slap-stick may require a revolution in our way of looking at the arts; having taken thought on how we now look at the arts, I suggest that the revolution is not entirely undesirable.

—Gilbert Seldes, "The Keystone the Builders Rejected"

We must all involve ourselves and participate in creating the new kind of humor, in filling in a new page in the world history of laughter.

—Sergei Eisenstein, "Bolsheviks Do Laugh (Thoughts on Soviet Comedy)"

Contents

Acknowledgments

It is a pleasure to recognize all those who have contributed to this book. I could not have completed it without the support and advice of numerous friends, students, and colleagues. While I was teaching at Gettysburg College, Elizabeth Duquette and Len Goldberg managed to find time in their hectic schedules to scrutinize and comment on portions of my developing manuscript. Since arriving at the University at Buffalo, I have continued to benefit intellectually from among so many others: Damien Keane, David Schmid, Cris Miller, Carrie Tirado Bramen, and Steven Miller, as well as Josh Lam, Jesse Miller, and Justin Parks. I am also grateful to Daniel Nasset of the University of Illinois Press for his encouragement through the various stages of this project. Jeremy Braddock's insights and encouragement have also been absolutely indispensable. An earlier version of a section of the introduction appeared as "Second Technologies: American Modernism and Silent Comedy," in *Interdisciplinary Studies: A Journal of Criticism and Theory* (Spring 2005): 66–91. A portion of chapter 6 is taken from "Slapstick Modernism: Charley Bowers and Industrial Modernity," in *Modernist Cultures* 2.2 (2006): 170–88. My most profound debt is to my wife, Molly; my son, Eliot; and my parents, Eric and Irene Solomon. It is only because of their presence in my life that I was able to see this book through its many incarnations to its end.

Introduction

The Origins of Slapstick Modernism

> It goes back to those crazy days before World War II when [. . .] our fathers wore straw hats like W. C. Fields. It goes back to the completely senseless babble of the Three Stooges, the ravings of the Marx Brothers [. . .] to Laurel and Hardy in the Foreign Legion[. . . . T]his had begun to disappear around the end of World War II [. . .] when suddenly it began to emerge again."
>
> —Jack Kerouac, "The Origin of the Beat Generation"

In 1955 a minor event occurred in the field of US literature that augured a major upheaval in the nature of cultural production in this country. In this year (the same one that William Gaddis's *The Recognitions* first appeared in print and that Olympia Press published J. P. Donleavy's *The Ginger Man* and Vladimir Nabokov's *Lolita*), the seventh volume of *New World Writing* contained excerpts from two pivotal works in progress. Attributed to "Jean-Louis" and titled "Jazz of the Beat Generation," the first selection in the volume, composed by Jack Kerouac, included materials that would be integrated either into the writer's Beat-generation classic *On the Road* (1957) or into his still underappreciated experimental masterpiece *Visions of Cody* (published posthumously in 1972).[1] Located near the end of the same collection was Joseph Heller's "Catch-18," the first chapter of the book that, when it appeared in print six years later, retitled *Catch-22*, would be swiftly embraced as one of the quintessential achievements of American black humor. That the latter text is a marvelous mélange of Louis-Ferdinand Céline and Mack Sennett, of Franz Kafka and the Marx Brothers, is a commonplace of literary history.[2] Yet few critics have remarked on the degree to which the slapstick film tradition of silent and sound comedy helped shape the portraits and incidents depicted in Kerouac's autobiographical fiction. The numerous comparisons of the book's hero, Dean Moriarty, to memorable slapstick comedians—

"He [Dean] did this, crouched low to the ground like Groucho Marx, his feet carrying him with amazing swiftness out of the bar, like an apparition, with his balloon thumb stuck up in the night. [. . .] These were the first days [. . .] which would lead to the strange, ragged W. C. Fields saintliness of his later days" (*On the Road* 112–13)[3]—establish that the character was indeed intended to serve less as the epitome of a cool hipster than as the latest in a long line of verbose reprobates whose prototypes had appeared on screen during Kerouac's Depression-era youth.[4] With this in mind, it is plausible to take the renaming in the book of Allen Ginsberg as Carlo Marx as an indication that the former has been reenvisioned as Harpo, to whom Kerouac would pay tribute in a 1959 poem ("To Harpo Marx").[5] This in turn leaves only Chico, the faux Italian, as the primary touchstone for the book's narrator, Sal Paradise (though when hired as a "special policeman" and on his way to his "first night of work," he feels as if he is "flapping around like Charlie Chaplin" [*On the Road* 58]).

This book is a study of a process of cultural transformation that, beginning in the early decades of the twentieth century, led to the rise after World War II of the phenomenon I call slapstick modernism. Manifesting itself in literature, (underground) film, and popular music, the rise of slapstick modernism signaled the coalescence in cultural practice of the artistic experimentation associated with high modernism and the socially disruptive lunacy linked to the comic film genre. What for the most part had remained separate throughout the 1920s started to converge in the 1930s (albeit mainly in Europe) and then came together in explosive fashion in the United States in the post–World War II era. While the appearance in the 1950s and '60s of a slapstick modernism has not gone entirely unnoticed, it has yet to receive adequate theorization. This is partly due to the insufficiency of the terms initially used to capture the specificity of this new, hybrid cultural entity. The category of black humor, for example, remains an ill-defined one, and its use in the early '60s as a marketing strategy has further compromised its conceptual value.[6] But the remapping of the field in the mid-1980s in accordance with the idea of postmodernism has also played a role in obscuring the phenomenon whose historical formation I investigate below. I remain wary of this totalizing category in part because periodizing usage of it dictates the identification of a simple break where I discern a complex genetic process (involving the inheritance of traits across cultures or between media). Moreover, Fredric Jameson's still influential account of postmodernism (*Postmodernism*, 1992) strongly implies that the functional imperatives governing modernist projects were dissolved or abandoned in the decades following World War II. In insisting, in defeatist fashion, on the weary recognition of a past failure, Jameson's model casts into the shadows the sustained investment in formal or aesthetic innovation (considered, however idealistically, to be a socially beneficial endeavor) that endured at least through the mid-1970s in this country. My central claim, then, is that the pursuit of a slapstick modernism constituted a progressively oriented modification of the creative impulses that animated artistic practice earlier in the century. Richard Kostelanetz captured something of this when, in an introduction to a 1967 collection of short stories, he characterized the materials he had gathered together as "an extension of the modern revolution, on modernism's terms," one that "takes off from, rather than reacts against, the most fruitful decade for [. . .] fiction in America, the 1920's" (16).[7] In other words, if Morris Dickstein was correct to assert that the 1960s witnessed "the second coming of modernism in American fiction"—and I think he was—my claim is that the modernism that returned to the United States in these years did so with the physiognomy of a slapstick comedian (*Gates of Eden* 92).[8]

There is another reason that the growth and development of a slapstick modernism has evaded critical and scholarly articulation, one that does not lay the blame for its invisibility on the inattentiveness of literary historians. Few of those participating in the rise of the phenomenon self-consciously formulated their agenda to bridge the gap between aesthetic innovation and comic hijinks. No programmatic declaration of policy and aims along these lines was ever generated. Slapstick modernism had no manifesto of the sort that mobilized the various avant-garde ventures of the early decades of the twentieth century.[9] The closest one is going to come to such expressions of motivation are the isolated admissions—widely scattered in minor critical essays, interviews, public talks, or book prefaces—of certain authors who can be said to have participated in the cultural mutation under investigation. Henry Miller, for instance, acknowledged in "The Golden Age" (1939) his exposure to and enduring (albeit nostalgic) admiration for the "thousands of slap-stick, pie-throwing Mack Sennett films"; for the "bag of tricks" of "Charlie Chaplin"; and for "Fatty Arbuckle, Harold Lloyd, Harry Langdon, Buster Keaton, each with his own brand of monkey shines" (54). However, he makes no mention here of the impact of this film genre on the persona he constructed in his groundbreaking semiautobiographical comedies. Eudora Welty's comments late in life in the context of a public lecture are closer to the mark, but they too hardly indicate that the affection she felt for silent comedy resulted in a deliberate effort to commingle the two cultural endeavors: "In devotion to Buster Keaton, Charlie Chaplin, Ben Blue, and the

Keystone Kops, my brother Edward and I collapsed in laughter. My sense of making fictional comedy undoubtedly caught its first spark from the antic pantomime of the silent screen, and from having a kindred soul to laugh with" (36). Similarly, Nabokov's response to an interviewer's question about the kind of motion pictures he enjoyed is intriguing but inconclusive: "I went to the corner cinema about once in a fortnight and the only kind of picture I liked, and still like, was and is comedy of the Laurel and Hardy type. I enjoyed tremendously American comedy—Buster Keaton, Harold Lloyd, and Chaplin. [. . .] The Marx Brothers were wonderful [. . . and] Laurel and Hardy are always funny; there are subtle, artistic touches in even their most mediocre films" (quoted in Appel 153–54).[10] And in the prologue to the aptly titled *Slapstick* (1976), admittedly one of his weaker dystopian fictions, Kurt Vonnegut dedicates the novel to "slapstick film comedies, especially those of Laurel and Hardy, of long ago" on ethical grounds: "they did their best with every test. They never failed to bargain in good faith with their destinies, and were screamingly adorable and funny on that account" (1). Yet such assertions are inconclusive, merely offering suggestive points of departure for further inquiry as opposed to illuminating declarations of practical intent.

Kerouac's "Jazz of the Beat Generation," however, supplies valuable insight into the shift in aesthetic priorities the slapstick modernists persistently sought to enact, for the piece is perhaps the earliest indication of the extent to which the writers (and filmmakers) involved sought analogies for their innovative endeavors in the field of popular entertainment. It takes little interpretive pressure to read the numerous descriptions of live music the piece contains allegorically, as reflexive figurations of what the writer aspires to do. The following account of a saxophone player's use of his instrument is simply one of several cases in point: "He was very simple in his ideas. Ideas meant nothing to him. What he liked was the surprise of a new simple variation of chorus. He'd go from 'ta-potato-rup, ta-potato-rup' repeating and hopping to it and kissing and smiling into the horn—and then to 'ta-potatola-dee-rup, ta-potatola-DEE-rup!' and it was all great moments of laughter and understanding for him and everyone who heard" (12).[11] If improvised sound takes precedence over discursive sense here, so too does the power of (typed) words to make readers feel happy, to induce states approaching ecstasy, and to displace more traditional concerns with crafting autobiographical representation. "We seek to find new phrases; we try hard, we writhe and twist and blow; every now and then a clear harmonic cry gives new suggestions of a tune, a thought, that will someday be the only tune and thought in the world and which will raise men's souls to joy" (16).

Appearances notwithstanding, referentially verifiable portraiture yields the stage at this historical moment to what John Dos Passos had endorsed almost three decades earlier in a review of an E. E. Cummings play as "a style of writing that might be called oblique in the sense that it attempts to generate feelings and ideas [. . .] and direct in that it aims to express sensations rather than tell about them. People trying to 'understand' such writing according to the method of plain narrative are likely to get seized with a sudden panic, to close their eyes tight and say it's all nonsense" ("Mr. Dos Passos" 110).[12] That the Beats turned to music for compositional inspiration is of course a critical commonplace, one that Kerouac himself would subsequently codify in essays like "Essentials of Spontaneous Prose." Nevertheless, the appeal remains a significant one in the present context, for it constitutes a revealing attempt to invest literature with the expressive force and affective intensity that are customarily associated with more performance-based practices. Crucially, the tendency to draw on nonliterary amusements as sources of formal (and functional) inspiration frequently led artists in the 1950s and '60s to look back to the cultural materials they had enthusiastically consumed in their youth. Hence Allen Ginsberg's 1959 declaration in the liner notes to a recording of *Howl* that his primary ambition in the poem had been to create a "tragic custard-pie comedy of wild phrasing, meaningless images for the beauty of abstract poetry of mind running along making awkward combinations like Charlie Chaplin's walk" ("Notes" 29).[13] And elsewhere (in a letter to William Carlos Williams included in *Paterson*), Ginsberg offered as an example of his effort to "make contemporarily real an old style of lyric machinery," "a mad song (to be sung by Groucho Marx to a bop background)" (Williams, *Paterson* 173–74). Moreover, in another missive to the older poet, Ginsberg proclaimed that he was ready to "make big political speeches" with as his twin guides "W.C. Fields on my left and Jehovah on my right" (*Paterson* 210). But when exactly did all of this begin?

Triangulating Modernism

> Read as a Chaplin-like comedy, Eliot's Prufrock makes ready sense. Prufrock is the complete Pierrot, the little puppet of the mechanical civilization that was about to do a flip into its electric phase.
>
> —Marshall McLuhan, *Understanding Media*

It was in the spring of 1912 in a London tea shop that Ezra Pound first employed in conversation the term *les imagistes* in reference to Hilda Doolittle and Richard Aldington. In November of that year Pound declared—this time in print—that the future of literature was in the hands of this new school of poetry, which had T. E. Hulme as its most immediate forerunner. By 1913 the aesthetic principles that Pound intended the movement to adhere to had been formulated and announced publicly in "A Few Don'ts by an Imagiste." In addition to expending his critical energies on this new cultural enterprise, he also sought to make a practical contribution to its growth and development by sending ostensibly exemplary works to *Poetry*, the US–based magazine for which he had assumed the position of "foreign correspondent." And indeed the first dozen pages of its April 1913 issue were taken up by twelve of his lyric poems, including "In a Station of the Metro." Shortly thereafter Pound continued his campaign by editing an anthology titled *Des Imagistes*. The compilation, which contained materials produced by, among others, William Carlos Williams, Amy Lowell, James Joyce, D. H. Lawrence, and Ford Madox Hueffer, came out in February 1914 (a broken printing press delaying publication for several months). In sum, it was in large part due to the promotional and editorial labors Pound initiated in 1912 that Anglo-American literary experimentation "began to gain a sudden and considerable strength" (Levenson 69–70).[14]

In the summer of this same year Mack Sennett left Biograph and his mentor D. W. Griffith to form the Keystone Film Company with Charles Bauman and Adam Kessel, a move that helped to ignite a blaze of "furious, improvisational comic activity" in the film industry (Mast 44). The studio's first theatrical release, a split reel containing *Cohen Collects a Debt* and *The Water Nymph*, appeared in September of that year, thus marking the beginning of what James Agee characterized as the glory years of screen comedy ("Comedy's Greatest Era" 4). Keystone quickly gained a reputation for having revived the tradition of film humor in this country, and demand for its well-received product was sufficiently high that by June of that year Sennett had seven directors making three single reels a week and a two-reeler every month (Lahue 72).[15] In addition to the ensemble cast constituting the Keystone Kops, the studio's early roster of comic talent included Mabel Normand and Fatty Arbuckle, who often teamed up on screen. In late 1913 Sennett hired Charlie Chaplin away from Fred Karno's English music hall troupe. The comedian's first movie performance was in *Making a Living*, a February 1914 film that was followed shortly thereafter by *Kid Auto Races*. Throughout the three-year period that Keystone most actively reshaped the field (lasting roughly until 1915, when Sennett joined Griffith and Thomas Ince to create the Triangle Film Corporation and Chaplin started work for Essanay), "laugh after laugh" poured out the "Fun Factory's" doors (73).

By 1912, as the Imagist movement was consolidating and slapstick film taking off, the time-and-motion studies of the sort Frederick W. Taylor had codified in *Principles of Scientific Management* (1911) were helping to refine the production process at another industrialized workplace. Opened in January 1910, the Ford Motor Company's Highland Park factory quickly responded to consumer demand for the Model T by inventing and applying recently devised techniques for increasing output. Conveyor systems and gravity slides were put in place to facilitate the smooth flow of materials through the shop. In April 1913, as innovation in the economic realm continued, the first assembly line was installed, one well-known effect of which was to further regulate the movement of the working body in order to continue eliminating wasteful gestures. By 1914 magneto coils, transmissions, and car chassis were being put together in standardized fashion through the use of moving assembly lines. The endless chain quickly replaced manually pulled ropes and windlasses as the most efficient way to bring parts to workers, and in 1915 company output approached 400,000 vehicles a year (up from 20,000 in 1910).[16] Rationalization and mechanization had transformed the automobile plant "into a kind of super-machine in its own right, with both human and mechanical parts" functioning together in this highly efficient and widely influential method of manufacturing automobiles (Wollen, "Modern Times" 36).

Although the preconditions for the coterminous set of events recounted above extends back into the nineteenth century, the intensification of innovation that occurred at the beginning of the second decade of the twentieth century in the economic and cultural spheres remains striking. How, then, can we investigate together this remarkable burst of new ideas and practices in literature, motion pictures, and systems of manufacturing in general? How can we heed interpretively Gertrude Stein's insistence in "Portraits and Repetition" that "any one is of one's period and this our period was undoubtedly the period of the cinema and series production. And each of us in our own way are bound to express what the world in which we are living is doing" (177).[17] My guiding premise is that the differences and similarities between modernist writing and slapstick film can be measured most effectively when both are understood in critical relation to the socioeconomic forces of capitalist modernity.

This book therefore assumes that the integration of slapstick film into commodity production did not necessarily eliminate that power of this form of comedy to put dissident energies into circulation. Certainly the making of such movies was a commercially profitable enterprise, but the films themselves consistently maintained an ability to contest the disciplinary ramifications of urban-industrial modernity. Hollywood's implementation in the 1920s of rationalized production methods and increased reliance on standardized narrative patterns notwithstanding, "many of the unruly elements of film's origins in popular performance culture survived, especially in comedy" (D. E. James, *Most Typical Avant-Garde* 20–21).[18] Moreover, as Raymond Durgnat noted long ago, although the "shift in stress, by Sennett, from the music-hall's older comedy of character to the comedy of mechanized man, parallels the invention, not many years before, of time-and-motion study by Frederick W. Taylor," these same films parody such analytic operations by "concoct[ing] a universe where authority, routine, and the monotony of factory days are shattered." Whereas Keystone comedies "register [. . .] the spreading concept of man as an impersonal physical object existing only to work rapidly, rhythmically, repetitively," they depict such transformations hyperbolically, thereby veering "towards revolt," creating "an orgy of disorder, a Saturnalia of chaos" (Durgnat 71). And if they accept "the shock of speed and mechanization [. . .] as conditions of life," they nevertheless turn these into "a source of festive disorder," achieving "a revenge which is a brief mental liberation from its oppressive aspects. It hoists the 'enemy'—the system—with its own petard" (73). As Siegfried Kracauer succinctly put it in 1926: "One has to hand this to the Americans: with slapstick films they have created a form that offers a counterweight to their reality. If in that reality they subject the world to an often unbearable discipline, the film in turn dismantles this self-imposed order quite forcefully" (quoted in M. B. Hansen, "America, Paris, the Alps" 373). (A year later Walter Benjamin voiced a more qualified endorsement of the emancipatory potential of slapstick comedy. Aligning its "superiority" with the "cinema of the Russian Revolution," he argues that the genre is tendentious, that its target is technology, and that it is comic "only in the sense that the laughter it provokes hovers over an abyss of horror. The obverse of a ludicrously liberated technology is the lethal power of naval squadrons on maneuver, as we see it openly displayed in *Potemkin*" ["Reply" 17]).[19] A linguistically structured sight gag in Buster Keaton's *Playhouse* (1921) is telling in this regard. After waking from his dream of becoming a theatrical performer, a young stagehand is sent by his boss on break. He approaches a time-keeping mechanism and then, physically punning on the instructions posted on it to "punch clock," defiantly smashes his fist through the device's face.

Recent commentary has not been quick to attribute a comparable capacity to resist the status quo of capitalism to literary experimentation in the interwar years. The "presumably adversarial relationship of the modernist aesthetic to the myth and ideology of modernization and progress, which it ostensibly rejects in its fixation upon the eternal and timeless power of the poetic word," has repeatedly been "put in question." Many have argued that modernism was "deeply implicated in the processes and pressures of the same mundane modernization it so ostensibly repudiates" (Huyssen 56).[20] Though they are entirely legitimate, such assessments, in dissolving the tensions between art and (dominant) society, suggest a critical resignation; there is little reason to inquire further into the potentially volatile interplay between the two domains insofar as modernism failed to attain the autonomy for which it presumably yearned. A key premise of this study is that by attending to the functional ambitions of literary modernism alongside silent comedy, we put ourselves in position to recapture a sense of the social aspirations informing both. Well before the coupling that gave birth to slapstick modernism, the literary and cinematic progenitors of this countercultural phenomenon struggled to situate themselves in opposition to the discourses and practices of urban-industrial modernity. The specificity of this period is that in it literary modernism and silent comedy remained institutionally distinctive enterprises and are therefore best comprehended as adjacent yet nonidentical cultural undertakings. But they may nonetheless be productively considered when situated as coeval (and mutually illuminating) attempts to find solutions to a historically unique set of problems. What experimental writing and slapstick filmmaking had in common at the time is that each addressed and hoped to invent methods of handling such pressing matters as the mechanization of bodies and minds and the anxiety-inducing conditions of existence in the city. The artists and entertainers involved were motivated to register, and in certain cases sought to alleviate, the emotional and somatic effects of inhabiting a dramatically altering environment, one in which the rationalization of the labor process and of everyday life was perceived to be the cause of collective despair.

Miriam Hansen formulated the methodological reorientation in question more than a decade ago in the opening section of "The Mass Production of the Senses: Classical Cinema as Vernacular Modernism." For her, taking the juncture of cinema and modernism into consideration in effect dislodges previous disciplinary fascinations with "single-logic" genealogies and jettisons the timeworn binary oppositions that previously structured the field (59). Rather than track developments within a specific artistic medium or concern herself with the distinction between autonomous and mass culture (the "high" and the "low"), Hansen, following Benjamin, favors a broader approach that "situates artistic practices within a larger history and economy of sensory perception" (60). Registering the importance of how art was produced, consumed, and transmitted in the mid-twentieth century, she valuably frames the study of "modernist aesthetics to encompass cultural practices that both articulated and mediated the experience of modernity" (60). However, my project does not fit perfectly into what she terms a "vernacular modernism" (extending from the 1920s through the 1950s), since, save for a few pivotal exceptions, slapstick modernism was a predominantly post–World War II phenomenon. It was the fusion of elements of modernist writing and aspects of slapstick film that accounts for the emergence of my ultimate object of inquiry. A revitalizing mutation of the overall cultural field occurred as a result of the eventual commingling of literary experimentation and cinematic comedy.

Sketched out by Hansen, the virtues of the critical model on which I rely has been demonstrated by critical scholars focused on the interplay between film and literature in the interwar years. Specifically, Susan McCabe's *Cinematic Modernism: Modernist Poetry and Film* (2005) and David Trotter's *Cinema and Modernism* (2007) have profitably addressed the long-standing problem, as Jonathan Crary has put it, of "how to understand the ways in which film and modernist art occupy a common historical ground" (*Suspensions of Perception* 5).[21] Although Trotter takes issue with McCabe's strategy, and explicitly articulates his focus (following Garrett Stewart in *Between Film and Screen: Modernism's Photo Synthesis* [1999]) on "parallel histories" in opposition to what he calls her tendency to argue by analogy, his approach is much closer to hers than he wishes to acknowledge, for both depend heavily on third terms to justify their linkage of cinematic and modernist materials (Trotter 4). As McCabe sees it, avant-garde film and innovative poetry may be conceptualized together, since both evince a preoccupation with corporeal fragmentation and, by implication, with the feminine as well. Her book is thus arranged as a series of examinations of defensive reactions to and ecstatic embraces of images of somatic disarray or physical dislocation. Writers and filmmakers alike may be judged according to the ways they attended to socioeconomically or technologically determined threats to idealized models of bodily wholeness or integrity, and thus to dominant notions of masculinity. Put differently, psychoanalytic discourses (as well as the work of contemporaneous experimental psychologists) mediate McCabe's various juxtapositions; with this in mind it is not surprising that hysteria and masochism, among other pathologies, appear as the crux of specific chapters of her book. While Trotter adopts a more philosophical orientation, drawing for the most part on assorted strains of existential phenomenology, he too relies on a set of third terms to negotiate his varied investigations of the relationship of British and Irish modernist writing to early cinematic achievements. What allows him to move between Eliot, Joyce, Lewis, and Woolf on the one hand and Chaplin and Griffith on the other is that they all addressed themselves to aspects of their contemporary surroundings, confronting issues like the elusive tangibility of things, the appeal of involuntary or automatic modes of being in the world, as well as the paradoxical play of absence and presence that the use of mechanical recording apparatuses entails. To the degree that urban-industrial modernity is generally accepted today as the conceptual category that best encompasses most of the topics McCabe and Trotter engage, they may be said to employ a triangulated critical approach to their topic. Situating cinematic and literary materials as contemporaneous responses to the conditions of existence in a particular historical situation reduces the importance of discovering the way one influenced the other, which in turn frees the critic to track their formal and functional complementarities without insisting on a causal relationship. Here, I take a similarly triangulated approach, although causality as double causality returns in my overarching contention that slapstick modernism was the historical product of silent comedy and experimental literature.

In contrast, in *The Tenth Muse* (2007) Laura Marcus concentrates on the *direct* interplay between early twentieth-century film and modernist literature, attending as well to the struggle to develop a critical discourse that would be adequate to the representational properties and aesthetic dynamics of the newer medium. Similarly, Daniel Kane's *We Saw the Light: Conversations between the New American Cinema and Poetry* (2010) explores the interaction between contemporaneous filmmakers and experimental poets in the 1950s and '60s. In *The Cinema and the Origins of Literary Modernism* (2012), Andrew Shail, redefining influence as "generative causality," also addresses the impact of the new medium on the older one (4). The critical merits of his scholarly investigation are apparent in his analysis of narrative cinema's investment in a "continuous present" as a determining factor in high modernist formal innovation in the United Kingdom. For Shail, narrative cinema took shape around 1911 in the context of the discursive construction and practical implementation of a distinctive "image regime" (93–145). My different preoccupation is with the impact on literary modernism of what Shail calls, following André Gaudreault, "kine-attractography," the performance-based aesthetic that the institutionalization of narrative cinema for the most part displaced, though crucial aspects of it managed to survive in slapstick comedy.

The study closest in spirit to mine is Michael North's *Machine-Age Comedy* (2009), which locates assorted modernist artists (Wyndham Lewis, Samuel

Beckett, and Marcel Duchamp) as being engaged, like popular film figures (Chaplin, Keaton, and Mickey Mouse), in a dialogue with their environment. Though they themselves are products of mechanization, the cultural materials North examines nevertheless served as a means of reflecting on "industrialized life" (23). Moreover, in showing us what we all have in common somatically and psychically—mechanization and the tendency to repeat—they carry us beyond Bergson's classic understanding in *Laughter* of comedy as being grounded in the difference between the organic and the technological. The hope embedded in machine-age comedies derives from the fact that in enabling us to recognize our shared automaticity, they make it feasible that we will better accommodate ourselves to our surroundings. Works of art supply the knowledge we require to inhabit reality without despair. Manufacturing processes and the robotic gestures their rhythms enforce may foster "the imaginative powers necessary for people to manipulate" (12) and thereby regain control over machine technology. Thus, in his reading of Keaton's film *The Cameraman* (1928), North aligns the performer with the Soviet documentarian Dziga Vertov on the grounds that the projects of both intimated that "a new kind of comedy might emerge from the collaboration of human being and machine," one "tied to mechanical reproduction and yet finding in it both freedom and novelty" (31).

Although he confronts the question of "the revolutionary promise of technology" (52), and at times draws on Benjamin's Depression-era speculations on this topic, North's pursuit of a theory of comedy that is adequate to modernity, of what makes mechanization funny, leads him to swerve away from the German thinker's urgent preoccupation with the potential social functions of cultural practice. For Benjamin the most promising aspect of silent comedy (and, later, Disney animation) was its capacity to serve as a means for large groups of disenfranchised people to adjust in an empowering fashion to the pressures of everyday existence in the city as well as to the burdens of mechanized labor. Adopting in (the second version of) "The Work of Art in the Age of Its Technological Reproducibility" (1936), a dialectical outlook on the issue, Benjamin proposed—through the interlocked concepts of "innervation," "second technology," mimesis, and play—that silent comedy had the potential to further an evolutionary process whereby those who were suffering from oppression might attain corporeal mastery over their surroundings. The manner in which this was to occur was through the formation of a prosthetically enhanced collective body, one that would have "its organs in the new technology" (124).[22] Ultimately, Benjamin's idiosyncratic account of slapstick film contained two Aristotelian strands: (1) the idea of it as a "perfecting mimesis" that could compensate for the inherent insufficiencies of natural beings, and(2) the notion that it facilitated cathartic releases, thereby alleviating the psychic anguish engendered by machine technology.

So, whereas North focuses on the *cognitive* benefits of machine-age culture, Benjamin speculates more daringly on the technical media as the basis for practices that facilitate *affective* relays, thus enabling the embodied masses to acclimate to their environment not by way of self-consciousness, but via physiologically and neurologically invigorating transfers of energy. The task that slapstick film (and literary modernism[23]) had been assigned by its situation in history was to help the subjects of urban-industrial modernity acquire the skills they needed to survive in a potentially deadly setting. We may get a preliminary impression of the kind of resistance Benjamin found so worthwhile in slapstick film by looking at one of Chaplin's indispensable short films.

Reverse Motion Studies: Chaplin vs. Gilbreth

> Humor saves a few steps, it saves years.
> —Marianne Moore, "The Pangolin"

In this section I treat Chaplin's *Pay Day* (1922) as an effort to comically undermine the kind of time-and-motion studies pursued by one of Frederick Taylor's disciples in the field of production engineering: Frank Gilbreth. After this I examine "Chaplinesque" (1921), Hart Crane's poetic tribute to the slapstick comedian, alongside one of Ezra Pound's early articulations of his vocational criteria, "The Serious Artist" (1913). The goal of this latter discussion is to obtain a preliminary impression of an affective modernism, of a mode of linguistic play that, inspired by silent screen comedy, deviated from the priorities informing communicative expression. Together these two case studies begin to establish the complementary relationship of modernist writing and slapstick film in the 1920s as critical responses to the governing principles of economic rationalization as these pertain to work processes and to discursive labor.

Pay Day, a two-reeler, was the penultimate movie (of eight) Chaplin made for First National, the company with which he was associated from 1918 to 1922. The first half of the film focuses on the antics of the Chaplin character at the building construction site where he is employed; the second concerns the character's struggles to make his way home to his wife after a night of heavy drinking with friends at the "Bachelor's Club." The critical thrust of the film derives not from a preference for leisure over labor, but from the way it inscribes the disruptive values of play into a disciplined workplace.[24]

After an opening title that frames the scene as a portrait of "hard shirking men," we are shown assorted workers casually digging and transporting materials around the site (one is even smoking) while the oblivious foreman sits reading the newspaper and soaking his foot in a bucket of steaming water. Disgusted when he looks up with the lack of productivity, the foreman (Mack Swain) barks a series of commands and the men begin scurrying about frantically, climbing up and sliding down ladders, dashing along ramps, and sweeping furiously. The use of fast-motion photography adds a manic edge to the scene, the reprimanded workers now moving at an extraordinarily quick pace. Charlie arrives shortly thereafter—late, though with a flower, which he flirtatiously offers to the foreman, hoping to make amends. As the latter stares at him, Charlie confidently approaches a hole in the ground shaped like a grave, removes his coat, selects a pickax, swings it high in the air, and then plunges it down into the ditch. A previously unseen worker leaps up, as if raised from the dead, and shouts in complaint while stomping off and rubbing his possibly punctured rear end. Moderately chagrined, Charlie switches to a shovel and, as the perplexed foreman looks on, expends tremendous physical energy removing what turns out to be less than a handful of dirt from the hole. Predictably exasperated, the foreman yells at Charlie, reminding him he is "working by the hour—not the ounce." Turning back to what looks like the digging of his own grave, Charlie manages to get a more respectable load the next time but then flings it behind his back into his boss's face.

The frustrated foreman having left, his daughter (Edna Purviance) arrives with lunch. While looking for her father, she hops over the ditch. As she moves off, we see Charlie's head pop up, perhaps aroused by the vision of the girl that he obtained from below. Charlie follows her to the scaffolding for a bit more voyeuristic fun; perverse desire is thus introduced into the workplace as a distraction interfering with the demands of productive labor. In contrast, in the remarkable scene that follows, Charlie presents himself as a kind of super worker, an expert at stacking bricks. So perfect are the skills he exhibits that it becomes evident that Chaplin's antic exaggerations are aimed at both the ideal of the worker as a smooth-running, hyperefficient mechanism and at Gilbreth's use of the cinema for cognitive purposes in his time-and-motion studies.

Before setting to "work," Charlie "takes the vaudeville-balletic stance that announces a stunt in the offing," an implication that is confirmed when Charlie takes a bow (Kerr 186). Flourishing a handkerchief, he wipes his hands and then drops it from the platform. By throwing it back, the worker positioned below now appears as the assistant to the theatrical performer who is about to do his routine. The directly addressed viewer is thus made aware that what is coming is a magical spectacle, an illusory performance designed to amaze and delight rather than to depict accurately, much less inform. Any concern with documentary verisimilitude, with the neutral recording of an action, is to be set aside, at least temporarily, so that something impossible can be shown. Next Charlie turns his back to the camera and bends over so that his bottom becomes the focal point of the spectator's gaze, the anonymous-looking rear end replacing the individualized face. As bricks fly up to him, Charlie catches each one with exceptional grace. At first he uses both hands without looking at the projectiles, as if the act of catching has become automatic. He then expands his repertoire, employing all four limbs as well as the small of his back and his chin. And when the foreman arrives and instructs another man to participate, Charlie effortlessly maintains the accelerated pace, never dropping a brick while managing to stack them neatly in piles. The three men laboring in unison in effect become the parts of a wonderfully organized, smoothly flowing machine. (However, when the lunch whistle blows, Charlie lets a brick go, "accidentally" bouncing it off the foreman's head, as if in protest against Charlie's physical transformation into a mechanical component.) The character will briefly display his abilities again after lunch, but it is a cinematic trick—reverse photography—that enables his virtuosity. The skillful act of catching bricks tossed from below is a special effect and thus a referentially untenable (non)representation of the inverse process of dropping them. As North aptly puts it in his comments on the film, "cranking backward" makes the camera "a machine that turns work into play" (*Reading 1922* 169).

This comic deployment of the cinematic device takes on critical force when set alongside the contributions to scientific management made by Gilbreth, who, in his quest to standardize labor practices and improve efficiency, focused his early research efforts on the bricklaying trade.[25] Though it is important to apply "motion study to our office and field forces and to many of the trades," the "results on bricklaying are the most interesting, because it is the oldest mechanical trade there is." Purportedly in a condition of perfection "before we applied motion study to it," Gilbreth nevertheless claims to have "revolutionized" bricklaying, successfully overcoming the costs and output limitations stemming from poorly directed, ineffective, or unnecessary movements (8). By pushing the rationalizing ambitions of the production engineer to a ludicrous extreme, Chaplin in effect upends them, rendering them laughable.

Chaplin's performance also establishes the status of the cinematic apparatus as a site of conflict between science and entertainment. For Gilbreth, film had the potential to help further refine the labor process. The recording device was to be an instrument with which, through the analytic breakdown of physical movement, the best method of working could be discovered and then communicated to the worker. The epistemological value of film as a medium was that it could accumulate knowledge that was unavailable to ordinary or natural vision—that it could furnish, in Benjamin's terms, a means of access to the "optical unconscious" of the workplace (*Selected Writings* 3:117). Therefore, in the final chapter of *Motion Study*, Gilbreth asserts, "The arts and trades of human beings should be studied, charted, photographed, and motion-pictured" (99). For, like the stereopticon, "motion picture machines" "enable us to observe, record, and teach as one never could in the past" (103).[26] Such pedagogical employment of film technology is precisely what Chaplin seeks to counter in the brick-catching scene by disrupting the medium's claim to perceptual accuracy. Whereas Gilbreth's cognitive plans for the motion-picture camera depend on the referential verifiability of what it depicts, Chaplin deploys the device to generate an amusing spectacle that also cautions against trusting one's cinematically mediated sensory perceptions. For Bryony Dixon, on "the very few occasions where Chaplin tried trick photography," he was guilty of "cheating with the camera" in a manner that betrayed "film's inherent realism." Performing feats impossible in the actual world is "intolerable and strictly the preserve of juveniles" (29). Yet such a harsh condemnation misses the fact that in fooling around in this fashion the slapstick comedian manages to expose precisely what the scientific engineer's use of motion-picture technology obscures: that the cinematic acquisition of knowledge must repress or ignore the capacity of the medium to play tricks on the eye.

According to Gilbreth, a key principle underlying the training of workers is that "in most cases the direction of motion that is most economical is the one that utilizes gravitation the most" (74). "The determination of the path which will result in the greatest increase of output is a subject for the closest investigation and the most scientific determination. Not until data are accumulated by trained observers can standard paths be adopted. The laws underlying physics, physiology, and psychology must be considered and followed" (82). Engaging in a "light-hearted defiance of the laws of gravity" (Dale 45), Chaplin's cinematic levity upends the knowledge of physics that the engineer depended upon in his efforts to quicken the labor of masons. Moreover, in undermining the representational trustworthiness of the medium, bringing forth by way of his impossibly economic movements the medium's epistemological unreliability, he offers the proletarian masses that "fill the cinemas" the opportunity "to witness the film actor [and director] taking revenge on their behalf [. . .] by placing [. . . the] apparatus in the service of his triumph" (Benjamin, *Selected Writings* 3:111).

An Unserious Artist: Hart Crane

> Poetry [. . .] is a forceful, intensely serious occupation. Serious to be interpreted say as might be Chaplin's studies to amuse.
>
> —William Carlos Williams, "For a New Magazine"

The detection of homologies between work processes and innovative writing techniques goes back at least as far as Rebecca West's 1913 introduction in the *New Freewoman* to some of Ezra Pound's new verse: "Just as Taylor and Gilbreth want to introduce scientific management into industry, so the *imagistes* want to discover the most puissant way of whirling the scattered stardust of words into a new star of passion" (86).[27] The parallel between modernism and modernization is especially evident in a critical essay by Pound from the same year. "The Serious Artist," which Frederick J. Hoffman long ago called "one of the most important documents in the history of modern 'experiment'" (193), explicitly draws on the discourse of science to justify contemporary poetic undertakings. Pound's defense of poetry articulates an ideal of aesthetic rationalism that in turn specifies the acquisition of knowledge as the shared imperative according to which literary and labor practices can be equated.

Much as the stress within scientific management falls on instructing workers in ways to accomplish their assigned tasks as precisely as possible, without superfluous physical gesture, Pound encourages poets to aspire to perform their designated assignments as accurately as they can, without excessive verbiage.[28] Correlatively, if skill in labor requires mastery over one's tools, literary superiority demands a comparable excellence in language: "Good writing is writing that is perfectly controlled, the writer says just what he means. He says it with complete clarity and simplicity. He uses the smallest possible number of words" (Pound, "Serious Artist" 50). Time is of the essence in both spheres: "The author tries to communicate with the reader with the greatest possible despatch" (though Pound qualifies this by immediately adding "save where for any one of forty reasons he does not wish to do so" [50]), much as for Taylor the goal was swifter modes of production. The motivation behind literary invention therefore logically resembles the goal of experimentation in the factory: both are oriented toward the fashioning of the quickest, most economical means of achieving a specific end. The "part of the work [that] is good," that deploys "rhythm, cadence, and the arrangement of sounds" in effective fashion, is appropriately sedimented as "'technique'" (51). And since "technique consists precisely in doing the thing that one sets out to do, in the most efficient manner, no man who takes three pages to say nothing can expect to be seriously considered a technician. To take three pages to say nothing is not style, in the serious sense of the word" (54). In sum, of the "several kinds of honest work" (55) into which literary activities can be divided, the poetic will always strive for a "'maximum efficiency of expression,'" by which Pound means "the writer has expressed something interesting in such a way that one cannot re-say it more effectively" (56).

Reference to Pound's embrace of the tenets structuring economic rationalization as a model for innovative writing helps mark the idiosyncratic dimensions of Hart Crane's "Chaplinesque," a lyric poem that reflexively aligns the silent screen performer and the modernist poet on the grounds that they are participating in a shared artistic endeavor: to preserve the capacity to feel intensely in an environment that threatens to extinguish the power to experience strong emotions. "Chaplinesque" is a singularly important achievement for my purposes, since it presages the post–World War II rise of slapstick modernism as an affectively charged force in the world.[29]

Composing the poem in 1921, shortly after viewing Chaplin's first feature film, *The Kid,* Crane makes a case for the virtues of unserious artistry by associating his eccentric literary technique with Chaplin's physical style and ethical integrity. The scene the poet takes as his point of departure is no doubt the first one in which Chaplin's character the Tramp appears. Out for his morning promenade, the Tramp dodges bricks as they are tossed out a second-floor window, only to have a bunch of loose refuse from another apartment dumped on him. Undaunted, he pauses near a garbage can to smoke a butt and discovers a swaddled infant abandoned in a corner of the alley. After looking for an easy way out of his predicament, he eventually accepts the burden that chance has imposed on him and decides to raise the child himself. Taken together, the image of the actor's corporeal agility alongside his personality traits (compassion, perseverance, and cleverness) provided Crane with a way to formulate the imperatives structuring his linguistic dexterity on the page. The aesthetic virtuosity each artist displayed in his respective medium had a common purpose: survival in a hostile milieu.

We make our meek adjustments,
Contented with such random consolations
As the wind deposits
In slithered and too ample pockets.

For we can still love the world, who find
A famished kitten on the step, and know
Recesses for it from the fury of the street,
Or warm torn elbow coverts.

We will sidestep, and to the final smirk
Dally the doom of that inevitable thumb
That slowly chafes its puckered index toward us,
Facing the dull squint with what innocence
And what surprise!

And yet these fine collapses are not lies
More than the pirouettes of any pliant cane;
Our obsequies are, in a way, no enterprise.
We can evade you, and all else but the heart:
What blame to us if the heart live on.

The game enforces smirks, but we have seen
The moon in lonely alleys make
A grail of laughter of an empty ash can,
And through all sound of gaiety and quest
Have heard a kitten in the wilderness.
("Chaplinesque" 11)

Crane's correspondence provides a useful background for comprehending the obscure poem. In a letter dated October 17, 1921, Crane mentions the affinity he feels for Chaplin as being the consequence of the manner in which both are compelled to react defensively to their contemporary surroundings. Alluding to the first line of "Chaplinesque," he writes:

> I am moved to put Chaplin with the poets (of today); hence the "we." In other words, he, especially in *The Kid*, made me feel myself, as poet, as being "in the same boat" with him. Poetry, the human feelings, "the kitten," is so crowded out of the humdrum, rushing, mechanical scramble of today that the man who would preserve them must duck and camouflage for dear life to keep them or keep himself from annihilation [. . .] and in the poem I have tried to express these "social sympathies" in words corresponding somewhat to the antics of the actor. (Weber 68).

Conflating art and emotion as comparably endangered enclaves, Crane proposes that the dodging movements of the film star's body parallel the verbal elusiveness the writer deploys to handle the same sociohistorical predicament. A letter written at the beginning of the same month confirms Crane's ambition to match linguistically Chaplin's performative fluency: "My poem is a sympathetic attempt to put in words some of the Chaplin pantomime, so beautiful, and so full of eloquence, and so modern" (Weber 65). A few weeks later, Crane accounts for the pleasure his achievement has given him on the grounds that he has produced a poetic equivalent to the skillful escapes he has observed on screen: "It is because I feel that I have captured the arrested climaxes and evasive victories of his gestures in words, somehow, that I like the poem as much as anything I have done" (Weber 69).[30]

The description of Chaplin's physical successes doubles, then, as a self-conscious account of the poet's accomplishments, and what conceptually binds the two together according to Crane is that both practice an art of avoidance.[31] But if the poem is an "allegory of poetic vocation," and the poet is figuratively engaged in a series of "acrobatic duckings," what exactly does he wish to evade, what climax does he desire to arrest? (Sitney, "Poet as Film Viewer" 7, 17). In *The Kid* Chaplin manages to steer his body clear of falling trash, the arm of the law, and the fists of a neighborhood bully. In "Chaplinesque" such swerving corresponds to Crane's ability as a writer to render meaning vague or ambiguous and thus to prevent the reader from reaching a satisfying and expected conclusion, from determining the significance of the verse. Crane's skill is utilized less to convey information than to puzzle, to produce obstacles for those whose goal is to understand, a demand that appears in the poem as a threat to existence. The personification of death in the third stanza thus inscribes the reader, in fragmentary form, into the text: the smirking entity intent on finality corresponds to the prospective reader intent on cognitive gratification. The doom portended by "that inevitable thumb / That slowly chafes its puckered index toward us" occurs when the artwork is consumed, when it is grasped properly. The poet's ambition, then, is to annul the power of the reader to crush the mortal object. Granted that the parts of the hand and face metonymize the general reader, the black-and-white character of Chaplin on screen takes on the status of a trope for the written page. And what the letters on the latter must dance away from is the narrow and obtuse vision, the "dull squint," of those who look for stable semantic content. The poem's linguistic maneuvers are designed to counter the expectations of those who dislike surprises and want clear-cut messages instead. Such postponements are neither commercially motivated ("no enterprise"), nor are they merely disingenuous exhibitions of aesthetic elegance ("pirouettes of a pliant cane") for its own sake. They are a way to stay alive, for to endure the artifact must frustrate Fate, must stave off its destiny as an object of knowledge. The task is not a duplicitous one, "the collapses are not lies," because there is a subjective truth governing the fabrication of a poetics that slides away from discursive coherence: the poet does not want to pass away.

Here we approach an explanatory justification of the notorious difficulties that Crane's corpus contains.[32] Indeed, his verbal sidestepping repeatedly causes stable meanings to fall down ("fine collapses"). For instance, in the last line of the first stanza the use of "slithered" in conjunction with "too ample pockets" sneaks, snake-like, the impression of "a narrow cut" into a descriptive term that refers to something else entirely. Correlatively, in stanza 4, lateral or contextual associations add the meaning of obsequiousness or humble to "obsequies," the latter having a vague etymological link to the former.[33] Blurring the boundary between the two discrete words generates too much meaning, the semantic excess potentially complicating rather than enhancing the significance of the poem. In the previous stanza, the "slow" chafe of the "puckered index" has the odd (in light of the ordinary usage of "index") effect of conflating two digits; the mischievous poet's manipulation of words brings together what should remain separate, in the process blocking the reader's ability to hold on to what is being said. Conversely, the elliptical structure of the preceding line generates confusion, the incomplete syntax rendering unclear how we are to fill in the blank or missing piece. (Are we to read "More than the pirouettes" as "Anymore than they are the pirouettes," or are we simply supposed to insert a missing "Or"?) Worse, this elided "Or" has already made a surprise appearance at the start of the fourth line of the second stanza, where logic would dictate an "In." The motive for the seemingly gratuitous substitution of a conjunction for a preposition may have been to increase the assonance of the line, yet the pleasant sound effect is secured at the expense of discernible sense, the grammatical aberration converting a straightforward statement into an enigmatic pronouncement.

One of the text's more peculiar yet revealing tactics is to punningly insert the author's proper name into the text. The repetition of "heart" in the last lines of stanza 4 evokes both art and Hart, suggesting the centrality of the former to the existence of the latter ("What blame to us if the heart live on"). This surreptitious self-designation retroactively allows the "cane" that ends line 2 of the stanza to evoke the author's last name. The effect of this procedure is to inscribe the poet in the poem in grotesque fashion as a detached bodily organ and a prosthetic extension. The inanimate thing (the cane) also suggests the writing implement by virtue of which Crane executes his linguistic twirling (on the balls of his poetic feet). Although it is difficult to decide whether this pun is deliberate or aleatory, is a planned result or accidental effect, it is evident that Crane's dazzling style does not preclude the poet's retaining a sincere degree of concern for humanity. Crane's linguistic tramping may result in, as Sitney puts it, "a negation, or at least a retardation of the instantaneous transmission of meaning" ("Poet as Film Viewer" 17), yet such aimless semantic wandering does not entail a rejection of sentimental compassion for others: "For we can still love the world."[34] Feeling survives due to a series of unapologetic swerves away from the lucid conveyance of thought.

Elaborating the financial resonance that the first stanza suggests, we may say that the semantic currency the reader assumes he will obtain turns out to be of minimal cognitive value. Rather than acquiring a wealth of meaning, the baffled (or short-changed) reader must adjust—as the poem's protagonist and the poet have already learned to—to a situation of relative dispossession. All must adapt and accept whatever chance, in the form of the wind, randomly offers as partial compensation for the grand prize (of profound meaning) that cannot be won. If linguistic impoverishment is equivalent to a lack of money, "no sense" the same as "no cents," then the baggy trousers of the Tramp image an internal emptiness that is applicable to the poem as a verbal void, one to which the writer has resigned himself in willful opposition to the demands of the ordinary reader.

The poem's final stanza proposes, however, that there are considerable rewards for those who have the courage to reject the generically prescribed promise of intelligibility.[35] While many people will dismiss the kind of game playing in which Crane indulges as frivolous and irrational, the non-cynical writer and his inspirational cinematic ally have witnessed (if not caused) magical events such as the conversion of "an empty ash can" into a legendary object of desire—a "grail"—invested here with the power to induce a fulfilling state of joyful happiness, one that causes laughter.

Nevertheless, "Chaplinesque" does not stand as a full-fledged example of slapstick modernism.[36] This is largely due to Crane's desire to elevate the popular entertainer whom he admires, if not idolizes, to the status of gifted artist. The result of this aspiration is that Chaplin gets included in a sharply circumscribed set of the privileged few, of the exceptionally compassionate inhabitants of urban modernity who seek protection and solace together in relative isolation from the cruelty of others.[37] Hugh Kenner would employ roughly this same tactic many years later, albeit in the field of literary criticism, when he pointed out in *The Counterfeiters: An Historical Comedy* that

Buster Keaton's "great creative period [. . .] 1921–1927" was also "the age of *Ulysses* and "The Hollow Men" (68–69). Kenner's manner of locating Keaton among his peers on the grounds of their shared self-consciousness about their artistry in turn set the stage for Garrett Stewart's critical readings in the late 1970s of *Modern Times* and *Sherlock Jr.* Still high-water marks in the interpretation of silent (and partially sound) comedy, Stewart's emphasis on the two filmmakers' reflexive attentiveness to the materiality of their medium makes a convincing case for our retrospective ability to discern modernist elements in at least selected slapstick films.[38] But he draws no conclusions about the implications of such liaisons for our general understanding of the relation of artistic modernism to silent screen comedy, especially as this might pertain to the cultural ethics or politics of the post–World War II period in this country. Both McCabe and Trotter repeat this gesture, assimilating silent comedy (in the form of Chaplin and Keaton) into the realm of modernist artistry and thereby missing the chance to speculate on the future emergence of a genuinely populist—that is, a slapstick—modernism aimed at bridging the gap between formal invention and progressive social function.

The final section of this introduction offers a preliminary glimpse of the kind of postwar figures we will meet at the study's end, many of whom strove to appeal, as Chaplin and many other slapstick comedians had previously, "to the most international and the most revolutionary emotion of the masses: their laughter," and were determined to take advantage of rather than abandon the heritage of modernist experimentation (Benjamin, "Chaplin in Retrospect" 224).[39]

The Slapstick Modernist as Mad Scientist

> There is a social literature through filmic pantomime, that is, non-verbal comedy satire; a "comic-ominous" image that pertains to our time and interests which Hollywood and the commercial cinema are ignoring.
>
> —Stan VanDerBeek, *Visibles*

In his 1966 "manifesto and proposal," "Culture: Intercom and Expanded Cinema," the American filmmaker Stan VanDerBeek (who claimed to have coined the term "underground") states with considerable urgency that he believes it is the duty of the innovative type of cinema he envisions to help ensure that humankind does not obliterate itself. Noting that as "the current growth rate risk of explosives to human flesh continues, the risk of survival increases accordingly," he declares that it is "imperative" that motion pictures serve as a means "to counter-balance technique and logic." The preservation of the species requires that avant-garde artists in his medium find a solution to the current crisis in "world communication" (15), for the fact that life is "an experiment on earth has never been made clearer" (16). An "Ethos-Cinema" must come into existence that will "make motion pictures into an emotional experience tool that shall move art and life closer together" and in so doing will reestablish a lost equilibrium between "man" and the machines he has made: "Technological research, development and involvement of the world community has completely out-distanced the emotional-sociological (socio-'logical') comprehension of this technology" (15). The best way to solve this cognitive and affective predicament, VanDerBeek says, is to invent "a new world language," "a non-verbal international picture-language" (16). Since "language and culture-semantics are as explosive as nuclear energy," research into the possibility of utilizing "existing audio-visual devices" as an "educational tool," as what he calls "an experience machine" or a "culture-intercom" must get under way immediately (16).

Describing the various ways the otherwise dangerously forceful flow of images and sounds could be effectively presented to a public that desperately needs to "re-order" itself, that must attain another level of self-awareness, VanDerBeek predicts that "cinema will become a 'performing' art [. . .] and image-library" (18), its pedagogical task to make contact via its "visual 'power'" with "any age or culture group irregardless [*sic*] of culture and background" (18). This "totally new international art form" would probe "for the 'emotional denominator'" that if found might ward off the catastrophes that ongoing miscommunication between the world leaders of heavily armed nations entails. Speaking with words is too slow to rectify a situation in which "the logical fulcrum of man's intelligence [is] so far outside himself that he cannot judge or estimate the results of his acts before he commits them" (16). Unfortunately, "man does not have time to talk to himself [. . . nor does he] have the means to talk to other men [. . .] the world hangs by a thread of nouns and verbs" (16).

That VanDerBeek sought in several of his own films to meet the social demand his manifesto identifies is evident in the program notes he composed to explain the purpose of his films. For instance, VanDerBeek describes "the social ambition" of his "experimental comedy," *Science Friction* (1959), a ten-minute collage animation (one that influenced Terry Gilliam of Monty Python's Flying Circus), as being "to help disarm the social fuse of people living with anxiety, to point out the insidious folly of competitive suicide (by way of rockets)." In his films VanDerBeek was "trying to evolve a 'litera-graphic' image, an international sign language of fantasy and satire" (*Visibles* 4).[40] Motion-picture comedy must employ laughter to generate the energy required to get the masses thinking skeptically about the decision-making capacities of their leaders. (Indeed, late in the film a cut-out Dwight D. Eisenhower dances around gleefully after pushing the button that triggers an atomic disaster.) To alert the American populace to the violence through which the industrial media shapes opinion, VanDerBeek has a sharply pointed tip of a rocket burst through a television screen and puncture a skull with a target on it. Elsewhere we see a monkey operating a giant computer, the densely wired apparatus an image of the technologically sophisticated ways in which the public psyche is programmed. The film also indicts modern psychophysics as a practice contributing to the degraded state of human beings. An early shot shows a patient strapped to a chair in a doctor's office being hit in the face with a hammer, after which a dog's face is superimposed on the blank space left by the tool's blow. American citizens are analogous to the reflexologist Pavlov's animal test subjects. We have all been trained through repetition to behave on command, have been taught to respond physiologically to specific stimuli. To challenge such scientific procedures, the avant-garde artist must behave like a mad scientist. Thus we observe VanDerBeek himself in a laboratory insanely combining various liquids contained in beakers and vials. He then drinks the concoctions, as if he must first test the new chemical compounds to determine their effects. This is easily read as an allegory of the compositional process governing the film's construction: the thought-provoking juxtaposition of curious images. As he put it with regard to a scene in the similarly motivated *Breathdeath*: the comic catalyst was the mixing of an "unexplainable fact (Why is Harpo Marx playing harp in the middle of a battlefield?)" with an "inexplicable act (Why is there a battlefield?)" (*Visibles* 5).

Many of the elements that constitute a slapstick modernism thus come together in VanDerBeek's oeuvre. While expressing a semi-nostalgic devotion to the memory of silent screen comedy and its performance-based or shock aesthetic, he maintains an ethical commitment to improving the conditions of existence of the masses and a political inclination to protest against their ideological manipulation. His sustained investment in artistic invention constitutes a way to meet scientific and technological advances on their own ground, so to speak, and in so doing he hopes to ameliorate their more pernicious effects on society. His interest in disrupting ordinary (or efficient) modes of communication and his sense of the pertinence of experimenting with language (verbal or not) are crucial components of his enterprise. And, last but not least, VanDerBeek's critical antagonism toward the persuasive force of the discourses of the industrialized media—advertising and print journalism especially—is grounded in his conviction that these tend to serve as agents of capitalist modernity, not to mention its prolongation in the military-industrial complex.

The first chapter of this study investigates W. C. Williams's and Mack Sennett's respective investments in the 1920s in destructive enterprises, comically excessive violence amounting in both to a repudiation of the values that inform economic rationalism. In the former's *The Great American Novel* (1923) critical reflexivity and collage experimentation constitute acts of resistance to narrative signification; in the latter, the symbolic dismantling of the Model T serves as a gesture of defiance aimed at Fordism.

Chapter 2 brings Sergei Eisenstein's concept of "the montage of attractions" to bear on John Dos Passos's *Manhattan Transfer* (1925). The crux of Eisenstein's approach (the inspiration for which he locates in silent comedy as well as the circus and amusement park rides) is that it subordinates the representational dimensions of the image to its capacity to impact the spectator's emotional disposition. Rather than passively depicted, reality is actively assembled into a spectacular construct designed to affect the audience (ideologically), to make them feel intensely. *Manhattan Transfer* has customarily been misunderstood by critics as an attempt to record in an impartial, emotionally detached, and therefore epistemologically reliable way the sights and sounds of everyday life in the city. But achieving descriptive accuracy was not the novelist's main priority; on the contrary, his montage technique was part of an attempt to make the reader loathe the effects of monopoly capitalism. From this perspective, *Manhattan Transfer* may be considered to have been a "novel of repulsions," its series of juxtapositions organized to galvanize collective protest against the current state of the nation.

Chapter 3 picks up the conceptual thread of "attraction" while addressing the film oeuvre of the "third genius" of silent screen comedy: Harold Lloyd. This time it is the manifesto-like claims of Eisenstein's theatrical collaborator, Sergei Tretyakov, that provide the theoretical point of departure. I argue that Lloyd, in conjunction with his producer Hal Roach, grasped the virtues of athletic performances on screen as a means of helping to train the masses somatically in order to handle the demands of life in threatening urban settings. The actor's thrilling performances were meant to invigorate spectators emotionally and to enable them to acquire the neurological skills and physiological dexterity they needed to inhabit the world safely. Here again the status of the image is not that of a copy of a preexisting reality; rather, it was designed to play a formative role in the life of the spectator, who in identifying with a cinematically projected other was guided toward the attainment of the hand-eye coordination and quick reflexes necessary to survive in dangerously mechanized surroundings.

Chapter 4 takes the concept of "becoming-child" from Gilles Deleuze and Félix Guattari's study of Franz Kafka in order to account for the peculiarity of Harry Langdon's screen persona. The bizarrely babyish acting style of Langdon, the all but forgotten fourth star in the constellation of silent screen comedians, offers a valuable point of access to one of the fundamental traits of the genre as a whole: its sustained appeal to immature behaviors and correlative rejection of adult standards of behaviors as well as the normative sexual roles these tend to enforce. What emerges here is one of the strongest links between slapstick film and the counterculture generation's affirmation of youthful irreverence as an oppositional stance.

Chapter 5 moves into the Depression era in order to track the initial emergence abroad of a slapstick modernism in the novels of Louis-Ferdinand Céline and Witold Gombrowicz. Justifying his comically outrageous undertaking medically as a revitalizing remedy for the sicknesses of contemporary existence, Céline ultimately pursued cathartic effects that would take place at the level of the word as well as the body and mind. His powerfully emotive technique was oriented toward the purification of the signifier via the elimination of the signified. Language for Céline, like machine technology for Benjamin, was both curse and cure. Gombrowicz's first novel, *Ferdydurke* (1937) is a key piece in the global or transnational puzzle that slapstick modernism ultimately constitutes. Its significance for my purposes derives from the fact that it both thematizes and formally enacts the volatile process of becoming child, thus establishing a strong compositional link with the brand of cinematic lunacy that had flourished in the United States in the previous decade.

Chapter 6 tracks the full-fledged rise of slapstick modernism in this country in the late 1950s and '60s. After surveying this field with help from Jack Kerouac's tribute to the Three Stooges in *Visions of Cody*, I look to Joseph Heller's *Catch-22* for insight into the sociopolitical importance of technically mastering the rhetorical dimensions of language, verbal tropes in particular. Heller's Marx Brothers–like humor, I claim, made an essential contribution to the development of a countercultural sensibility, for in his novel jokes serve as the means of carving out a space for alternative attitudes toward ideologically coercive notions such as patriotism and sacrifice. The clever deployment of figures of speech thus seeks to generate a skeptical intelligence and in so doing to contest the dreadful impact of military officers' demands on their woefully naïve subordinates. Wit emerges as a forceful mode of countermanding the orders that when accepted send gullible soldiers to their doom. The coda to this chapter touches on the achievement in the late '60s of an American proto-punk band: Iggy Pop and the Stooges. Here I propose that it was in the aural media that the project initiated earlier in the century by modernist writers and silent comedians alike came to (partial) fruition. Amplified instrumentation in the high-energy field of popular music provided the precondition for the production of an electrically empowered collective body, one that was ideally attuned to the rhythms of the "mechanosphere" in a non-debilitating, non-subservient manner.

PART I

1920s

1

The Work of Art in the Age of Mechanical Transportation

It was as though, despite his lifelong ramrod-stiff and unyielding opposition to, refusal even to acknowledge, the machine age, Grandfather had been vouchsafed somewhere in the beginning a sort of—to him—nightmare vision of our nation's vast and boundless future in which the basic unit of its economy and prosperity would be a small mass-produced cubicle containing four wheels and an engine.
So he bought the automobile.

—William Faulkner, *The Reivers*

Henry Ford's fiercely prescriptive, religiously impassioned adherence to the disciplinary principles of economic rationalism is on display throughout the first volume of his autobiography, *My Life and Work*, first published in 1922. Vigorously defending hard labor as the "natural thing to do" and as the primary means of obtaining "prosperity and happiness," he also identifies it as the indispensable basis of a moral existence, as the condition of "our sanity, salvation and self-respect" (3, 120). Arguing at times with prophetic fervor, Ford proclaims that commercial enterprises are worthwhile not because they furnish the owner with profits, but because the businesses contribute to the well-being of everyone: "There is something sacred about wages [. . . and] there is something just as sacred about capital which is used to provide the means by which work can be made productive" (163). The spread of merchandising endeavors across the globe is desirable, since "what will happen when the world is put on a production basis" is that the quality of life will be improved for all. It is essential that problems in industry be solved scientifically and that work get done "better and faster" (98), for "the purpose of a factory is to produce, and it ill serves the community in general unless it does produce to the utmost of its capacity" (107). Manufacturers thus justify their existence as "instruments of society" when they increase "the degree of comfort of the people at large" (135), a task best accomplished by the elimination of waste and controlled use of the wealth they have accumulated for the collective good. "The highest use of capital is not to make more money, but to make money do more service for the betterment of life" (194). For Ford, then, the fate of modern civilization rests on the willingness of the masses to believe in the effort to mechanize work as an admirably inspired collective project: "What this generation needs is a deep faith, a profound conviction in the practicability of righteousness, justice, and humanity in industry" (105).[1]

This chapter examines the degree to which William Carlos Williams's *The Great American Novel* (1923) and two Mack Sennett films—*Lizzies of the Field* (1924) and *Super-Hooper-Dyne Lizzies* (1925)—endorsed values that were diametrically opposed to those the successful businessman promoted. Both the motion pictures and the literary text indicated their ethical opposition to the priorities informing economic rationalism by integrating the Model T into decidedly destructive undertakings. Canonically associated with the development of the assembly line, and thus with a highly systematized mode of manufacturing commodities, the vehicle obviously served as a touchstone for Sennett's ongoing expression of his disdain for the governing criteria of Fordism. In contrast, Williams's articulation of his defiance of capitalist modernity was more tangential; yet the aggressive dismantling of the automobile in the comic films mentioned above ultimately finds an aesthetic and ideological corollary of sorts in Williams's critically oriented cancellations of the generic conventions of the novel, as well as in his brutal dismemberment of discourse at the level of the sentence and the word. This is not to say that the sociocultural interventions in question were identical, for whereas Sennett's films featured numerous representations of the sacrifice of the Tin Lizzie to the gods of wild play, Williams's almost unreadable enterprise went much further, sacrificing representation as such in the name of artistic integrity. Indeed, his extreme acts of linguistic negativity occurred at the expense of communicative coherence; the cost of his trying to do something entirely new was that his work barely made sense. However, as partial compensation for his destructive labors, he managed to make a vital contribution to the development of an arguably more sophisticated rhetorical technique—collage—one that has proved indispensable throughout the twentieth century as a means of contesting the persuasive force of discourses designed to delude and manipulate unsuspecting persons.

Importantly, although late in life Williams described *The Great American Novel* as having been "a satire on the novel form in which a little (female)

Ford car falls more or less in love with a Mack truck," the formally recalcitrant text is not especially funny, and this fact might seem to exclude it from a study devoted to the growth and development of a slapstick modernism (*Autobiography* 237). My argument, however, is that a historical investigation of this phenomenon must first reckon with the fact that in the 1920s the two cultural practices (silent comedy and experimental writing) tended to coexist without commingling, Crane's "Chaplinesque" being a singular exception to this rule. Only by attending to this initial state of affairs can we properly understand the significance of what began to happen in the Depression era when certain modernist writers began to incorporate into their novels aesthetic traits that were associated with the popular type of cinematic entertainment. One reason for this eventual convergence was undoubtedly that slapstick filmmakers and modernist writers alike were seeking viable solutions to the set of problems that urban-industrial modernity perpetually posed to its inhabitants.

Notably, it was also in the 1930s that Georges Bataille began to reflect on the social significance of certain types of artistic wastefulness in ways that prove applicable to both Williams's avant-garde venture and Sennett's popular (and commercially profitable) enterprise. For instance, in "Notion of Expenditure" (1933), an article influenced by Marcel Mauss's *The Gift: The Form and Reason for Exchange in Archaic Societies* (1925), Bataille praises a kind of poetry that goes beyond the regulatory "principles of classical utility" and in so doing stands in excess of socioeconomic procedures narrowly oriented toward the necessities of acquisition and conservation (Bataille, "Notion of Expenditure" 116). The primary investment of such poetry, he continues, is in that "immense travail of recklessness, discharge, and upheaval" that constitutes the "most appreciable share of life" (117). Existentially essential gestures of this sort are liberating in that they dispense with "the ordered and reserved forces" that have pertinence only within closed and well-balanced systems of production and exchange. Enthusiastically embracing ostensibly dangerous states of disequilibrium, acts of unconstrained consumption give free rein to the "irresistible impulse to reject [the] material and moral goods" that it would otherwise be "possible to utilize rationally" (128). Such a perspective readily brings to mind critical assessments of Sennett's output as having "in an era of determinedly materialistic values [. . .] celebrated the orgiastic destruction of goods and possessions, of cars and houses and crockery" (Robinson 43). More recently, Rob King has reiterated this evaluation. Invoking the mechanization of the labor process at Ford's Highland Park automobile plant, he describes Keystone Studios as having "supplied compensatory spectacles of disorder, of bodies unable to perform according to the requirements of a task"; for King, the film studio's "carnivalesque resistance to the industrial virtues of discipline and orderliness" amounted to a "cheerful proclamation of the values of disorder and spontaneity (*Fun Factory* 48). Somewhat similarly, David Jarraway once referred to *The Great American Novel* as a textual "potlatch" (26). That Bataille's ideas resonate with claims made on behalf of Sennett's version of silent screen comedy *and* with attitudes toward Williams's initial foray into "high" modernist prose suggests that certain formal and functional affinities did indeed structure the relationship of the two cultural practices even before they began to coalesce.

Mack Sennett's Visions of Slapstick Excess

> This was still that fabulous and legendary time when there was still no paradox between an automobile and mirth [. . .]
>
> —William Faulkner, *The Town*

In *The Comedy of Philosophy: Sense and Nonsense in Early Cinematic Slapstick*, Lisa Trahair convincingly demonstrates the feasibility of applying Bataille's philosophy of laughter (as unknowing) to silent screen comedy. The opening chapter of her study draws on Jacques Derrida's "Restricted and General Economy: A Hegelianism without Reserve" to elucidate Bataille's concept of the comic as a sovereign operation, and this paves the way for her analysis in subsequent chapters of portions of Keaton's cinematic oeuvre. Trahair's guiding thesis through the first half of her inquiry is that the categories of restricted and general economy may be respectively correlated with (while also complicating) the distinction—central to previous critical discussions of slapstick film—between narrative and gag. For her, the dialectical procedures of narrative belong to the realm of restricted economy to the degree that narrative is a "form of exchange that makes meaning possible" (36). Arranging events in space and time in causally coherent fashion, narrative as it logically unfolds allows the existential conflicts it dramatizes to be overcome or synthesized intellectually. Conversely, although gags do not serve exclusively as devices interfering with orderly narration, they do tend to function in accordance with the conditions of general economy ("sacrifice, waste, play, excess, and expenditure without return" [103]), thus instigating nonsensical slapstick processes that in effect transgress the conceptual closure that narrative representation seeks to impose on material reality.

One can find additional support for Trahair's assertion that Bataille's thought is well suited to the practice of silent comedy at the end of his "Sacrifice," an essay drafted in the late 1930s. At the start of the piece he acknowledges that he should explain his previous assertion that "the bloody fantasies of sacrifice" possess a "meaning" (61). He admits that in making such a claim he runs the risk of legitimating such ritualized cruelty, but this is not his intent, for he believes that it is possible today to satisfy in less savage ways the needs that this custom fulfilled in antiquity. Nevertheless, due to his commitment to inducing a sense of the "sacred horror" that remains outside the emotional range of those invested in the ethos of rational production, Bataille feels compelled to interpret the enigma that "massacres of men and beasts" pose to contemporary humanity. To be reasonable and to attain a state of rest in the world, one must first confront the appalling fact that through mutual agreement living beings were put to death in the past. Identifying what "forced men to kill their own kind in religious ceremonies" may disclose the secrets of "human existence" (62). The problem of sacrifice, then, has to do with group living, with social or collective being, or rather with the tension between the self and a community of others. If death is a warning to the "I" that the conviction that the self alone matters is a falsehood, then the tragic consequence is that "I" can live only by "relinquishing this life of mine" (66). "Each man must consider both confining himself in isolation and escaping from that prison." Torn between these "irreconcilable poles," man must endure on a daily basis the dispute "between tiny enclosure and free space," between a "selfish and empty," because solitary, existence and fusion with a world "of communicating elements" (66). Importantly, but perplexingly, "the bottleneck" connecting inner being with the external realm of the many is said at this point to be "rarely death itself, but always its adumbration or its image" (66).

The essay's final section, titled "Laughter," proposes to clear up the mystery of sacrifice, albeit via a circuitous path that twists through silent screen comedy. Having already mentioned laughter in the context of communicative processes through which individuality is superseded, Bataille reiterates this point decisively: "Barriers collapse, and the convulsive moments of those laughing break free and reverberate in unison. Not only does each man participate in the limitless streaming of the universe but his laughter mixes with that of others, so that a room will contain not several laughs, but a single wave of hilarity. The icy solitude of each laughing individual is, as it were, refined: all lives are waters flowing into a torrent" (69).[2] Nevertheless, according to Bataille, laughter remains "a facile form of communication" when compared to "major" sorts such as violent sacrifice (68). To explain this curious distinction he returns to the classic example employed in so many theories of comedy: the sight of someone tumbling to the ground and the mirthful reactions such a spectacle engenders in the spectator. Here we are told that the "man who unwittingly falls is substituting for the victim who is put to death," and "the shared joy of laughter is" therefore "that of sacred communication" (68). Revelation and ecstasy occur when we burst into "a full, remorseless, laughter" at the expense of someone else; in such circumstances of overwhelming emotion or communal "transport" (69), we become "one" with those around us, which in turn enables us to penetrate "into the secret place of things" and thus partake in "the joy of living" (70). The suffering that gravity causes to another releases a wave of guiltless hilarity in which the witnesses of pedestrian awkwardness come together as a harmoniously unified entity. Bataille then adds a crucial component to his model of comedy: to the extent that laughter begins when anguish arises, the former can be understood as a method for dispelling the paralysis that feelings of distress might otherwise cause. Concocting a misogynist (and ageist) scenario to convey his point, Bataille imagines a scenario involving reckless driving rather than inept walking: "If, in a car, I laugh on reaching maximum speed, it is because within me the pleasure of going fast is far greater than the valid anxiety about danger (I would not be laughing if I were more accustomed to speed or if wholly closed to fear). I can laugh a lot, if it is not my fear that is involved, but that of someone else, such as a pretentious old lady, wholly antithetical to that world of intense movement which is to my taste." The more the woman protests, the faster Bataille drives the imaginary car, for the "anguish at stake" is something he could feel, but because of his "hostility" it remains something that belongs to "another" (70). Exuberant happiness derives from the capacity to frighten someone else by making her anticipate a disastrous accident. An act of aggression aimed at scaring an elderly woman allows the youthful operator of a motorized vehicle to transcend his own worries about the possibly grievous consequences in the future of rapid spatial movement.

Bataille turns next to a scene he recalls from Chaplin's *The Gold Rush* (1925); the philosopher's ostensible purpose is to address the effects of artificially as opposed to naturally generated laughter, but reference to the motion picture also provides him with an opportunity to refine his overall argument by distinguishing subtly but sharply between the awfulness of serious acts of sacrifice and comically inflected depictions of terrifying events.[3] The scene, in which the Tramp and another character are said to fight each other inside a shack that is teetering on the edge of a precipice, exemplifies a case in which "the convulsion of uncontrollable laughter impels him who has provoked it to go to the limit, to the point of vertigo, of nausea" (71).[4]

As the characters flail about endeavoring to keep the precariously balanced shack from plunging off the cliff, the laughing members of the audience are presumably propelled into a state of mind that shatters illusory notions of individual particularity. The threat of capsizing uproots the viewer, forcing him toward a "beyond" in which "he is no longer separable from death, from that which is mortal to him, since by an inextinguishable, rending laugh he has crossed the threshold, entered into this dreadful unison" (72). But Bataille then abruptly retracts his bold claim, confessing that this is not exactly what happens, for a "ruse was needed" to "lighten the anguish" such events inevitably entail. The trick or subterfuge rests on the fact that the potential catastrophe has been represented inside "the disparaged world of the comic," has been transformed into a comic spectacle, which allows the spectator to gain weight, so to speak, as he looks and laughs at the antics of the clownish performers imaged on the screen. The effect of the "redoubled laughter" the film solicits makes it seem as if the difference between lighthearted fun and serious agony has been eliminated, yet in truth the latter has been surreptitiously evaded. Consequently, there can be no "balance of accounts between profit and loss" (72). The momentum of the scene takes one "relatively far in the direction of loss," but in the end when viewing a comedy one consents to only a moderate degree of awareness of one's possible demise. To overdo the amount of consciousness one attains of the threat of self-destruction would be too displeasing, and to the degree that one does not reach the requisite level of affective torment one is *not* absorbed into the sacred sphere of the divine. Comic mediation is a makeshift maneuver in relation to the authentic experience of anguish, and this ensures that when one inevitably returns to a condition of seriousness the feelings in question will prove to have been "null and void." The impression while laughing of being "carried away into the 'immeasurable, limitless beyond'" is temporary, lasting for only a few, preciously irradiating moments (72).

Having formulated the irreconcilability of comic levity, which deludes the laughers into believing they can rise above their mortal predicament (and become God), with the dishearteningly gloomy awareness that this feeling of transcendence is comparatively an inferior mode of confronting human finitude, Bataille declares he is now prepared to "break open the enigma of sacrifice" (73). The spectacles of violence that comic enterprises such as slapstick film supply to onlookers are the ethically indispensable substitutes for the horrifyingly bloody, all but intolerable rituals carried out in ancient communities. Correlatively, realizing the capacity of the machine-age form of popular entertainment to cancel out or disperse anguish on a collective scale puts the anthropologically oriented philosopher into position to gauge by way of contrast the nearly unbearable emotional strength of the barbaric cultural practice that silent screen comedy had historically displaced for better not worse.

Peter Král's 1969 tribute to the body of work of a minor (though not uninteresting) silent screen clown, Larry Semon, further indicates the potential of Bataille's thinking to account for the resistance of silent comedy to the mandates of capitalist modernity. Early in the piece, Král praises the output of Keystone Studios in terms that directly recall Bataille's ideas on sacrifice: "Rarely has man's face been so actively illuminated from within by essential human anguish as in the films of the Sennett school (the humor of which is only a magical exorcism of this anguish)." Later Král locates in "the shorts produced by Mack Sennett a liberating, *quantitative* squandering (entire companies of cops and bathing beauties chasing solitary heroes, not to mention the cataclysmic accumulation of catastrophes)." This squandering is in turn "dialectically linked to a sense of the singular *quality* of certain elements and objects which perform a relatively constant role in Sennett's variable universe and give it the quality of an irrational *system* (custard pies, false beards, Model T Fords, hosepipes)" (109, 111; emphasis in the original).

A couple of more recent discussions of the significance of Sennett's achievement (and that of his many disciples) are roughly compatible with Bataille's stance, although it is doubtful these were influenced by his work. In the "Mechanics and Modernity" section of a 2010 essay collection, two important contributions address the relationship of the genre to the growth and development of industrial capitalism. Eileen Bowser's short but valuable piece "Mack Sennett vs. Henry Ford" identifies the symbolic antagonism between slapstick and the increasingly rationalized method of making automobiles. Whereas Ford, largely through his pioneering implementation of assembly-line strategies in the labor process, "brought us affordable cars for the common man," Sennett "gave us slapstick comedies that did their best to take apart, deform, and destroy the wonderful new machines" (108).[5] For Bowser, the conflict in question is a symptomatic manifestation of a basic ideological disparity in the national psyche: while the motion pictures "signify the nihilistic strain that existed in American life," the successful car manufacturer's "idealism, optimism, and ambition" expressed the other side of the country's collective sensibility (109–110). In "'Uproarious Inventions': The Keystone Film Company, Modernity, and the Art of the Motor," Rob King explains Sennett's penchant (beginning in 1915) for sensationalist spectacles featuring mechanical contrivances as evidence of the commercially savvy filmmaker's participation in the more encompassing project to exhibit potentially disturbing new technologies in ways that framed them as objects of pleasurable fascination. This strategy was designed to enable the motion picture company to expand its appeal, "to build a cross-class public for its films and draw filmgoers into a new world of mass culture." Comic films allowed people to comfortably negotiate what otherwise would have been distressing encounters with modern modes of transportation (automobiles, airplanes, motorboats, and even submarines) (115).[6] Abandoning its previous tactic of addressing working-class audiences via fantasies pertinent to their everyday lives, Keystone set as its primary task the construction of a broad social consensus. King conceptualizes this shift in approach as a decision to embrace an "operational aesthetic," which he defines as an attempt to stimulate (without satisfying) the spectators' desires to comprehend how the marvels of modernity work. The quasi-therapeutic goal of the cultural endeavor was to convert anxiety-inducing mechanical phenomena into thrilling sources of visual delight, thus alleviating dystopian fears of an eventual collective subordination to technology. The politically troubling dimension of this aesthetic compulsion resulted from its tendency to veil the causes of anxiety and to obfuscate the fact that real pain was often distributed in accordance with class distinctions, that members of the working class customarily suffered more from the rise of machine technology than those belonging to the middle classes. "At Keystone [. . .] the image of the world as a crazy machine was a fetish for the modern era, in which cogwheels, levers, and gears meshed to such exhilarating ends that there remained not the slightest gap for confronting the costs of a mechanized environment" (127).

Marshall McLuhan had suggested a similar point of view back in the 1960s in a chapter of *Understanding Media* devoted to the motorcar's impact on the subjects of urban modernity. Speaking initially of the Depression era, he asserts that "emotionally the violence of millions of cars in our streets was incomparably more hysterical than anything that could ever be printed. All the rhinos and hippos and elephants in the world, if gathered in one city, could not begin to create the menace and explosive intensity of the hourly and daily experience of the internal-combustion engine. Are people," he then asks rhetorically, "really expected to internalize—live with—all this power and explosive violence, without processing and siphoning it off into some form of fantasy for compensation and balance?" He then takes note of the fact that in "the silent pictures of the 1920s a great many of the sequences involved the motorcar and policemen. Since the film was then accepted as an optical illusion, the cop was the principal reminder of the existence of ground rules in the game of fantasy. As such, he took an endless beating" (196).[7] Yet, as is often the case with McLuhan, a lively discussion of an intriguing topic trails off before the analysis is satisfactorily completed. Nevertheless, his situating of slapstick film as a reaction to the anguish of everyday life in densely populated and heavily trafficked areas is a useful one, for it draws our attention to the cathartic dimension of cultural practice that seems to have informed Bataille's outlook on comedy and tragic sacrifice (not to mention his attitude toward matters pertaining to political economy).

Whether understood medically or philosophically, as affective purgation or intellectual purification, physiological cleansing or dialectical cure, bringing the concept of catharsis to bear on silent comedy alerts us to the collective purposefulness of the cultural phenomenon (if only at the level of structural intention). Could consuming such visual materials have a remedial effect on the spectating masses? Walter Benjamin appeared to believe this was the case when in the 1930s he asserted that the images of lunatic behavior that "American slapstick comedies and Disney films" put on display had the potential to "trigger a therapeutic release of unconscious energies" in the audience. "Collective laughter" was thus characterized by him as a "preemptive and healing outbreak of [the] mass psychosis" that technological change in repressive civilizations tended to cause ("Work of Art," 2nd version 118).[8] Given the paucity of empirical data, such a provocative hypothesis is destined to remain unverified. Still, it is worth pursuing the speculative notion that the cinematic genre sought to perform such a socially worthwhile task. To do so I attend to a very small sample of the plethora of scenes of automotive destructiveness from this era: *Lizzies of the Field* and *Super-Hooper-Dyne Lizzies* were both directed by Del Lord (who went on to direct numerous Three Stooges shorts and in the process helped shape their unique style of violent knockabout), and each stars Billy Bevan and Andy Clyde.[9]

Film historians generally agree that Sennett's distinctive output was most vulgarly rowdy between 1912 and 1915, before he joined forces with Thomas Ince and D. W. Griffith in the ill-conceived founding of the Triangle Film Corporation.[10] As King recounts it, the business venture was doomed to failure not only because of its leader Harry Aitken's inept financial management of the project but also because of the misguided nature of his vision. Aitken's aspiration to fashion an exclusively "highbrow" or genteel film culture both grossly underestimated the commercial dynamics structuring the modern leisure economy and demanded that Keystone sever its grounding ties to working-class and immigrant communities, who could barely afford the expensive prices the theaters showing Triangle pictures charged for tickets.

More important, the plan to cultivate the wealthy required that Sennett make many compromises at the aesthetic level, resulting in a new tolerance of standard models of sentimentality and acceptance of many elements of musical comedy, such as an interest in depicting luxurious lifestyles (King, *Fun Factory* 143–79). By mid-1917, Ince, Griffith, and Sennett had all abandoned the enterprise, with the latter signing a distribution deal with Paramount to release "Mack Sennett Comedies." This association lasted until 1923, and Sennett then contracted with Pathé Exchange through 1929. If the films he supervised tended after the First World War to be less inspired than during his heyday, the bizarre films mentioned above have been singled out as partially controverting the narrative of qualitative decline. Simon Louvish, for instance, considers *Super-Hooper-Dyne Lizzies* to be a revitalizing return to the basics of Keystone's trademark manic mobility, one that prefigures the strangeness of Salvador Dali and Luis Buñuel's avant-garde collaborations (232).[11]

The opening sequence of *Lizzies of the Field* is easily read as a reflexive prelude, as a self-conscious invocation of the commonplace equation of the act of dreaming and of viewing a motion picture. What we see at first (after a quick shot of a posted flyer for an upcoming road race) is a shot of Bevan, who an intertitle will soon identify as Bud Gasket, rocketing down a residential street gripping a steering wheel while wearing a sleeping cap and nightgown. Because the curious image is framed at waist level, we have to wait until a longer shot reveals what we had suspected: that the vehicle he is driving is his bed, or as the intertitle puts it, he is "snorting along at 40 H.P. in his Snoozenberg." As he arrives at a more pastoral setting, Bud's seemingly motorized bed stalls, so he must get out and restart the engine; after a few cranks, we see a puff of smoke and off he goes again. Having entered a more rugged terrain, the camera then shows us from a low angle the bed teetering precariously on the ridge of a hill. The screen briefly goes black and then predictably returns us to reality, albeit a relatively odd one: still clutching the steering wheel, Bud, we now realize, has been slumbering the entire time in a bed located on an elevated platform inside a car repair shop. Rocking dangerously, the poorly designed bed finally dumps him on the floor, whereupon he wakes in a daze. The subtle implication of the extended gag is that the recognition of the possibility of bodily injury, if not death, is realer for the (dreaming) subject of the unconscious than for the semiconscious individual; in contrast to the former, the latter is too stunned to appreciate the fact that he has just had an encounter with human finitude. More significantly, we are encouraged to align conceptually the comic film with the dream, to comprehend both as ways individuals are enabled to obtain (without risk of genuine injury) more affecting experiences of corporeal vulnerability than they are customarily able to maintain in their everyday affairs. The physical pain of actually tumbling to the ground notwithstanding, the inhabitant of modernity may feel the threat of grievous injury or of their own mortality more intensely when images of the suffering that machine technologies can cause are projected on a screen.

After the prelude we are presented with a few standard bits of comic foolishness revolving around automobiles. Just before these we are informed that Bud's boss, Nick Pliers, the proprietor of the Black Cat Garage, is "pinched for money" and that many believe his daughter, Polly Pliers, would make a "charming couple" with young Tim Fender. The connotation of the proper names, which figure people as either car parts or tools, is that in this weird world there is an intimacy or indiscernibility between inanimate things and animate beings. This quasi-ontological motif is then picked up in the following scene, in which Tim and Polly go for a walk together. Because the camera again tightly frames the space the characters occupy, we have to wait a moment for a longer shot to reveal that they are not (as we might have assumed) pushing a baby in a stroller, but that the handles we have glimpsed belong to an odd-looking contraption on wheels with the longest of its several hoses looping around at the top of the device. While we are still processing this peculiar sight, Ben Davis, Tim's villainous rival for Polly's affections, speeds by in a race car, which is surprisingly equipped with a passenger seat that extends outward so that Davis can scoop the girl away from her boyfriend. However, when Davis attempts to molest her in a tunnel, he gets what he deserves, for as they emerge from the darkness, Polly is now in the driver's seat and it is clear from his wounded face that she has pummeled him.

Davis, we soon learn, runs the Red Dog Garage, located directly across the street from Tim's father's business. As the two battle each other for customers, they literalize a couple of dead metaphors. After Davis tries to "pull in" clients with a ship's anchor, Bud suggests they rope them in with a lasso. Snagging a motorist, the competitors use their cars to yank at his in opposite directions, stretching the automobile's body until a passing roadster cuts the immobilized vehicle in two, one half of which crashes through the side wall of Pliers' garage. To compensate his boss for the property damage his scheme has caused, Bud agrees (as will Larry Semon in *Kid Speed*, a similarly structured film released in the same year as *Lizzies*) to enter the aforementioned road race, advertised in a telling double entendre as "free for all." In this spectacular event, the destructive catastrophe augured in Bud's dream is realized, albeit in a comically delirious fashion that renders the emotional thrills and sensorial excitement that are associated with mechanically accelerated movement through space laughable rather than terrifying.

Even for a contemporary viewer the depiction of the race is experienced as an onslaught of difficult-to-process visual stimulation, an aesthetic strategy that further undercuts any lingering claims in *Lizzies* to verisimilitude. Not only does Bud's team vehicle look outlandish at rest—it is trapezoidal in shape with zebra stripes angling across its body and has black and white spirals painted on its wheels—but when stared at in motion it has a dizzying effect that is analogous to what happens when one stares at certain optical toys. The race itself begins chaotically, Bud's automobile accidentally hooking the pyramidal platform on which the race officials are standing high in the air. As the vehicle drags them along, the exuberant crowd roars with delight, cheering at the plight of the frantic officials, who manage at the last second to escape impending doom by clambering onto a bridge, only to be almost run over by a passing trolley. The rapid editing, which mirrors the velocity depicted in the film, leaves the spectator no time to contemplate the epistemological feasibility of the near disaster it has just witnessed. Without a moment's pause, a panning (and slightly under-cranked) long shot from a distant hill yields to a traveling close-up taken from a vehicle traveling alongside the hero's speeding car; this in turn is succeeded by a visually rollicking shot filmed from behind. The latter is particularly notable because as the trailing automobile swerves down a sharply curving road, the camera repeatedly swings wide of its ostensible target on both sides. Whether the result of clumsiness or deliberation, the technique effectively produces both an intense awareness of the mechanical device as a condition of seeing and a state of extreme unrest as the spectator feels jostled from one side to the other. Cinematographic crudeness thus generates a sense of embodied and mobile immersion. The subsequent inclusion of a couple of timeworn gags, one of them a substitution trick, jettisons any lingering representational investment in *vraisemblance* in favor of spectator amazement. First, to retrieve a lost tire, Bud jumps on a bicycle and in a cartoonishly impossible burst of speed passes the motorized vehicles; later, one of the racers slams into a log being carried across its path, and after the smoke clears we see the implausible sight of men staggering around with piles of chopped wood in their arms.

That the increasingly extravagant car stunts contained in the second half of the film foil the efforts of a road construction crew is hardly surprising given Sennet's trademark tendency to invert the priorities governing rationalized labor processes. Whereas the efficient building of new roads was of obvious importance within an economy organized in large part around the production of inexpensive automobiles, in *Lizzies* acts of motorized play are repeatedly shown as interfering with the hard work of converting a relatively rough terrain into a navigable space across which one may drive comfortably. For example, as the race progresses, a nicely choreographed scene shows a line of vehicles rhythmically speeding over a man digging a ditch with a pick, the oblivious worker fortunately managing each time to avoid being torn in half, though the last of the moving vehicles snags his tool and drags him out of his hole. Next, the villain and his assistant seek to gain an unfair advantage over Bud and his partner by switching two adjacent road signs, one of which has an arrow directing racers to detour left, the other warning them not to go right and enter a "blasting zone." Fooled by the cheaters, Bud and Tim barrel into the forbidden area and mistake the frantic flag-waving of the safety crew as an indication that the finish line is near. So our heroes proceed to "step on it!" and of course the explosive device detonates at the exact moment they pass over it. When the cloud of smoke disperses, we learn that the metal body of the vehicle has been completely shredded, that the men's clothing is in tatters, and that they have thus barely escaped a brutal death. Although the car manages to keep going, we observe from behind that it is dropping assorted parts as it rolls unsteadily down the road. Then, in the climactic scene, the other racers, though presumably having taken the correct route, find themselves plunging down a steep hill and off an unfinished wooden ramp as members of the road crew stand by helplessly. The slight use of slow motion adds a touch of gracefulness to the spectacular sight of several of the cars soaring through the air, one of the last of which managing to do a near somersault before crashing on top of a steadily increasing pile of wrecked vehicles. Far behind and unaware of the mechanical carnage ahead, Bud and Tim decide to insert a lit stick of dynamite into their car's gas tank to make up for lost time. The extra force does indeed propel them to victory, launching them over the tangled mass of injured bodies and damaged machines and just across the finish line, where they land in a heap.

The film's depiction of road racing as a form of destructive fun that interferes with the labor of a road building crew furnishes the basis for a critical distinction between two types of destructive activity. When guided by the interests of automobile manufacturers, destruction tends to serve a utilitarian purpose, functioning as a means to the serious end of constructing new or improving existing roads. In contrast, in *Lizzies* destruction appears in a comic context as an entertainingly irrational waste of time, energy, and available resources. Fittingly, the expended energy *in the film* does not result in financial gain. Though they have won the race, Bud and Tim cannot collect the $25,000 purse, because the starter declares that he has fired his gun too soon. To achieve their goal, then, they will have to do the whole thing over again. (This thematic outcome, of course, stands in sharp contrast to the lucrative nature of the cinematic enterprise itself, Sennett having excelled at the art of making film comedy a highly remunerative commodity.) But there is more to be said about the social significance of slapstick film's enduring penchant for scenes of automotive mayhem.

In his book *Inventing Autopia* Jeremiah Axelrod floats a reasonably penetrating thesis, diagnosing slapstick filmmakers' fascination with car crashes as a symptomatic reaction to a historically determined epistemological crisis. For him, the widespread preoccupation through the 1920s—in film and elsewhere in Los Angeles—with the menacing aspects of traffic accidents was a collective expression of the distress that inhabiting a dramatically changing environment had caused. As the city expanded during this transitional era from a small to a mid-size urban entity, neighborhood ties were loosened and the communal order seemed to be collapsing; consequently everyday life became cognitively disorienting, with the use and abuse of the private automobile having exacerbated this unsettling process of change. (This state of confusion would only worsen when, after World War II, the area emerged as a thoroughly decentralized asphalt megalopolis structured around the freeway as the dominant system of mass transportation.) Taking this as his premise, Axelrod proposes that the extensive newspaper coverage of the "Saturnalia of death" taking place in the city streets may be considered to have been a manifestation of the agitation that the increased illegibility of one's visible surroundings was engendering (73). The discursive proliferation of nightmarish visions of the milieu as a potential graveyard for pedestrians due to the irresponsible lack of caution of speeding scofflaws; the ubiquitous reportorial accounts of grisly episodes of bodily injury; as well as the tabulation of casualties and printing of a "death toll" in the daily press were reflections of a panic rooted in the shared experience of a world that had ceased to yield to totalizing understandings (73). Terror about automobile crashes had as its hidden source a social situation in which relationships with others and with the landscape were becoming increasingly difficult to comprehend.

Axelrod then analyzes the disturbing flip side of collective anxieties about the possibility of suffering corporeal harm in the busy streets of the city. The "perverse pleasure" that many people took in the images of motorized disaster that were then in circulation signaled that an erotic evasion of a horrifying condition of existence was occurring (77). The motion picture industry therefore stands accused of having appealed to the prurient sensibilities of those living in Southern California, the excitingly wild car chases they screened mobilizing illusory gratification to deflect audience attention away from the epistemological uncertainties plaguing it outside the movie theater. This helps explains why there was such enthusiasm for silent screen comedy at the time.[12] As Axelrod explains, as the city expanded dramatically away from its "compact downtown core," it became harder to comprehend as a single entity. "This illegibility manifested itself ludically in a visual language of uncontrolled movement," with cinema showing the inhabitants of the area what they had become accustomed to on a daily basis as a cause of emotional distress. Silent comedy "made light of chaos and helped translate anxieties over the social, topographical, and demographic change that urbanites saw all around them into an obsession with sheer movement as a force in itself" (81).

Two of Bataille's ideas make it possible to further refine our sense of the virtues rather than the drawbacks of silent screen comedy as a socially meaningful cultural practice. The first derives from the primary thesis of his book *The Accursed Share*: that the excess energy (wealth) that social formations accrue must ultimately be spent lavishly without return (21). Such a claim goes against the plans informing rational economic organizations, in which all excess is envisioned as being absorbed in future operations and therefore as contributing to the acquisition of greater profits. For Bataille, it is essential to recognize the importance of acts of sumptuous consumption, for to ignore this fact is to involuntarily undergo what could otherwise be brought about deliberately. The former case had been epitomized in the recent past by the two world wars, with the threat of a nuclear holocaust its future corollary. In short, Bataille interprets catastrophic destruction on a massive scale as the inevitable consequence of situations in which developed nations fail to dissipate accumulated energies in "glorious" fashion. The tragic outcome of such international strife demonstrates the necessity of searching for practical solutions to the problem, which technological innovation exacerbates, of possessing an accumulated surplus that must be released. If military conflagrations show what happens when nations reach the limits of economic growth, the practice in ancient societies of obtaining relief from blockage in festivals suggests the fundamental importance of unproductive expenditures as a way of reducing collective tensions. From the broad perspective of general economy, the comically exaggerated style associated with Sennett of dismantling the built world may thus be contemplated as having been a mode of popular entertainment designed to keep explosive pressures "below the danger point" (40).

The second of Bataille's ideas that is pertinent to critical reflection on the functions of silent comedy is a claim he formulates in part two of *The Accursed*

Share, in the context of a discussion of the Aztecs as an exemplary manifestation of a society devoted to consumption and ritual sacrifice as opposed to productive enterprise and regularized work. The intended effect of past forms of violent cruelty, he argues, was to restore to the sacred realm what mundane modes of labor had rendered profane and debased. "Servile use has made a *thing* (an *object*) of that which, in a deep sense, is of the same nature as the *subject*, is in a relation of intimate participation with the subject" (55; emphasis in the original). Destruction took aim not at the thing as such but at its utilitarian degradation; communally affirmed acts of negation were carried out in the hope of rediscovering or illuminating a connection with things that their status as possessions or property had veiled. Consecration demanded the transfer of things from the "real order" of moderation, reason, and lucidity into the antithetical domain of immoderation, madness, and intoxication (58). The practice of impassioned, ecstatic consumption also promised to open up lines of intense communication between separate beings. A concern for collective existence thus justified the victimization of fellow beings (or their animal or plant substitutes). A surplus drawn from the sphere of useful wealth, the sacrificed being was put to death to save the community from ruination, the desire to unite and preserve being motivating gestures of sumptuous wreckage. The meaningfulness of such delirious operations (rarely if ever entirely successful) and the suffering they entailed was to eliminate "the weight introduced [. . .] by the avarice and cold calculation of the real order" (61).

If we modify these notions to fit existence in the machine age, we may posit the brutal treatment of the Model T in particular (and the automobile in general) in slapstick film as a comically tempered type of sacrifice. Correctly recognizing "that the car *is* the commodity form as such in the twentieth century" (Ross 19; emphasis in the original), silent comedy repeatedly took destructive aim at this emblematic article of exchange, one typically used in a subordinate way that is compatible with the criteria of a productive economy (as a highly regulated means of transportation). Perhaps the aspiration underlying such gestures was the hope of reestablishing a lost intimacy not just between the individual members of a given society but also between animate people and the inanimate things with which human beings have daily contact in urban-industrial modernity. The first reel of *Super-Hooper-Dyne Lizzies* supports this contention marvelously.

Like the Hal Roach studio product *It's a Gift* (featuring Snub Pollard), released two years earlier in 1923, the Bevan-Lord collaboration (from a script by Frank Capra) takes as its topic the ambition to find an alternative source of power for automobiles. In *Super-Hooper-Dyne Lizzies*, Andy Clyde plays a seemingly crackpot inventor named Burbank Watts, whose zany project (an intertitle tells us) is to replace petroleum-based gasoline with the "hot air wasted on radio speeches," which is to say he hopes to convert the waves enabling audio transmissions into electrical energy and use the latter to get cars going. The film opens on a presumably empty room containing a cabinet resembling a safe with a sign posted on it that reads "DANGER HIGH VOLTAGE." Suddenly an explosive blast occurs, whereupon a befuddled Watts tumbles out of the enclosure tangled up in a thick cable and holding a charred and still smoking wire. In the next shot his handyman helper Hiram Case (Bevan) pops his head out from behind a table on which there rests a miniature Model T with a peculiar diamond-shape antenna stuck on the hood. Pushed against the wall of the shop is a gigantic machine with assorted odd-looking parts; and as the two men twist a few dials and flip a couple of panel switches on the contraption, the toy vehicle starts moving in a circle, indicating that they have finally discovered a remote control system of driving.

The massive machine also contains a device called a "radioscope," which is evidently a telecommunication instrument, for when Watts pushes one of its many rectangular components, he is able to videoconference (to put it anachronistically) with his daughter, Winnie, who is in the process of sending him a distress signal after running out of gas somewhere across town. Case rushes to the rescue, but before he can get there the scoundrel T. Potter Doam, "the biggest oil can in the industry," arrives. (The thematically fitting allusion is to the then recent government bribery scandal involving the secretary of the interior in the Harding administration and oil company executives.) Doam creates a distraction (by kicking over a gas can, the contents of which spill down the street, igniting an explosive device that injures and infuriates a couple of workers, who then confront Bevan) and spirits Winnie away. The businessman plans to do the same with Watts's clients, to grab them as he has grabbed his daughter. He is of course defeated, and the gas merchant is soon on the verge of bankruptcy. Meanwhile—and this is the focal point of the film—widespread enthusiasm for the use of "radio power" via Watts's gadget has set the stage for a considerable amount of automotive pandemonium. Experimenting with assorted wire connections in his shop, Watts mistakenly tunes in to the wrong frequency, which diverts the electrical charge flowing through overhead power lines (and from nearby towers) directly to the cars of those who have purchased his "super iodine antenna." (The otherwise invisible beaming of the current is crudely drawn on the celluloid in zigzag fashion.) In the ensuing bedlam, the driverless vehicles, as if possessed of minds of their own, run wild, knocking their owners to the ground and then defying the rules of the road by smashing through vegetable carts at crossroads and plowing through residential backyards before taking off for destinations unknown.

A couple of wealthy investors who are interested in purchasing the rights to Watts's invention arrive at his shop, and (like the spectator of the film) witness in the radioscope perhaps the most telling of the comically uncanny visual gags the film features. Cleverly extending the alternate consumption motif, the gag depicts a driverless vehicle breaking through a farm fence into a pasture. Several famished calves give chase, having evidently mistaken the car for their mother. While trotting along they manage to nurse successfully from a leaking set of teat-like stopcocks extending from the udder-shaped fuel tank. Presenting gas as a viable substitute for milk both humorously diminishes the difference between animals and automobiles and suggests the benefits of appropriating existing technology in unexpected (and in a sense unlawful) ways to satisfy existing needs. The latter notion is especially apt in a motion picture that evokes the virtues for a local community of do-it-yourself science as an effective method of frustrating the greed of agents of corporate capitalism. More generally, the notion is relevant to slapstick film's customary treatment of the Model T; smashing Tin Lizzies to bits for visual entertainment is not exactly what Henry Ford intended when marketing them as well-designed yet low-priced means of engaging in recreational travel.

Silent comedy's subversive style of destructively consuming automobiles is also on full display in an earlier scene in *Super-Hooper-Dyne Lizzies*. Here it is a human organism that functions as the force that moves numerous mechanized vehicles to their eventual doom. Left with the task of getting Winnie's car back to the shop, Hiram begins pushing it slowly from behind, remaining oblivious to the fact that after a few blocks his load has increased seven- or eightfold. Staggering up an incline, he unwittingly knocks the stolen and now wrecked property of others off a ledge into a dirt pit below (the outraged owners arrive at the construction site seconds too late to stop him). If such a comic dismantling obviously cancels the possibility of using the automobile rationally as a servile thing, it does not appear to do so in the name of reinvesting the demolished object with a sacred aura. On the contrary, such amusing imagery gestures toward a collectively empowering embrace of machine technology, as if cinematic modes of affectively charged play might help supply the energy and courage required to precipitate a genuine upheaval in existing social relations.

This is not to say, however, that the cultural intervention Sennett spearheaded was without contradiction. As King explains it in a section of *Fun Factory* titled "'A Peep Behind the Scenes': Rationalization, Irrationality, and the Founding of the Keystone Film Company," the cinematic entrepreneur's tendency to characterize his studio as the site of riotous play, as opposed to hard work, was to a considerable extent a promotional strategy. At the same time (in 1912) that he was declaring his irreverent disdain for "rationalization and efficiency experts," Sennett (at the behest of his financial backers) was taking the advice of and even hiring the kind of specialists in factory-style management that had propelled the rise of capitalist modernity (34–35). Two years later the studio's "publicity apparatus" was still speaking "out against the very tenets of industrial rationalization" that it "had implemented" (37). Moreover, by the mid-1920s Sennett had accrued a personal fortune estimated to be around fifteen million dollars before losing most of it in the stock market crash at the end of the decade (Louvish xi–xii). Such an obvious discrepancy between the studio's ideological orientation and its economic integration into the structures of monopoly capitalism is less a cause for censure than a condition of commentary on slapstick cinema in general as a historical phenomenon.[13]

The Ethics of Destruction in W. C. Williams's *The Great American Novel*

> This loose linking of one thing with another has effects of a destructive power little to be guessed at.
>
> —William Carlos Williams, Prologue to *Kora in Hell*

Trahair's explication of Derrida's reading of Bataille hints at the specifically comic dimension of the sustained act of critical destruction that Williams carries out in *The Great American Novel.* If, as she asserts, "what constitutes the comic is the disruption of discourse" via "the subjection of meaning to a certain nonmeaning" (32–33), then the American writer's over-the-top employment of epistemologically aberrant tropes justifies a definition of his project as a comic one. *The Great American Novel* (cited as *GAN*) is indeed a travesty not just of the novel but also of the quintessentially modernist desire to achieve cognitive control over one's art through linguistically self-consciousness acts of figuration. Williams's literary enterprise is laughable to the extent that none of its metaphors hits the mark, the farcical proliferation of incompatible comparisons cancelling out the possibility of ascertaining exactly what writing is (or words are) like.[14]

The most striking aspect of the text is undoubtedly the exorbitant number of reflexive figurations it employs, which in turn are responsible for the unusual text's remarkable density. In his first foray into prose fiction, Williams generates a disorienting series of tropes, the bulk of which refer to some aspect of language (most frequently either to the materiality of the signifier or to the semantic dimension of words). His oft-cited strictures against the use of figures of speech notwithstanding,[15] Williams's nonsystematic self-consciousness is inextricably bound up with the use of an inordinate number of tropes, the effect of which is a loss of stable meaning and reliable reference to the world.

Registering the degree to which the text repeatedly folds back on itself requires little interpretive subtlety; its critically formalist preoccupations are apparent from start to finish. The novel's third paragraph is one of many cases in point:

> To progress from word to word is to suck a nipple. Imagine saying: My dear, I am thirsty, will you let me have a little milk—This to love at first sight. But who do you think I am, says white goldenrod? Of course there is progress. Of course there are words. Because I am thirsty, one might add. Yes but I love you and besides I have no milk. Oh yes, that is right. I forgot that we were speaking of words. Yet you cannot deny that to have a novel one must have milk. Not at the beginning. Granted, but at the end at least. Yes, yes, at the end. Progress from the mere form to the substance. Yes, yes, in other words: milk. Milk is the answer. (*GAN* 159)

Despite the disconcerting effect of our being positioned as the listener of a dialogue taking place between two unspecified speakers, one of whom appears to be a flower, it is immediately evident that the feeding of a baby serves here as a figure for an ideal relation between reader and text. A biological process, the primary orality required for the healthy growth and development of the child, furnishes a metaphor for the demands the typical novel yearns to gratify: though it may take awhile, the reward for reading is the nourishing attainment of meaning ("milk"). Correlatively, the instinctive hunger, or thirst, of a newborn functions as a trope for the need of the ordinary reader to obtain the life-sustaining content that words (as breasts) purportedly contain.[16] The immediate rejection of the equation is predictable, for it is a restatement of the metaphorical invocations of the mother as source that organized the discursive production of romanticism around a transcendental signified.

Commenting on the epistemological break that allowed for the birth of German poetry, Friedrich Kittler locates the emergence of this new model (or "discourse network") in Goethe, or rather in Faust's initial aspiration to experience the act of reading as the sucking on "'breasts' or 'Wells that sustain all life'—an elementary and infantile form of consumption" (*Discourse*

Networks 7).[17] From this point of view, Williams simply updates the notion that the "[absolute] origin of language" is "maternal gestation" (Kittler, *Discourse Networks* 25) by mingling (in a disorienting fashion) components of an episode in which the protagonist of the novel, a doctor, makes a house call and, after passing by a local power plant along the way, delivers a child. The "high pitched singing tone of the dynamos endlessly spinning" fill "the room where the bed of pain stood with progress. Ow, Ow! Oh help me somebody! said she. UMMMMM sang the dynamo in the next street" (Williams, *GAN* 162). And again a paragraph later, as he is heading home, his thoughts still on the boy's birth, he sees through "great doors [. . .] open to full view of the world," a power house "lighted from the interior" in which "in rows sat the great black machines saying vrummmmmmmmmmmmm. Stately in the great hall they sat and generated electricity. [. . .] Here is progress—here is the substance of words—UMMMMM" (163). Conflating the inner organs of the mother with the electrical generators of an industrial facility offers a machine-age version of the roots of poetry in the voiced yet presignifying sounds or tones emitted by the maternal body. If, in the romantic tradition, the gift of the mother to her children "is language in a nascent state, pure breath as a limit value from which the articulated speech of others begins" (Kittler, *Discourse Networks* 27), here the vibratory hum of the feminized generator as muse, in conjunction with an actual mother's anguished expression of her suffering, is the precondition for the poetic discourse of (male) humanity.[18] Writing accomplishes what the murmuring that issues from the maternal lips cannot, with use of the typewriter (rather than the stylus) facilitating the reproductive transmission of "unembellished accents from the profoundest regions of the soul as clearly as direct speech would sound" (64).

That both the natural and the technological versions of this oral-based model are anachronistic is precisely the point, for the text as a whole is animated by its urge to answer the fundamental questions it poses about writing and reading as graphic practices that do not overlook the power of the letter in favor of speech. This is why, in the seventh paragraph of *The Great American Novel*, Williams had already introduced an architectural metaphor that contests the promise of semantic fullness that the biological analogies had suggested: "There cannot be a novel. There can only be pyramids, pyramids of words, tombs" (160). Here, the structure of the linguistic sign renders the goal of the literary enterprise unattainable; in giving the word concrete shape as a hollowed-out dwelling, as the final resting place of a mummified cadaver, Williams negates the previously conveyed impression that words, like a part of the maternal body, contain a life-sustaining substance. Confusingly, the presumably rejected figure is now reintroduced and oddly conjoined with a new, vehicular trope: "Their warm breasts heave up and down calling for a head to progress toward them, to fly onward, upon a word that was a pumpkin, now a fairy chariot, and all the time the thing was rolling backward to the time when one believes" (160). The latter trope implies that the verbal disillusionment under investigation is a historically conditioned disenchantment. Our faith in the capacity of words to transport us elsewhere is a fairy-tale notion, and our belief in the magical power of words to cast spells cannot survive the brute realization of the empirical facts of spelling. Words are not in truth "indivisible crystals," for they can indeed be "broken" via the disarrangement of their constitutive elements: "Awu tsst grang splith gra pragh og bm" (160). Next, words are compared in an again disorienting fashion to, among other things, the wheels of a moving vehicle and a decaying body buried in the earth. (These reflexive figures seem to have arisen as metonymical derivatives of the previous metaphors.) "Words are the reverse motion. Words are the flesh of yesterday. Words roll, spin, flare up, rumble, trickle, foam—Slowly they lose momentum. Slowly they cease to stir. At last they break up into their letters—Out of them jumps the worm that was—His hairy feet tremble upon them" (160). The collapse of words into their component parts allows for something to leap into view, but exactly what the image of a parasitical animal—a word worm—devouring a rotting corpse stands for in this linguistically self-conscious allegory is not easily ascertained.[19] However, for my purposes translating exactly what the novelist as critic wants to say is less important than registering the figural extravagance of how he says it.

Admittedly, the text's investigation of its own formal properties also takes place straightforwardly as the discursive or literal articulation of more or less axiomatic principles. We are told, for instance, in the second paragraph that the material traits of writing cancel out the possibility of modeling the act of reading on the sensory perception of extratextual reality: "Words are not permanent unless the graphite be scraped up and put in a tube or the ink lifted. Words progress into the ground. One must begin with words if one is to write. But what then of smell?" (158). But such declarations are consistently placed in close proximity to a disparate array of self-referentially oriented images that indirectly comment on the same basic set of issues. Consequentially, the reader cannot help wondering whether the presumably narrative portions of the text are in truth extensions of the reflexive inquiry. For example, the second half of the first chapter (titled "The Fog") appears to be an ordinarily representational episode in which two people depart together in an automobile after having attended a meeting of the Mosquito Extermination Commission. A heavy fog arises, rendering the windshield of the vehicle "opaque," which makes it almost impossible to drive safely. So they pull over and the passenger hands the driver something "like a handkerchief," and the latter proceeds to wipe the glass "on both sides, the top and the bottom pane and then returns "the cloth [. . .] to the owner—who put it back where it came from not seeming to mind that it was wet and dirty. But of course the man is a mechanic in a certain sense and doesn't care" (161).

Even if the (first) readers could not know that Williams would a decade later applaud the "great pleasure" Marianne Moore "gets [. . .] from wiping soiled words" (317), the suspicion still arises that the story proper has not yet begun, that the seemingly realistic depiction may be another metalinguistic passage. Indeed, earlier in the chapter the exasperated writer had conflated the weather conditions, language, sensory perception, and the operation of a motorized vehicle: "Fog of words. The car runs through it. The words take up the smell of the car" (159). With this in mind it is hard not to think that the description of the opacity of the windshield in the later section is meant to function as an acknowledgment of the verbal obstacles hindering either the writer's or the reader's efforts to discern (with eyes or nose) the natural world outside the text, to see or smell through language to reality. (Moreover, chapter 3 opens with an unattributed critical distinction between Williams's work and that of James Joyce: "The difference being [that in the former there is] greater *opacity*, less erudition, reduced power of perception" [167; emphasis mine].[20]) It is as if the author has bifurcated himself into, on the one hand, an artist who is interested in composing an autobiographically inflected novel about his daily activities and, on the other hand, a critic ("a mechanic in a certain sense") who is responsible for keeping in working order the components of the machine on which his creative collaborator must rely to move his project forward. From this point of view, the following account of the final portion of the trip allegorizes the blinding complications that the visually or phenomenologically oriented aspect of the literary enterprise has (and will intermittently continue to) run into: "On the highway they began to encounter fog. It seemed in the rush of the car to come and meet them. It came suddenly, with a rush and in a moment nothing could be seen but the white billows of water crossed in front by the flares of the headlights. And so it went all the way home, sometimes clearer, sometimes so thick he had to stop"(161).

Discerning the status of the fog here is not easy. It may signal the clouding over of a previously transparent discourse. Alternately, it may connote the misty or mystified state of mind of a naïve reader whose tendency it is to mistake linguistic reference for extratextual reality and who wishes to ignore the empirical fact of inscription in favor of the imaginary world the text purports to depict. Either way, whenever the image of fog reappears, it does so at the expense of the demand for illusory realism that generic expectations would dictate the novels seek to satisfy.

Williams's related reservation about the capacity of his critical labors to accomplish the task he has set for himself—to release words from the referential or semantic burdens others have imposed on them—is evident in the prematurity of the narrator's declaration in the text of literary success. At the end of chapter 2 the speaker announces that he has "understood the fog" and that, correlatively, after "long practice [the words] had come to be leaves, trees, the corners of his house" (167). Because he has done what seemed impossible, he can now be "alone in the air with the words of his brain" and is free to breathe "the pure mountain air of joy." "Everything had been removed that other men had tied to the words to secure them to themselves. Clean, clean he had taken each word and made it new" (167). The triumphant claim that he has invested words with the ontological status of natural entities, real or actual things in the world, and that in so doing he has "added a new chapter to the art of writing," is ironically undermined by its position near the beginning rather than the end of the text.

Rather than attempt to survey the range of tropes that Williams draws on in *The Great American Novel* to reflect critically on his novelistic undertaking, I concentrate my commentary on the most puzzling yet consistently thought-provoking of the many reflexive figurations incorporated into the text: driving an automobile. As we will see below, one interesting point about the use of this rhetorical motif, considering writing as a system of transportation, is that it enables Williams to broaden the horizon of his critical reflexivity to encompass the mechanized tool upon which he will increasingly come to rely at this stage of his career: the typewriter.

Chapter 3 of *The Great American Novel* begins with a conversation on the central importance of invention in literary composition (as epitomized by Joyce). The narrator suddenly detours away from this exchange to provide a short account of an unidentified driver's skillful ability to pull his motorized vehicle into his garage without causing any damage. After having started the chapter by setting up a dialogue in which he is probably both of the interlocutors, the would-be novelist henceforth issues a challenge to himself to show his "originality": "NOW let me see what you can do with your vaunted pen" (168). His immediate response is to declare once again "that literature is a matter of words," that Joyce's "vaunted invention is a fragile fog," that "his method escapes him," and that the Irish author's most "important service" to the aspiring American was to have "in a great measure destroyed what is known as 'literature'" (169). It is in the midst of this critical digression that Williams inserts two curious paragraphs on the completion of a nighttime drive:

> At that the car jumped forward like a live thing. Up the steep board incline into the garage it leaped—as well as a thing on four wheels could leap—But with great dexterity he threw out the clutch with a slight pressure of his left foot, just as the fore end of the car was about to careen against a mass of old window screens at the garage end. Then pressing with his right foot and grasping the handbrake he brought the machine to a halt—just in time—though it was no trick to him, he having done it so often for the past ten years. (169)

That the driver has been training himself physiologically to habituate his limbs to the demands of the machine for a decade is suggestive given that *The Tempers*, the first volume of Williams's poetry that he deemed worthy of being included in his collected works, appeared in print in 1913. Such a parallel is admittedly insufficient to support the notion that the riding machine is a writing machine, that the description of "the familiar gesture of a motorist in the modest act of shifting gears" is an authorial expression of the pride he takes in having attained the tactile dexterity that effective use of his equipment demands.[21] However, in the foreword to his autobiography Williams did testify to the role the timesaving device played in his therapeutically oriented way of handling his hectic everyday existence. Recalling that he kept a typewriter in his office desk, and that he could hide it whenever a patient arrived at the door, he explains that he "developed a technique" so that when "something growing inside [. . .] demanded reaping," he would bring out the machine and "bang out ten or twelve pages. In fact, I couldn't rest until I had freed my mind from the obsessions which had been tormenting me all day" (n.p.). Moreover, Williams's biographer, Paul Mariani, mentions the furious pace at which the writer typed while putting *The Great American Novel* together in the early 1920s, and Neil Baldwin reports that around 1930 "he [Williams] built a hideaway in the attic [. . . and] when he really got moving on a poem or a story, he banged his foot on the floorboards in time to the staccato rhythm of the typewriter keys, [. . . his sons] knew to keep their distance. The house trembled with their father's nervous energy" (quoted in Mariani 188).[22] Significantly, just before the scene in question ends, the narrator attributes to "the trusty mechanism" the capacity to generate in verse form a reflexive variation on a traditional nursery rhyme. The lights of the car "flare intimately against the wooden wall as much to say" that "good poetry [is] made [. . .] / Of rats and snails and puppy-dog's tails" whereas "bad poetry [is] made of everything nice" (Williams, *GAN* 169). As the anthropomorphized vehicle's owner then shuts it off ("The engine sighed and stopped at the twist of the key governing the electric switch"), leaving the "idle car behind him to its own thoughts" (170), one suspects we have just caught a glimpse, under figurative cover, of the domestic component of Williams's means of literary production. Appropriately, after further discussion of the state of contemporary writing, the chapter ends with the speaker's acceptance of the fact that his pursuit of his aesthetic goal may have a destructive outcome resembling an automobile wreck: "To me it [beauty . . .] is discovery, a race on the ground. / And for this," his interlocutor replies, "you are willing to smash—/ Yes, everything" (171). (The presence of the keyboard also rises to the surface in "Novelette" [1932]: "This is the alphabet qwertyuiopasdfghjklzxcvbnm. The extraordinary thing is that no one has yet taken the trouble to write it out fully." Later, the narrator tellingly links two seemingly disparate sounds: "The click of the keys. The squeal of the car on the hill" [Williams, *Imaginations* 282, 300].)

For Kittler, it is the conjoined impact of the invention of the three major technical media—the phonograph, film, and the typewriter—that set the stage for the rise after 1900 of "a high literature" in which "'the word' becomes something 'too conspicuous,' that is, it becomes a purely differential signifier" (Kittler, *Discourse Networks* 248). He then cites an argument made by Hugo von Hofmannsthal at the turn of the century that anticipates the critical perspective Williams insisted upon throughout the 1920s. Dismissing, as Kittler puts it, "the basic concepts of classical-romantic Poetry" as "so much blabla in relation to the material of the word," Hofmannsthal wonders "whether all the tiresome jabbering about individuality, style, character, mood, and so on has not made you lose sight of the fact that the material of poetry is words.[. . .] We should be allowed to be artists who work with words" (249). Given the importance of pedagogical reform in Kittler's inquiry, it is fitting that Williams's most emphatic and unequivocal definitions of literature as a matter of words appear in *The Embodiment of Knowledge* (1928–1930), the educational tract he dedicated to his sons. Especially informative is the section titled "Modern Primer," where he credits Gertrude Stein and James Joyce and before them Lewis Carroll with having demonstrated that "words are real and are realized to be the material of letters" and that "false reliance on emotion and idea" must continue to "be whittled away." "The province of letters," therefore, "is that realm of the intelligence in which words and their configurations are real and all ideas and facts with which they deal are secondary. It is the complement of all other realms of the intelligence which use language as secondary to the reality of their own materials—such as science, philosophy, history, religion, the legislative field. Hence in letters the prevalence of fiction and the predominance of poetry" (18–20).

Structured, as so much of the text is, as a jagged montage, chapter 4 of *The Great American Novel* juxtaposes passages of linguistic criticism against a peculiar vignette in which a small automobile expresses an eroticized attraction to a large truck. The (metonymical) contiguity of the two motifs also allows the fiction involving machine love to be taken as a metaphorical articulation of the novelist's politicized endorsement of American literature on the grounds that its experimentation opposes more traditional, reactionary defenses of narrative conventions. That the "conscious desire" surging in the breast of the little "runabout" as it rolls "with fluttering heart" by the massive vehicle is invested with such reflexive significance is not immediately evident, yet the oddness of the personification encourages the reader to presume that something more than literal description is at stake in the feminized Ford's "secret hope" that "somehow he would notice—HE, the great truck [. . .] would come to her" (171). The subsequent inclusion of remarks on the current state of the novel, attributed to H. G. Wells, retroactively hints at the meaning of the tiny mechanism's wish for recognition from the gigantic one. (Wells, we are told, has rebuked, in imperialist terms, the impulse toward generic innovation as an offense against thematic integrity: "No new form of the novel required. Lack of substance always takes the form of novelty mongering. Empire must be saved!" [172].) The tone of mockery confirms Williams's hostility to the defensively antiformalist stance he quotes, but the effect of his restating it in such close proximity to the impassioned car-truck affair is that "the great machine," which we are informed has "Standard Motor Gasoline" written "in capital letters" on its side, becomes associated with Wells insofar as he is inclined toward the maintenance of both traditional literary standards and historically established forms of political domination. He is, in sum, "FULL of gas," and the admiration of the "little dusty car" at the sight of this emissary of power (corporate and political) must be resisted, the appeal to a relative unknown of conforming to an ostensibly superior generic model notwithstanding. In other words, the American writer has seized on the two differently sized vehicles to work through—in gendered fashion—his ambivalence toward stiflingly proprietary approaches to the novel. It is hardly surprising that the womanly car suppresses her longing and heads off without acknowledgment from the paternalistic Other. "Puh, puh, puh, puh! Said the little car going up the hill. But the great green and red truck said nothing but continued to discharge its gasoline into a tank buried in the ground near the gutter" (173). In contrast to Wells and his conservative ilk, who seek to store large amounts of fuel for future use, Williams persistently expends his smaller supply of energy, with the stuttering of the automobile's combustible engine as it struggles to get somewhere emerging in this light as a trope for his strenuously mechanized attempt to generate something new, to make innovative poetry or prose out of initially insignificant syllables like "puh."[23]

As most interpreters of *The Great American Novel* have noted, in the latter portions of the book Williams introduces collage into his repertoire of unconventional compositional strategies. It is as if an intense preoccupation with the critical purification or renewal of words has given rise to its dialectical antithesis. Out of a minimalist attentiveness to the basic particles of writing, a more encyclopedic ambition to compile old documents has emerged. The latter procedure is reflexively figured in the text on at least two occasions: first, in the description interpolated into chapter 13 of how Native Americans of the Southwest weave their blankets by unraveling found fabrics and then twisting together the loose strands to fashion a different artifact; and, second, in the account inserted in the final chapter of how shrewd yet unscrupulous rag merchants make "shoddy" clothing by recycling the wool from previously worn items. Commentators have noticed as well that the rhetorical transition in question is anticipated in the first chapter of the novel when the "hero" becomes enraged upon realizing that his spouse "has penetrated his mystery." While the two are in bed and she is reading an article in *Vanity Fair* to him, she suddenly stops, informing him that he can't fool her, that she has discerned that "he was stealing in order to write words" (161). His secret is out now: the would-be liberator of words has been chained all along to the discursive past. The modernist who placed his faith in the promise of creative originality must resign himself to the status of an archivist or copier, whose labors remain dependent on the work of anonymous others. All he can do now is move or transport extracts from one textual site to another.[24]

But this is not necessarily a disempowering situation for the progressively oriented artist. As the "Newsreel" sections of John Dos Passos's *USA* would effectively demonstrate in the next decade (as would Muriel Rukeyser in *The Book of the Dead* [1938]), collage techniques have had the potential to function as a means of making subversive interventions into existing discursive environments. His inventive "device" showed how one may seize on the detritus of mass culture and the news media to instill in readers the skepticism required to resist the coercive force of industrially distributed information. And the importance of the trilogy for William Burroughs's widely influential cut-up method is a well-established fact of literary history.[25] One of the finest evocations of the political promise of such a formal innovation appears in Clancy Sigal's little-known but compelling 1962 novel, *Going Away*. Toward the end of the fictive memoir, the autobiographical protagonist takes a job cleaning 16-mm film for a company that syndicates and distributes the prints to television stations. One day he discovers how to engage in a glorious act of cultural sabotage: "I then cut through the film with my razor blade, took up two feet of film, cut through again, cemented the ends, dropped two feet of amputated film into a trash bin at my side, and rolled on." The narrator ecstatically contemplates the disturbed reaction of "the Late-Late-Viewers as they bumped and jolted through a more than normally incomprehensible story." This vision brings tears of joy to his eyes, even though he acknowledges that to us, the reader, his tactic of mutilation "may sound vicious, or hostile, childish even. Such is the fate that awaits all great seminal actions of a revolutionary character" (482–83). From this day forward, the protagonist's job—bolstered theoretically by his pseudo-scholarly speculations on "the Possible Merits of Cultural Luddism in the Twentieth Century"—becomes genuinely meaningful to him; correlatively, in the late 1950s the countercultural deployment of collage emerged as a crucial feature in the work of several protest-oriented underground filmmakers. VanDerBeek, Bruce Conner, and Ken Jacobs are the most distinguished comic exemplars of this tradition, with the latter's lengthy (and only recently completed) *Star Spangled to Death* a particularly stunning achievement in the field of cinematic radicalism. Crucially, collage as a method presupposes the initial loss of meaning that was at the center of Williams's critical poetics in the 1920s. The negation of semantic or referential certainty, the detachment of words from things and ideas, the elimination of the signified from the signifier, is the sine qua non of the kind of ironic juxtapositions that have flourished in leftist film and literature throughout the twentieth century.

From this perspective *The Great American Novel*, especially at its most satirically focused, merits recognition as one of the lesser-known precursors of a once vibrant tradition of countercultural dissent. The best case in point of this is the novel's penultimate chapter, which ironizes the persuasive force of narrative paradigms that are ideologically complicit with the dictates of capitalist modernity. The chapter starts with a series of quoted stories about "successful immigrants" whose triumphant careers are said to "read like romances" (220–21). The tales of those "whose names are linked with the great strides in science, commerce, finance and industry" are claimed as "living proof that America, besides breeding great men, imports them" (221). The sarcasm is impossible to miss here, as is Williams's palpable loathing for the type of myth of economic gain that one associates with Horatio Alger (and that would be subsequently savaged by Williams's friend Nathanael West in *A Cool Million,* Henry Miller in *Tropic of Capricorn,* and Hunter S. Thompson in *Fear and Loathing in Las Vegas.*) Next, Williams inserts a self-aggrandizing advertisement issued by the editor of the *Atlantic Monthly.* Here he both mimics and mocks the selective labors of the magazine functionary, who claims to find on his desk a mass of materials that make it "one of the most interesting spots in America." The wide assortment of article submissions from which he is free to choose are said to contain "all the qualities" that powerfully affect people—"joy, sorrow, romance, ambition, experience" (221–22). "Radiating from every nook and corner of the world," these thrilling items inevitably arrive at the central location his office desk constitutes, and individuals who "think of life as the supreme adventure" should therefore subscribe to the journal. Next in the metonymic display is a New Jersey railway company's letter to its patrons (and to the Board of Public Utility Commissioners) defending its decision to raise its rates, followed by a department-store catalog hawking its merchandise as good Christmas gifts (222–23). Taken together, the excerpted materials convey an authorial hostility not merely toward enterprises predicated on making a profit but also toward the myriad discourses that sustain modern commerce by seeking either to bilk customers or seduce buyers.

Collage, however, is only part of the solution to the problem of how to fashion a cultural practice that is capable of performing tasks of social importance. Immoderate modes of festive play, in which desires are dissipated and energy expended without limits, are another. Thus, it is proclaimed in chapter 12 (with an allusion to Vachel Lindsay) that what America requires "to save her soul" is "flamboyance," and the "strange and often uncatalogued ways" the country "tries to satisfy this need" include spectacular amusements such as the circus, jazz, the Follies, and various film genres. With feigned dismay the speaker declares that people go "*en masse*" to watch trapeze performers, clowns, and animals under the big top and to see women tastelessly dressed "in orange and green gown[s] and war-paint of rouge" cavort on stage (200). "Even the movies, devoid as they are of color in the physical sense, are gaudy, in the imaginations of the people who watch them; gaudy with exaggerated romance, exaggerated comedy, exaggerated splendor of grotesqueness or passion" (200). The impassioned adornment of an otherwise drab world is an existential necessity, and the public's demand that "splendor," "beauty and infinite depth" be added to life must not be denied. Vivacious forms of communal fun are in turn the expression of a faith that there is a surplus of energy available to meet this demand: flamboyance "is a shout of delight, a declaration of richness. It is at least the beginning of art" (201).

Conversely, the end of art is epitomized by the pursuit of knowledge about the scandalous behavior of overstimulated young people. The sardonic insertion into the text of a lengthy promotional review of *Flaming Youth*, a contemporaneous best seller by Warner Fabian (the pen name for Samuel Hopkins Adams), condemns the mind-set behind "scientific" investigations of collective revelry. Endorsing the fiction as the product of research into facts that will reveal the "truth" about the super-flapper, the review encourages readers to take the book as a psychological portrait that will bring about "a gradual return to sanity" (201). Its dramatization of female licentiousness is intended to function as a cautionary tale, one that in rendering a case of emotional frenzy in comprehensible form makes it possible for others to overcome such an impassioned condition. The contiguity of an advertisement for a medical compound to the review doubles the irony while reiterating the main point. Endorsed as "the most efficient agent for the treatment of local inflammation," DIONAL, when "applied locally over the affected areas," is said to act "promptly, with prolonged effect." *Flaming Youth* is thus implicitly figured by the sarcastic author of *The Great American Novel* as a "Drugless," "Non-irritant," "Non-toxic," remedy designed for those who are otherwise subject to states of hysterical excess.

How, then, to compose a novel that would forego cognition in order to affect readers as powerfully as do native forms of collective entertainment, but without abdicating the ethical responsibility of the socially conscious artist to improve the conditions of existence of the masses? How might one invigorate rather than pacify readers while maintaining an interest in urgent political matters? This is the burden of Dos Passos's *Manhattan Transfer* (1925), an episodic novel that decisively rejects the narrative tradition of realist illusionism. Moreover, for inspiration in constructing what he envisioned as an ideologically compelling spectacle, the increasingly radicalized modernist carried literature closer than it previously had been to the kind of high-energy public attractions that would also serve as a resource for slapstick filmmakers and performers through the 1920s.[26]

2

The Politics and Poetics of Attraction I

Dos Passos

What also stimulated his cogitations?
[. . .] the infinite possibilities hitherto unexploited
of the modern art of advertisement [. . .] of magnetizing
efficacy to arrest involuntary attention, to interest,
to convince, to decide.

—James Joyce, *Ulysses*

In a recent reading of Alfred Doblin's *Berlin Alexanderplatz* (1929), Stefanie Harris invokes Sergei Eisenstein's ideas on cinematographic montage in order to frame his work as an example of a "Literature of Attractions." In so doing she carries us to the threshold of a critical breakthrough in our understanding of a particular strain of modernist prose in this era as the product of a sequence of authorial investments in sensationalist forms of mass entertainment. However, Harris fails to take full advantage of her insight when she goes on to argue that Doblin's innovations served primarily to generate alternate ways of *representing* the modern metropolis. For her, Eisenstein's "cinema style" jettisoned traditional narration in the hope of "recording" everyday life in the city with greater visual immediacy. Harris's account of John Dos Passos's technique in *Manhattan Transfer*—one of the pivotal novels in the historical development of a slapstick modernism—adheres to this same circumscribed outlook; there she describes his project as an experimental effort to match the new, nonprint media's ability to store the rapid flow of perceptual data or capture the wealth of information circulating in a difficult to comprehend environment (Harris 95–147). What Harris's model of the literary text as a recording apparatus downplays (without ignoring entirely) is the degree to which the Russian director's and the American writer's respective turns in the early 1920s toward the realm of fairground amusement and theatrical spectacles (the cultural matrix from which silent screen comedy also sprang[1]) were comparably motivated by a desire to make affectively forceful interventions in the world. Eisenstein and Dos Passos alike sought to increase the aesthetic intensity and ideological persuasiveness of their art by appealing to performance-based methods of formal arrangement, thereby demonstrating "enough flexibility to use the tools that [. . . were] being discarded by dying circuses and vaudeville shows" (Dos Passos, *Major Nonfictional Prose* 120).

Eisenstein and Dos Passos: Theater, Cinema, and Literature

> Imitation is the way to mastery [. . .] But imitation of what?
> —Sergei Eisenstein, "Imitation as Mastery"

In his chapter on "Eisenstein's Aesthetics" in *Signs and Meaning in the Cinema*, Peter Wollen attributes the growing importance of the notion of shock in the director's thinking to his increasing interest in physiologically based models of reflexology. Strongly influenced in the 1920s by Ivan Pavlov's scientific research into methods of behavioral manipulation, Sergei Eisenstein turned away from his preceding theoretical (and theatrical) investment in the category of attraction: "As the idea of montage developed in his mind, he tended to replace the idea of attractions by that of stimuli, or shocks" (quoted in Wollen, *Signs and Meaning* 36).[2] Wollen considers this change of critical focus a reductive capitulation to the demands of political agitation or ideological provocation. Eisenstein in a sense agreed at the start of his filmmaking career to put on hold his enduring fascination with volatile states of ecstasy in which sexual pathology and religious passion commingle in order to participate in the misguided project of refining new techniques aimed at controlling the cinematic spectator's reactions. From this point of view, shock appears to be an aesthetically impoverished model in relation to his original, more promisingly "idiosyncratic approach to the emotional structure of works of art" (36), one in which a "'gesture [is] expanded into gymnastics.'" Initially dreaming of an art of somatically conveyed feelings, of corporeally communicated affects, Eisenstein's first goal was to create "'such emotional saturation that the wrath of a man would be expressed in a backward somersault from a trapeze'" (36).[3]

Although Wollen does not mention Walter Benjamin in his study, it is reasonable to suppose that the former had the latter's Depression-era investigations in mind when criticizing aesthetic procedures predicated on the possibility of producing shocking effects. The "Work of Art" would be particularly problematic for Wollen, given that the essay sets forth a quasi-scientific agenda for contemporary uses of the cinematic apparatus.[4] Yet I prefer to leave to the side any polemical insistence on the category of attraction as being somehow superior to that of shock in order to situate Eisenstein's and Benjamin's theoretical formulations as distinctive yet comparable attempts to delineate the (socially) functional potential of the new cultural medium. As Benjamin bluntly states in section 6 of (the first version of) the "Work of Art," the "exclusive emphasis" now placed on the "exhibition value" of artworks has established them as constructs "with quite new functions. Among these, the one we are conscious of—the 'artistic function'—may subsequently be seen as rudimentary. This much is certain: today, film is the most serviceable vehicle of this understanding. Certain, as well, is the fact that the historical scope of this functional transformation of art—which appears most advanced in film—allows for the methodological as well as the material confrontation with the primeval era of art" (18). The historical emergence of film is thus the precondition for anthropological insights into the purposefulness that has structured art since its inception in prehistory.

As a logical correlative to their shared privileging of social function in their critical thinking about artistic practice, both Eisenstein and Benjamin explored the virtues of film as a means for people to acquire the habitual skills that are necessary for survival in the world. For both men, art retained the potential to serve as a means of teaching collective entities how to adapt to the pressures of everyday life in their environment. As Eisenstein put it in the 1924 version of "The Montage of Film Attractions," film, as a "spectacle," was one of the "effective arts," and its primary function as an "agitational" force was to prepare individuals for the tasks vital to their existence. If motion pictures were a contemporary version of primitive magical practices, modern filmmakers were like the "sorcerers" of antiquity, their labors "directed much less toward the figurative tendencies ('for what purpose?') than towards the very precise training" of the present-day analogues "of the hunting and fighting instincts of the primitive audience." What merited further research, then, was the overall impact of performance on viewers, for it was out of such study that a "pure method of training the reflexes" would arise. The primary goal of the director was to refine the "imitative skill" of the spectator, and this ambition required that his work attain "the maximum emotional effect on the audience" (quoted in Taylor, *Eisenstein Reader* 44). The representational elements a given work of art might contain were simply the component parts of a pedagogical enterprise, one governed by the imperative of instructing the members of the audience as to how they might best contribute to the maintenance and well-being of the community.

Mimesis plays a key part in this process, yet not in the sense that the work of art or theatrical performance seeks to copy or imitate a preexisting reality; rather, (corporeal) mimesis occurs at the locus of reception; the viewing subject learns how to do things somatically by observing the impassioned movements of others, whether these appear to him in the form of images on the screen or in actuality. Jacques Rancière explains Eisenstein's achievement by reminding us that mimesis "is two things": (1) "the psychic and social power through which a word, a behavior, or an image prompts its analogue" and (2) "the particular regime of art that embeds this very power in the law of genres, the construction of stories, and the representation of characters acting and expressing their sentiments." Eisenstein's burden was therefore "to transform the powers of *mimesis* into a power of thought capable of producing, directly and within a specific mode of sensorialization, the effects that mimetic art had until then entrusted to the episodes of the stories and the audience's identification with the characters. This meant replacing the traditional effects achieved by identification with the story and the characters by the direct identification with the affects programmed by the artist." In sum, Eisenstein had "to wrench the psychic and social powers of *mimesis* from the mimetic regime of art" (Rancière 23–24; emphasis in the original).

Notably, in his early attempts to define the specificity of his innovative approach, Eisenstein looked to popular amusements in general and silent comedy in particular for guidance. In a 1923 essay titled "The Montage of Attractions," the director cites Chaplin's impact on his audience as an example of the confusion between psychological admiration and erotic appeal (or "charm") that film spectators frequently experience: "The lyrical effect of a whole series of Chaplin scenes is inseparable from the attractional quality of the specific mechanics of his movements" (30.) A year later (in the "Montage of Film Attractions"), the director again turns to the work of the silent comedian, this time to illustrate the comic tactic of interfering with a previously developed chain of associations. Thus Eisenstein describes a scene in which Chaplin devotes a great deal of footage to the seemingly complicated, laborious process of opening the lock of a safe, only to then incongruously bring to light its valueless contents; the point is that what looked like a desperate attempt to obtain a precious object turns out to be a simple act of cleaning the strongbox (37). Elsewhere in the same article Eisenstein locates "the American comedy film" as a formal inspiration for the future construction of "attractional schemas." Slapstick movies "provide inexhaustible materials for the study of [. . .] methods" because they utilize montage strategies deliberately, in contrast to the bulk of Russian motion pictures, which only "in fumbling fashion hit on successful combinations" (39–40).[5]

Eisenstein's film theory (and practice) may be understood as a politicized and rationalized version of the models of affective transmission that frequently informed late nineteenth-century entertainment practices. In *Why the French Love Jerry Lewis: From Cabaret to Early Cinema*, Rae Beth Gordon references the sociological work of Gabriel de Tarde (*Laws of Imitation*), as well as the psychophysical experimentation of Gustav Fechner, Charles Féré, and Charles Henry, to explain the development in the period of a physiological aesthetics premised on the notion that the feelings a given artist has in mind may be transferred to the spectator by way of involuntary acts of bodily mimicry. It was assumed that particular emotions could be ascribed to specific somatic poses or gestures, and that automatically copying the latter would convey the reverberations of affect from imitator to spectator: "Contagion" was thought to occur "through the transmission of the electric shock or 'jolts' (*secousses*) from performer to spectator" (7–12, 46).[6] Gordon also comments on the medical profession's faddish interest at the time on the magnetizer's capacity to transfix people. The apparent capacity of such showmen to exercise their will to manipulate members of the crowd (via the hypnotic casting of spells or simple use of their powers of suggestion) appeared to stem from the "fact" that they possessed a "superabundance of the magnetic fluid [which] spreads into his surroundings and penetrates people" (31). Gordon also points to Jean Epstein's pertinent assertions in "Magnification" (1921) that "the director suggests, then persuades, then hypnotizes. The film is nothing but a relay between the source of nervous energy and the auditorium which breathes its radiance. That is why the gestures which work best on screen are nervous gestures. [. . .] Chaplin has created the overwrought hero. His entire performance consists of the reflex actions of a nervous, tired person" (Epstein 238).[7]

This chapter proposes that Eisenstein's theatrical/cinematic concept of "the montage of attractions" illuminates Dos Passos's contemporaneous literary practice.[8] The Russian filmmaker's critical idea brings to light, I argue, both the formal procedures and the functional aspirations underlying the novelist's first major achievement: *Manhattan Transfer*. Admittedly, the association of Eisenstein and Dos Passos has become a cliché of cultural history, yet the repeated and often unproductive invocations of their affinities contain a kernel of profundity. One of the limitations of past commentary on this topic is its neglect of the question of "attractions" and correlative privileging of "montage" as such. This typically results in banal reflections on Dos Passos's cinematic multiplication of points of view, his use of "cross-cutting" techniques to weave various plot lines together, and his application of other film methods. Such critical perspectives almost without exception presuppose that representational accuracy remains the novelist's primary goal. Consequently, his juxtapositional strategies are grasped (incorrectly) as the means to a quasi-documentary end: the precise recording of objective reality. What gets overlooked is the most crucial aspect of his method: the radicalized writer's desire to forcefully affect his readers.[9] In truth, the rationale underlying Dos Passos's rhetorical innovation rests on the conviction that montage tactics can persuade readers to adopt a hostile attitude toward the environment they inhabit. The reason he arranges his text in unusual fashion is to generate feelings of emotional as well as intellectual repulsion, to make his audience disgusted at the quality of existence in urban modernity. The motive governing Dos Passos's carefully planned organization of myriad impressions or images of everyday life in the city was to strike readers initially at the level of their feelings, to cause them to react powerfully to the taken-for-granted fact that in a capitalist society people are expected to pursue wealth and are normally judged in accordance with how much money they have accumulated. Like Eisenstein, who reduced each shot to "its greatest tonal intensity in order to heighten the language of contrast," Dos Passos puts his disparate scenes together to shock his readers into an ultimately intellectual awareness of their economically determined degradation (Jameson, "Existence of Italy" 212).[10]

Tom Gunning's seminal essay, "The Cinema of Attractions: Early Film, Its Spectator, and the Avant-Garde" (1986), has made the notion of a "Coney Island of the avant-garde,—whose never dominant but always sensed current can be traced from Méliès through Keaton, through *Un Chien andalou* (1928) and Jack Smith"—readily available to cultural historians (61).[11] The essay also helps lead to a 180-degree shift in analytic approaches to the status of the image. By focusing on the exhibitionist appeal of turn-of-the-century cinema—its showman-like penchant for putting things on display—Gunning alerts us to the fact that images are as much active forces in the world as they are reflective duplications of a preexisting reality. In underscoring the willingness of filmmakers before 1906 to confront their viewers directly, Gunning recognizes the importance of exploring further the position of the spectator in cinematic relations. Asserting that turn-of-the-century materials aimed to generate sensory excitement and corporeal thrills reroutes critical attention, shifting it away from absorbing, verisimilar narrative fictions and dramatically expressive modes of characterization toward the nature of early film's address to its audience. Despite the numerous insights that Gunning's continuing work in this field has produced, it remains important to note that applications of his aesthetic model usually set to the side questions pertaining to the functional imperatives of cultural practices.

This tendency is already evident in Gunning's concentration on the erotic stimulus of early film materials. Making the partially disrobed female body the focal point of the spectator's interest implicitly links the cinematic attraction to a sensationalist form of theatrical fun—burlesque—as if the primary purpose of the performance were to sexually arouse the members of the audience. Early film actresses are thus positioned as striptease artists.[12] By concentrating on the libidinal appeal of early film's techniques of display, Gunning allows the functional agenda informing Eisenstein's appropriation of the formal technique to disappear. He does register the specificity of Eisenstein's "avant-garde" enterprise as an attempt to organize "popular energy for radical purposes" (60), but in restricting himself to the poetics and pleasures of mass entertainment Gunning misses an opportunity to deepen our understanding of how modernist cultural practice between the wars sought to mobilize the heritage of the fairground and the amusement park for politically purposeful ends. Hence the need to return to Eisenstein's critical work in the 1920s.

It was in 1923, while still involved in dramatic projects, that Eisenstein published in the journal *Lef* the aforementioned theatrical manifesto "The Montage of Attractions."[13] Its bold opening statement emphasizes that "the moulding of the audience in a desired direction (or mood) is the task of every utilitarian theatre (agitation, advertising, health education, etc.)." As an ideological apparatus, the cultural institution participates in a shaping process, and the "quality" it has in common with other such instruments of persuasion is the "*attraction*," which may be defined as "any aggressive moment in theatre, i.e. any element of it that subjects the audience to emotional or psychological influence, verified by experience and mathematically calculated to produce specific emotional shocks in the spectator in their proper order within the whole" (30; emphasis in the original). He then goes on to argue that the current theater should be primarily concerned with putting together an "effective show," thereby dismissing the accepted notion that directors should either strive to stay true to an authorial subjectivity or to picture the objective world accurately (31). Released from the burden of "'revealing the playwright's purpose" or of "'faithfully reflecting an epoch'"

(31), directors may look instead to the "music-hall/circus programme" for formal models as they strive to systematically organize a series of attention-grabbing performances. The traditional artistic pursuit of realistic illusions must be drastically curtailed, if not eliminated entirely. If one chooses to use conventional plot or story episodes, these should be inscribed into the textual whole via montage. Correlatively, the creation of lifelike characters who are capable of soliciting identification (or loathing) ceases to be privileged as the best way to maintain spectator involvement. Positioning the latter instead as the target of a violent assault, Eisenstein declares that directors must seek to deliver powerful blows, that they should take aim and try to strike the audience as powerfully as possible.

Even when the project requires the reconstruction of historical events in veracious fashion, the goal remains to impact the viewer as intensely as possible. As Eisenstein explained in "The Problem of the Materialist Approach to Form" (1925) in regard to his just-released motion picture *Strike*, the principal task of the filmmaker when depicting a previous act of collective protest is to devise a formal way of arranging the images so that they hit the spectating masses viscerally as well as mentally. The central concern for the revolutionary artist is to invent an approach that produces "the maximum intensification of the emotional seizure of the audience" (56). Cinematically induced modes of sensory perception must be profoundly shocking experiences that do affective justice to the collective uprisings they depict. In his polemical denunciation of the *Cine-Eye* (or *Kino Eye*; a six-reel film directed by Dziga Vertov and released in 1924 that sought to capture "life caught unawares") that follows soon after this statement, Eisenstein faults Vertov for failing to embrace such a brutally forceful "*utilitarian application*" (56; emphasis in the original) of art. Eisenstein accuses his rival's montage method of employing painterly tactics in too contemplative a manner; because Vertov randomly pieces together "*a set of montage fragments of real life*," Eisenstein judges him to be a "primitive Impressionist" (56; emphasis in the original). Vertov's mistake is to select images of things that delight him; what he should do instead is take his audience into consideration and make his choices on the basis of what will successfully "plough its psyche" (57). *Strike* thus demonstrates how to snatch "fragments from our surroundings *according to a conscious and predetermined plan calculated to launch them at the audience in the appropriate combination, to subjugate it to the appropriate association with the obvious ideological motivation*" (57; emphasis in the original). In conclusion, Eisenstein expresses his commitment to the controlled use of optically induced violence as a way to generate prescribed states of mind.

His slogan that a "Cine-Fist" is preferable to a Cine-Eye is one case in point, but more astonishing is the next trope he offers to express the effect he wants revolutionary films to have: "Soviet cinema must cut through to the skull" (59). More extreme than Walter Benjamin's well-known surgical analogy in "Work of Art," Eisenstein's conflation of doctorial and directorial operations conveys his desire to penetrate the psychic depths of his audience, to touch the emotional and intellectual core of its being.

Eisenstein justifies his artistic effort to managerially control the reactions of the spectator as a means of participating in the collective enterprise of building a new society. Progressive political commitments demanded that he seek to rationalize the process of jolting spectators via a planned series of stimuli. Not only did the two artistic practices (theater and film) have "a common (identical) basic material," but they also shared the same overall purpose: to influence "*this audience in the desired direction* through a series of calculated pressures on its psyche" ("Montage of Film Attractions" 35; emphasis in the original). Since the agitational task of either a utilitarian theater or a cinema of action was to mold the masses, it was imperative to invent an aesthetic that could subject the latter to often painfully intense feelings. To legitimate such a semi-torturous cultural endeavor, the director maintained the stance that his artistic procedures were designed to solidify and thereby strengthen an emergent social class. Selecting his addressee in advance, Eisenstein envisioned his undertaking as functioning in strict accordance with the goals of the Soviet Republic, where the audience was homogeneous and known (36, 52).

That Dos Passos shared many of Eisenstein's formal and functional aspirations (though his modified goal was to encourage collective dissent against the profit motive in the United States) is evident in the American writer's 1925 review of the production of his friend John Howard Lawson's new "jazz play." Though Dos Passos's occasional piece does not pursue the issues with the same theoretical rigor as do Eisenstein's early critical essays, the affinities between the two modernist artists at the level of motive and method is unmistakable. Published in *Vanity Fair*, Dos Passos's article, "Is the 'Realistic' Theatre Obsolete? Many Theatrical Conventions Have Been Shattered by Lawson's *Processional*," stakes out an anti-illusionist stance with regard to dramatic practices. Acknowledging that from an evolutionary point of view on cultural history, the stage has reached the brink of extinction, Dos Passos nevertheless praises it as "among the last survivors of what might be called the arts of direct contact" (75). Although in its current state the theater is not fit to compete with "the movies and radio and subsequent mechanical means of broadcasting entertainment and propaganda," there is a slight chance that it can regain its social vigor if it can figure out what it has to offer of value to its urban audience. In a profoundly sped-up environment, in a "century that has to snatch its hasty life furtively between time clock and alarm clock" (75), the theater must give "city-dwelling people" what they "need extremely, something matchless, that can't be found anywhere else." This rare commodity or "stimulant" will make up for what is missing "in the chilly fantasmagoria of the movies" and in other mass culture phenomena. This compensatory substance will remedy society's diminished affective capacities: "we have got to have some more organized and purposeful expression of our loves, fears, and rages" and require "some human externalization, warm and glamorous and passionate" (75). A renewed theater would be able to perform socially beneficial tasks, to overcome modern individualism by reestablishing properly communal bonds, by creating new, secular structures of collective feeling: "more than anything else [it] welds into a sentient whole the rigid honeycomb of our pigeonholed lives. Since religion has failed humanity, the theatre is the focus of mass emotion" (75).

Dos Passos vehemently denounces the modern theater's tendency to rely on paradigms derived from literature. This egregious error overlooks the historical fact that since antiquity the theater has "had various aims and motives, but none of them have been *literary*" (76; emphasis in the original) and veils the truth that plays have "had their real being [only] where they were acted and applauded and hissed by the populace as spectacular and emotional entertainment" (76). Worse, current attempts "to coax the American public into taking the theatre seriously" rely on anachronistic notions that belong to the "culture of a by-gone age"; consequently, plays are for the most part designed to satisfy the cravings of those who are possessed of considerable cultural capital but who fail to appreciate the latent power of the stage. What "literary-minded people" want are primarily narcotic effects: they "seek in culture a dope to make them dream that they live in Never Never Land" (76). The misguided solicitation of "sophisticated" audiences reinforces stupidly binary ways of conceptualizing the field, thus keeping in place "the idiotic schism between Highbrow and Lowbrow." Worse, the adoption of such a "non-theatrical state of mind," one that views it as art, short-circuits the more legitimate aspiration of "another sort of theater" to make the audience feel intensely, to wring "people's minds and senses and hearts" (76).

For Dos Passos, the most significant achievement of *Processional* is that it has initiated the process of searching for alternatives to illusionist representational strategies. For those who have been "brought up to believe" in the "invisible fourth wall," and who have retained their faith in the notion that "by the power of illusion" what one "sees going on on the stage really exists in the world of actuality" (76), Lawson's play proved startling. The skilled use of artificial conventions to produce the effect of verisimilitude has become passé. "The great triumph of the realistic theatre," to trick people so thoroughly that they "put their umbrellas up coming out of *Rain*" (76), is the kind of victory playwrights need no longer pursue. For "there is another sort of theatre," the genuinely energetic style of which has been preserved in burlesque, musical comedy, and vaudeville, and whose explicit aim "is to put on a show," to generate "in a hall full of people its own reality of glamour and significance." "Crude and comic," such a theater refuses to meet the demands of "Adult Entertainment" to have "real life honestly set down" on the stage, striving instead to "invade the audience's feelings by the most direct and simple means that come to hand" (77). To reinstate the theater as an authentically productive force in the world, one must guarantee that it will "move and excite" its spectators. However ungraceful the initial attempts in the medium "to find for itself a new function," it must continue to experiment in the hope of discovering new methods that are better suited to the needs of the public. It may "bungle [. . .] clumsily" at the start, even falling down in its preliminary efforts "to climb wholeheartedly out of the blind alley of realism," yet the task remains an essential one. For additional support, those participating in the enterprise should take into consideration recent breakthroughs in the sphere of popular amusement. Borrowing as does Lawson from the realm of mechanized recreation may prove nauseating to unprepared members of the crowd. Indeed, some in attendance at *Processional*'s opening night "had the face of a maiden aunt who has been unwillingly coaxed by a small boy to take a ride on a roller coaster. They felt sick and held on desperately and prayed that it would stop" (77). But such unpleasant reactions should not prevent the committed playwright from continuing to try out new techniques, for in time spectators who appreciate such innovations will appear: "as a trip to Coney Island on a Sunday afternoon will show you, there are a great many people in New York who are crazy to ride on roller coasters" (77).[14] Those who "genuinely desire motion" will be delighted to go to see plays like Lawson's, and such people constitute the "nucleus of the audience of a theatre that will have nothing to fear" from the challenge posed by technical media like the radio or movie. Such people will also presumably enjoy a novel like *Manhattan Transfer*, which E. D. Lowry aptly described decades ago as "a series of intense experiences, a chain of highlights and crises involving only crucial or pointedly revealing aspects of the theme" (1630).

A Montage of Repulsions: *Manhattan Transfer*

> Dos Passos very consciously uses this absurd and insistent illusion [that the novel is a mirror] to impel us to revolt.
>
> —Jean-Paul Sartre, "Dos Passos and *1919*"

D. H. Lawrence's appreciative review of *Manhattan Transfer* offers a superb point of access to the distinguishing features of the novel, in part because he completely misinterprets the rationale behind Dos Passos's decision to construct the text as a montage assembly of fragmentary images of everyday life in a changing urban milieu. As Lawrence mistakenly understands it, the novel's predominantly representational purpose is to match the storage capacity of the new technical media, to make language function as the means of recording and then reproducing flows of acoustic, optical, and other sensory data.[15] From this critical perspective, Dos Passos's motive was to write a book whose resemblance or correspondence to its extratextual referent would be guaranteed, as if the author's material surroundings could leave indexical traces in words in the same way that illuminated objects imprint their images on photographic film and the frequency curve of noises inscribe their wavelike shapes onto a phonographic plate. The merits of the novel stem, for Lawrence, from the innovative way it dispassionately recreates the sights and sounds (as well as the tastes and smells) of reality; it is therefore to be judged on the basis of whether or not it fulfills its representational task—to capture in a sensuously immediate and physically precise fashion the visible and audible (as well as olfactory, gustatory, and tactile) elements of the modern city—in an emotionally detached, mechanically exact manner. In Lawrence's view, *Manhattan Transfer* was "the best modern book about New York" he had read not only "because it furnished an endless series of glimpses of people in the vast scuffle of Manhattan Island" but also because it did so with the nonselective neutrality of the technical media: "If you set a blank record revolving to receive all the sounds, and a film-camera going to photograph all the motions, of a scattered group of individuals, at the points where they meet and touch in New York, you would more or less get Mr. Dos Passos's method." Amid the "rush of disconnected scenes and scraps," the "breathless confusion of isolated moments in a group of lives, pouring through the years, from almost every part of New York," that the novelist portrays, the reader gradually gets "to know the faces," and it is this that makes the book "like a movie picture," albeit one "with an intricacy of different stories and no close-ups and no writing in between" (Lawrence 642).

Lawrence thus praised *Manhattan Transfer* in terms cognate with those that Georg Lukacs would rely on to condemn it in "Narrate or Describe?" (1936). What for the former was the virtue of the text—that it was an episodic or descriptive reproduction of the shapeless, seemingly conflict-free chaos of everyday life in the early decades of the twentieth century as opposed to an epic or narrative organization of such material—was to the latter its principal vice (Lukacs 134–35). *Manhattan Transfer* is still customarily read within the narrowly epistemological confines of this aesthetic debate, as an attempt for better or worse to recreate in a referentially valid yet depthless manner the random movements of the subjects of urban modernity. Yet to regard the novel simply as a surface-level depiction—one that, instead of striving to disclose the significance of the events it exhibits, seeks to display the contingent trajectories of an assortment of fictive beings—is to overlook the author's determination to break this traditional conceptual framework apart by designing an affectively charged literary practice that would intervene forcefully in the world.[16] Indeed, common critical perspectives cannot be easily squared with the disdain for realist illusionism that Dos Passos voiced, in the same year that the novel in question was published, in the aforementioned essay on Lawson's *Processional*. For in the critical piece he insists on the culturally retrograde quality of dramatic attempts "to convince the audience that, by some extraordinary series of coincidences, they have strayed into a West Virginia mining town in the middle of an industrial war" (Dos Passos, "'Realistic' Theatre" 77). In light of such a statement, it is highly unlikely that he wanted to lead the readers of his own fiction to believe they had accidentally wandered into an urban metropolis, and that his goal as a (cinematically inclined) writer was to renovate the imitative tradition of novelistic representation.

Two short scenes in *Manhattan Transfer*—both of which focus on the act of reading—confirm Dos Passos's resistance to "naïve" or mystified ways of consuming narrative fictions. Both scenes feature Jimmy Herf, an obviously semiautobiographical figure, who in the first scene has come home from boarding school to New York City for the holidays. Staying in an apartment with his relatives because his mother has suffered a stroke, he recalls while alone in his bedroom a letter (reproduced in the text) his mother had previously written to him, expressing her regret at sending him away. Presumably in emotional pain, he then takes up the "thin leather book in his hand. The surf thundered loud on the barrier reef. He didn't need to read. Jack was swimming fast through the calm blue waters of the lagoon, stood in the sun on the yellow beach shaking the briny drops off him, opened his nostrils wide to the smell of breadfruit roasting beside his solitary campfire. Birds of bright plumage shrieked and tittered from the tall ferny tops of the coconut palms. The room was drowsy hot. Jimmy fell asleep" (82). An entirely unself-conscious reader, the drowsy youth enters a purely illusory or imaginary realm, perceptually immersing himself as swiftly and thoroughly in the fiction as the heroic protagonist does in the body of water he swims across. The words printed on the pages of the novel (*The Coral Island*) are nothing more than cues or external stimuli that trigger the mental act of daydreaming. The exotic landscape the boy fabricates provides him with a delightful and rewarding refuge from his distressing circumstances in urban reality, for it is in this substitute world that he can engage in athletic exercise and utilize his survival skills in nature.[17] His family-based anxiety, however, returns in the form of a nightmare variation on his daydream: "A fly the size of a ferryboat walks towards them across the water, reaching out its jagged crabclaws." The latter scenario ends abruptly when his aunt knocks on the door. Upon waking, the boy ("Jimmy was blushing") clearly feels as if he has been caught in the embarrassing act of letting himself get carried away. The shame he feels encompasses both the unconsciously produced dream and the made-up fiction, for in both cases he has allowed himself to fall into the realm of fabricated sensory impressions.

This same reflexive motif reappears when Jimmy is much older. At least a decade has passed (it is now 1915), and though Jimmy has found work as a reporter, he finds the currently apathetic state of the nation objectionable. "'Well perhaps you can tell me why in this country nobody ever does anything. Nobody ever writes any music or starts any revolutions or falls in love. All anybody ever does is to get drunk and tell smutty stories. I think it's disgusting'" (163). Before articulating his opinion, Jimmy had been reading, "with tightening gullet," one of the later volumes of Romain Rolland's recently translated *Jean-Christophe*. The description of Jimmy's absorption in the narrative resembles the earlier scene, although the critical point here is that he substitutes what he has read previously for his own lived experiences: "In his memory lingered the sound of the Rhine swirling, restlessly gnawing at the foot of the garden of the house where Jean Christophe was born. Europe was a green park in his mind full of music and red flags and mobs marching. [. . .] There was a knock at the door. Jimmy got up, his eyes blurred and hot from reading" (163). Nostalgia for an era of sociopolitical unrest that he imagines (or hallucinates) as having been a part of his personal past both conditions Jimmy's distaste for the present and offers him a means of fleeing it. His inability to focus visually on the actual world after the knock on the door interrupts his reading foregrounds the delusional aspects of the recollected (non)experience. Reading as a mode of identification diminishes one's capacity to see reality. (In the next chapter, Ellen Thatcher [whom Jimmy will eventually marry], at the time an up-and-coming Broadway actress, issues a comparable denunciation of the contemporary theater's manipulative dishonesty. Praised by her admirers for her ability to "put the passion and terror into" her performance, she yearns to confess that her emotional expressiveness on stage is entirely artificial, that it is simply a generically prescribed style: "'I hate it; it's all false. Sometimes I want to run down to the foots and tell the audience, go home you damn fools. This is a rotten show and a lot of fake acting and you ought to know it. In a musical show you could be sincere'" [180].)

An alternative model of reading, one that alerts us to the power of words to produce strong reactions, occurs earlier in the same chapter ("Tracks") and contains another negative lesson. The exemplary significance of this next scene derives from the fact that here Dos Passos depicts the capacity of material letters to trigger emotionally troubling affects in an embodied reader. Secretively grabbing a box of candy, Jimmy heads off to his room, taking from a bookcase as he passes it the first volume of the "American Cyclopedia." Again he starts to daydream, concocting an imprisonment and rescue scenario; he then switches to a maritime setting, where he appears as a sailor entering a cabin to give instructions to the captain. Having recited his prayers, Jimmy simultaneously bites into one of his treats, and then he opens the book: "His teeth broke through the chocolate into a squashysweet filling. Let's see. . . . A the first of the vowels, the first letter" (72). The intellectual substance the boy consumes proves to be a bit too much for him. After glancing at a picture of an aardvark, he suddenly encounters a series of overstimulating entries dealing with sex. The first article is rather mild, referencing an Egyptian prince (Abd-el-halim) born of a "white slave woman," the thought of which makes him blush ("His cheeks burned as he read" [73]). The next item is "Abdomen," which draws his attention to "the lower part of the body," "that of the pelvis." Worse, Abelard comes next and concludes with a description of Fulbert's "savage vindictiveness," which results in the latter gratifying "his revenge by inflicting on him [Abelard] an atrocious mutilation." After this come the "Abelites," who "denounced sexual intercourse as service of Satan"; "Abimelech," son of a "Sheshemite concubine, who made himself king after murdering all his seventy brethren"; and finally "Abortion," to which his shocked response is simply "No." Having taken in more information than he can stomach, Jimmy feels he might vomit: "his hands were icy and he felt a little sick from stuffing down so many chocolates" (73). If reading in this instance forecasts a painful initiation into the mysteries of copulation and procreation, it comes close to doubling as itself a symbolic rite of passage. Jimmy is not ready to assume castration as a precondition of manliness, but his textual encounter has put him in position to realize the price he must pay to attain this status.

The encyclopedia is not a perfect *mise en abyme*, yet it comes close to serving as a miniaturized version of *Manhattan Transfer*, for both are designed for educational purposes. Dos Passos, of course, will seek to harness for the purpose of persuasive social critique the affective force that the nonfictional text generates more or less accidentally. (Ellen's abortion, for instance, is intended late in the novel to compel the reader toward an awareness of the barrenness of everyday life in urban modernity.) The encyclopedia's alphabetic ordering principle differs from the juxtapositional system Dos Passos employs in *Manhattan Transfer*, and his goal is not to induce erotic excitement, but he does seek to devise a formal method of presentation that will affect his addressee powerfully, on a physiological as well as cerebral level. The writer's pedagogical task requires that he calculate how best to place his episodes in relation to each other so that his intended readers will feel so awful at the sight of current conditions of inequity that they will throw up. "All this material must be arranged and organized in relation to principles which would lead to the desired reaction in correct proportion" (Eisenstein, cited in Wollen, *Signs and Meaning* 39).

Returning to Lawrence's assessment of the novel, we find that despite misunderstanding its rhetorical strategy, he correctly specifies the major theme the reappearing characters convey: "they turn up again and again and again, in a confusion that has no obvious rhythm [. . . until] at last we recognize the systole-diastole of success and failure" (641). The part this motif plays in the novel, especially as it pertains to financial matters, is a crucial component of Dos Passos's literary enterprise. What he wants to do is generate anger toward a widely accepted system of values in which getting rich is the primary, if not exclusive, goal of the nation's inhabitants. His aim is to inspire feelings of disgust in his readers at the fact that in a capitalist society the measure of individual accomplishment is how much money one has made. Dos Passos therefore deliberately arranges the text's numerous lifelike segments to get his audience to loathe the debased attitudes of his fictive characters. He arranges his numerous vignettes to produce in his addressees a strong distaste for the rampant commercialization of daily life in this country. Jimmy's uncle Jeff is a repellent individual and the antithesis of a viable role model because he reprimands his nephew for not feeling "sufficient responsibility about moneymatters . . . er . . . sufficient enthusiasm about earning your living, making good in a man's world. Look around you . . . Thrift and enthusiasm has made these men what they are. It's made me, put me in position to offer you the comfortable home, the cultured surroundings that I do offer you" (*Manhattan Transfer* 100). Even Ed Thatcher, one of the few decent characters in the novel, finds it difficult not to give in to temptation and risk his savings on the stock market. Although he has "examined the books of too many bankrupts," he nevertheless dreams (in vain) of reaping the rewards of a quick score in the form of heightened prestige and prosperity: "The Fiduciary Accounting Institute, Edward C. Thatcher, President," "take a plunge they're all crooks and gamblers anyway . . . take a plunge and come up with your hands full, pockets full, bankaccount full, vaults full of money." "Dollars swarming up like steam, twisting scattering against the stars. Millionaire Thatcher leaned out of the window of the bright patchouliscented room to look at the darkjutting city steaming with laughter, voices, tinkling and lights" (93).

This is why most of the novel's numerous characters are profoundly unhappy, even those who are fairly well off. The state of despair they exist in is meant to discourage us from behaving as they do, from wanting what they want, for although the causes and severity of these fictive beings' moods of frustration are varied, the condition can always be traced back to the compromises they felt pressured to make in their paths to success (or failure) in their chosen vocations. For instance, when Ellen reflects on the costs of pursuing her goal of becoming the "Greatest hit on Broadway" (marriage to a talented yet homosexual actor and ceaseless badgering for dates from aging admirers) "a feeling of sick disgust suddenly choked her" (130–31). Similarly, Jimmy may have managed to become "a reporter on the *Times*," but to him it is "a hellish rotten job and I'm sick of it," for it requires him "to take all the stuff you have to take from people in this goddam town. I'm sick of playing up to a lot of desk men I don't respect" (209–210). He expresses this opinion during a conversation with his relative Joe Harland, formerly known as "the Wizard of Wall Street," whose spectacular fall from financial grace is one of the text's central illustrations of the precarious nature of achievement in the business world. Having frittered away the wealth he accumulated on the stock market in a haze of alcohol-fueled excess, Joe is shunned by his family and must depend on handouts until he gets a humbling job as a night watchman at a construction site. Yet he wonders whether his collapse was not to some extent a self-willed reaction to the ultimately unfulfilling life he had been leading. Thus he tells an envious young labor organizer that "funny things get into a man," that even with "women and that sort of stuff," one can "get kinder disgusted" (176). His interlocutor (Joe O'Keefe) finds it difficult to grasp "how a guy with enough jack can git disgusted," yet this is due to his inexperience. Later in life, when he learns what it takes to get ahead, he will agree to act as an informer, helping a company owner and corrupt politician negotiate with striking workers in ways that are unlikely to be in the best interests of labor.

Dos Passos, then, does not propose that simply hearing a knowledgeable person voice his disgust with capitalist society is enough to transfer the speaker's feelings to the listener. This holds both for interlocutors in the text and for the interchange between author and reader. An early episode, one of the longest sequences in the novel, illustrates this point. The action begins in an expensive restaurant, where Emile, after sneaking off the ship on which he was serving his military service for France, has found work as a waiter. Required to serve arrogant and vulgar customers in a deferential manner, he angrily thinks to himself, "When I make some money I'll show 'em" (26). He then watches as the revels of the intoxicated diners become increasingly outrageous. Late in the meal, Fifi Waters, a showgirl they have been waiting for, finally arrives and proceeds to kick a guest in the face while demonstrating her dancing skills. As blood and tears gush out of the wounded man's eye, the party breaks up, Fifi leaving with an older man, the Colonel, while her escort lies in the hall "vomiting into a firebucket" (30). A semi-scandalous incident that the daily tabloids might seize on to titillate their audience, and thus to exploit it commercially, is obviously intended in this context to repulse the novel reader. Yet the outrageous antics of the partying clientele fail to shake Emile free of his determination to make something of himself in the country. Later in the evening, when an acquaintance named Marco tries to convince him of the validity of revolutionary aspirations ("Police, governments, armies, presidents, kings . . . all that is force. Force is not real; it is illusion. The working man makes all that himself because he believes it. The day that we stop believing in money and property it will be like a dream when we wake up" [32]), the former's advice falls on deaf ears. The content of the aging speaker's radical discourse may be ideologically admirable, yet his ideas fail to penetrate the resistant consciousness of the troubled young man. "My God it's stupid," Emile thinks to himself as he goes to sleep. "Marco's gaga the old fool" (34).

Given the problematic lack of power of speech, the writer puts successive examples of individual suffering and hardship on display, his idea being that such cumulative exhibitions will result in a genuinely affecting demonstration of the difficulties impoverished persons confront in their struggles to survive in urban modernity. The miserable fate of Bud Korpenning, a young parricide from upstate whose experiences in the city are exceptionally brutal, is a case in point. Frightened that the law is after him and treated cruelly again and again by most everyone he meets, Bud winds up sitting on the rail of the Brooklyn Bridge in a state of severe emotional distress. With nowhere left to go, he envisions an unattainable future of wealth, respect, and happiness. Shutting his eyes, he imagines himself riding on his wedding day in a carriage full of diamonds to City Hall; sitting next to "his milliondollar bride," he is on his way "to be made an alderman by the mayor" (105). However, when he stops daydreaming and returns to reality, the brightly shining sun blinds him, whereupon he slips from his perch, dangles briefly by a hand, and then falls to his death, a yell strangling "in his throat as he drops" (105). Dos Passos locates this sad event at the end of the first section of the novel in order to maximize its impact, to ensure that the death will deliver an intense shock to the reader's conscience. In sharp contrast to the annoyed captain of the tugboat, who finds it exasperating that he must deal with the body once he has had it hauled on board, the reader should be profoundly moved and should appreciate that what happens to others in the city truly matters.

A comparably horrific incident occurs near the end of the novel. A young seamstress named Anna Cohen, whose fiancée is a radical activist, gets distracted while contemplating a glorious future. Though located in the stuffy back room of a dress shop, her fingers hard at work, her mind is elsewhere. "Equal Opportunity for All. Elmer says that's applesauce. No hope for the workers but in the Revolution. *Oh I'm juss wild about Harree, And Harry's juss wild about me.* . . . Elmer in a telephone central in a dinnercoat, with eartabs, tall as Valentino, strong as Doug" (337; emphasis in the original). So preoccupied is she with the confused fantasy of political triumph, of a left-wing parade in which her lover is a candidate for mayor who simultaneously morphs into two of the most celebrated motion-picture leading men of the era, Anna fails to notice that a fire has broken out around her: "Through the dream she is stitching white fingers beckon. The white tulle shines too bright. Red hands clutch suddenly out of the tulle, she cant fight off the red tulle all round her biting into her, coiled about her head. The skylight's blackened with swirling smoke. The room's full of smoke and screaming. Anna is on her feet whirling round fighting with her hands the burning tulle all round her" (337). The dramatic spectacle is not meant to serve as an opportunity for the reader to satisfy an indiscriminate craving for intense sensations. On the contrary, the intent is to produce as powerfully as possible feelings of horror at the social conditions that determine such corporeally devastating events. In this regard, Ellen, who happens to be in the store picking up a new outfit, serves as a negative surrogate for the reader. Though undeniably shaken by the gruesome sight she has glimpsed ("Out of the corner of her eye she sees an arm in shreds, a seared black red face, a horrible naked head" [337]), she can't understand why the incident has made her feel the way she does: "Ellen can hardly breathe. [. . .] She tries to puzzle out why she is so moved; it is as if some part of her were going to be wrapped in bandages, carried away on a stretcher. [. . .] Why should I be so excited? She keeps asking herself. Just somebody's bad luck, the sort of thing happens everyday. The moaning turmoil and the clanging of the fireengines wont seem to fade away inside her. . . . There's a horrible tired blankness inside her. O dear what shall I do? she whimpers to herself" (338).

Ellen's failure has less to do with a lack of sympathy for the other woman than with an inability to grasp the extent to which the predicament causing the latter's suffering encompasses her own. Leaving the dress shop, she heads off to meet George Baldwin, the unpleasant lawyer whom she has finally agreed to wed. An earlier scene has already disclosed to us that in her mind marrying him amounts to a reduction to the status of an inanimate thing. To him, she is merely an object of desire, the possession of which he presumes will fill an internal void ("'God if you knew how empty life has been for so many years. I've been like a tin mechanical toy, all hollow inside'" [319]). Worse, in giving in to his request, Ellen knows she is taking on her future partner's reified condition: "'Let's not talk about mechanical toys,'" she replies "in a strangled voice" (319). As he heats up with passion, she conversely becomes numb, losing her emotional and physical capacity to feel, which in turn guarantees that her degraded state will be permanent. "'By gad Elaine,' he said flaming up helplessly, 'you're the most wonderful thing in the world.' Through dinner she felt a gradual icy coldness stealing through her like novocain. [. . .] It seemed as if she had set the photograph of herself in her own place, forever frozen into a single gesture" (318). She recalls this previous rigidifying experience ("everything about her seemed to be growing hard and enameled" [318]) immediately after witnessing the aforementioned accident: "'George'll be mad when he sees me come breezing in like this. Likes to show me off all dressed up [. . .] like an Effenbee walking talking doll, damn him'" (338). Resigned to her future status as a trophy wife, Ellen still retains some sense that alternatives exist, but it is evident she will never pursue one of these: "'There are lives to be lived, if only you didn't care. Care for what: the opinion of mankind, money, success, hotel lobbies, health, umbrellas, Uneeda biscuits . . . ? It's like a busted mechanical toy the way my mind goes brrr all the time'" (339).

Ellen's dilemma is that she cares about the wrong things. She remains too concerned with material goods, with assorted things that, in being ready to hand, may, like an umbrella, protect her from confronting the impoverished state of her world and thus ensure that she will continue to live in accordance with the debased, ontic priorities of the masses. In contrast, Dos Passos's purpose is to compel the reader not to flee in this manner, to avoid being ensnared in an inauthentic kind of existence that tends to shut down one's awareness of the possibility of choosing to struggle toward a changed future. I have argued that the rhetorical method he employs to achieve this goal is to depict a vast number of emotionally disturbing incidents, under the assumption that repeated exposure "without opportunity for release of satisfaction" will result in "reflexes of struggle, and [a] heightening of the potential expression of class feeling" (Eisenstein on *Strike*, quoted in Wollen, *Signs and Meaning* 39). Indeed, we have witnessed a comparably horrific event at the beginning of the novel when Ellen's father, Ed, attracted by the bells of a speeding fire engine, joins the crowd of transfixed spectators gathered around a burning tenement building. As he watches, the flames consume numerous trapped residents. Even worse, a charred body drops "from a window" and lies "on the pavement shrieking" (13). Shaken by what he has seen, the stunned character trudges home. The gamble of the text is that the reader will respond without such resignation and that the quantitative accumulation of such events will produce a qualitative transformation, shocking the individual into a more resolute mood, one in which the threat that urban modernity ceaselessly poses to its inhabitants will be recognized as a situation demanding a collective response.

The intricately composed chapter headnotes frequently function as poetically compressed intensifications of the more prosaic materials contained in the main text. As such, they deserve to be compared to the montage sequences that Slavko Vorkapich, beginning in 1928, would supply for Hollywood films. Frequently referencing Eisenstein's writings, Vorkapich's theory was by "the mid-1930s [. . .] explicitly affective, predicated on the assumption of a determinate, Pavlovian link between specific techniques and psychological responses to them: 'it is possible to stimulate a spectator into various physiological and psychological reactions by means of certain visual irritations coming from the screen.' In his postwar lectures Vorkapich anchored the idea of physiological response to visual stimuli in Gestalt psychology and adopted the term 'kinethesia' to designate the shooting and editing practices that produce them" (D. E. James, *Most Typical Avant-Garde* 71[18]). A vivid illustration of the use of this kinesthetic strategy in *Manhattan Transfer* is the following headnote figuration of everyday life in terms of a thrilling amusement park ride: "*They pair off hurriedly.* STANDING UP IN CAB STRICTLY FORBIDDEN. *The climbing chain grates, grips the cogs; jerkily the car climbs the incline out of the whirring lights [. . .] Then the swoop. The sea does a flipflop, the lights soar.* [. . .] *The wind of their falling has snatched their yells, they jerk rattling upwards through the tangled girderstructure. Swoop. Soar. [. . .]* KEEP YOUR SEATS FOR THE NEXT RIDE" (201; emphasis in the original). Applied to existence in urban modernity, the sensorial trope visually conveys the idea that the city's inhabitants, whether they are prepared for it or not, are in for a series of dizzyingly rapid adventures. Taken in conjunction with the titling of a subsequent chapter, "Rollercoaster," the metaphorical imagery viscerally expresses the general historical thesis (absolutely central to the text as a whole) that what goes up inevitably comes crashing down.

Attraction and Advertising

> Like the advertising people [. . .] I'm concerned with the precise manipulation of word and image to create an action, not to go out and buy a Coca-Cola, but to create an alteration in the reader's consciousness.
>
> —William Burroughs, "Writers at Work"

Eisenstein's struggle to articulate a politically worthwhile physiological aesthetic can be situated as part of a much broader enterprise within industrial modernity to reconfigure subjectivity in light of one's ability (or lack thereof) to pay attention. As Jonathan Crary has demonstrated, from the late nineteenth century forward numerous investigators across a range of disciplines studied how people and social aggregates might maintain their concentration in a milieu made up of myriad distractions. Caught in an environment where the amount of sensory data seemed to be proliferating at an alarmingly high rate, individuals and groups experienced the need to process information more efficiently. Especially pertinent here is Crary's chapter on the modernist painter Georges Seurat, for the latter's aesthetic strategies are shown to coincide (but are not conflated) with a contemporaneous set of rationalizing discourses and practices. Predicating his labors on the notion that subjects act in response to outside suggestions "in a state of restricted awareness," and thus to a certain extent may be considered "psychic automaton[s]," Seurat's neo-impressionist undertaking participates in the break away from classical regimes of visuality (*Suspensions of Perception* 152). Hinging on the hypothesis that one might explain perceptual organization mechanistically, that it "could be quantified and predicted in terms of a stimulus-response circuit" (155), Seurat's creative method sprang from the same experimental physiology that influenced Eisenstein, the painter and the filmmaker both drawing on scientific ideas that had been in circulation since the latter half of the nineteenth century.[19]

After roughly two decades of inquiry focused on comprehending the reflex functions of the human nervous system and, correlatively, on measuring empirically behavioral reactions to various stimuli, it had become commonplace by the 1870s to deal with excitation and muscular contraction, and thus with questions pertaining to somatic redistributions of energy, when addressing issues of aesthetic reception. Treating the body as a complex organism and assuming that deliberate or involuntary movements could be studied as the effects of specific sensations, researchers set aside conscious thought in order to isolate the exact causes of motor expression in the perceiver (Crary, *Suspensions of Perception* 169). If their guiding imperative was to comprehend the drives or affects reductively, from a statistical or engineering standpoint, such goals were entirely compatible with the need of dominant society to increase its hold over its assorted members; the ability to foresee the levels of excitement produced in certain settings would supply a way to maintain control over the potentially unruly forces of the body politic (172). Viewing human beings as thing-like entities, such sciences made available techniques with the potential to, in effect, program people; collective cohesion could now be feasibly maintained via the use of laboratory-tested stimuli. Eisenstein's strategic employment of montage belongs to this historical field, as do the persuasive techniques that are skillfully mobilized by modern advertisers. The latter too were in the process of learning how to instill in psyches the desire for particular commodities, how to attract consumer attention to manufactured items.

Given Dos Passos's critical preoccupation with subjective states of distraction, with absentmindedness as a problematic condition of urban modernity, it is logical that *Manhattan Transfer* identifies advertising as one of its major rivals. That the author's most depressed characters frequently exhibit a tendency to lose themselves in a daydream is easily diagnosed as a compensatory reaction to the unbearable aspects of their mundane existence. Yet their enchanted reveries, in which they lead dazzlingly luxurious lives, in which they amass fortunes and attain social prominence, are to a considerable degree the result of the seductive power of the discourses and practices of modern advertising. Well aware that the public preferred images of "life as it ought to be," that it could be charmed into accepting dubious aspirations and persuaded to pursue false visions of future happiness, Dos Passos sought to counteract the spell that advertising's distorted mirror had the capacity to cast.[20] In this respect, *Manhattan Transfer* anticipates Raymond Williams's characterization of advertising as a "highly organized and professional system of magical inducements and satisfactions," one that in its flourishing modernized forms "operates to preserve the consumption ideal from the criticism inexorably made of it by experience" (185, 188). Indeed, the book recognizes that a (monopoly or corporate) capitalist regime "could not function without" (186) advertising insofar as the latter coercively sanctions hopes that remain ideologically in synch with a rapidly expanding economy. We can detect this understanding early in the novel in a real estate agent's enthusiastic exhortation to a potential client to take advantage of the opportunity to buy a lot in Queens. Purchasing this property, guaranteed to double in value given that all "these mechanical inventions—telephones, electricity, steel bridges, horseless vehicles"—must be "leading somewhere," is, the clients are told, a way to ride the "great wave of expansion of progress" (Dos Passos, *Manhattan Transfer* 14). To accomplish its assigned task, advertising frequently hones in on distracted individuals, aiming its suggestive appeals at those whose mental condition resembles that of a sleepwalker. As Marshall McLuhan puts it: "Ads are not meant for conscious consumption. They are intended as subliminal pills [. . .] in order to exercise an hypnotic spell [. . .] ads are carefully designed by [. . .] Madison Avenue [. . .] for semiconscious exposure. Their mere existence is a testimony, as well as a contribution, to the somnambulistic state of a tired metropolis" (*Understanding Media* 202–203).

McLuhan locates the crux of advertising as a cultural enterprise in its commercially motivated exploitation of widespread desires for collective existence. "The ad teams have billions to spend annually on research and testing of reactions, and their products are magnificent accumulations of material about the shared experience and feelings of the entire community. Of course if ads were to depart from the center of this shared experience, they would collapse at once, by losing all hold on our feelings" (203). Ads manipulate individuals in more or less facile fashion by convincing them that purchasing goods is the key both to social integration and emotional well-being. Directing its address to those who yearn for inclusion, the homogenizing force of advertising seeks to convince people that they can buy communal belonging. Roland Marchand marks the mid-1920s as the historical moment at which advertisers began to shift their attentions toward "the hopes and anxieties of the consumer" rather than continue furnishing "objective information about the product" (11). Advertisers increasingly sought to market future pleasure, attributing to objects for sale the benefits of "leisure, enjoyment, beauty, good taste, prestige, and popularity" (24). These "satisfactions" had in turn been "pre-sold" (or at least marketed) to customers, the masses having already bought the debatable notion that these are the "proper rewards for the successful pursuit of the American dream" (24).

An otherwise innocuous episode in the first chapter of *Manhattan Transfer* is significant in this regard because it introduces the text's competitive attitude toward modern advertising. A Jewish immigrant is walking past a set of filthy and crowded tenement buildings, in an agitated state, when an image in a corner drugstore window draws his attention. He stops and stares "abstractedly at a face on a green advertising card. It was a highbrowed cleanshaven distinguished face with arched eyebrows and a bushy neatly trimmed mustache, the face of a man who had money in the bank, poised prosperously above a crisp wing collar and an ample dark cravat. Under it in copybook writing was the signature King C. Gillette. Above his head hovered the motto NO STROPPING NO HONING" (9). The social connotations of the well-groomed visage in conjunction with the model's elegant apparel convince the "little bearded man" to enter the store, pay for the razors, rush home and clip "the long brown locks of his beard," and then shave (9). Pleased with his new look, his face now "smooth as the face of King C. Gillette," the father expectantly turns toward his wife and children, who have just arrived home. His daughters are stunned, their eyes "popping out of their heads," but his wife's reaction is most telling. Dropping "like a laundry bag into the rocker," she throws an "apron over her head" and moans in despair at her foolish husband's transformation. The writer's obvious concern is to alert his readers to the suggestive power of idealized appearances; they must be taught to resist the coercive capacity of ads to catch one's eye, for this then efficiently triggers mechanisms of identification predicated on the notion that imitation facilitates assimilation. If ads seize people emotionally in order to sell merchandise, an undesirable by-product of this process is the elimination of the traces of ethnic or religious difference. The task of the modernist novelist is to disenchant his reader, to counteract the epistemologically untenable associations that billboards endorse, to contest the fraudulent assumption that in obtaining "an object" you secure along with it "social respect, discrimination, health, beauty, success [and] power to control your environment" (R. Williams 189).[21]

By the 1920s the advertising industry had entered its corporate stage, an organizational process that included an increased reliance on scientific psychology for guidance in planning ad campaigns.[22] This growing dependence can be glimpsed in Arthur Judson Brewster and Herbert Hall Palmer's *Introduction to Advertising*, the first edition of which was published in 1924. Primarily framed as a textbook for classroom use, the authors propose that their articulation of the principles of advertising can also interest professionals in the business. In "The Appeal," chapter 7 of part 2, "How to Write Advertising," the authors acknowledge their debt to "the researches of psychologists" and assert that "we have learned something of how the mind behaves and how, to some extent, its action can be influenced by advertising" (76). Declaring that every "normal human being has certain fundamental needs and desires" and that along with these "go tendencies to react in definite ways, when the proper stimuli are present," the authors encourage students of advertising to learn as much as they can about such "desires and instincts" in order to figure out how best to appeal to potential buyers—that is, how to compose ads "which will cause a reaction in the mind of the prospective customer and result in a purchase either in the present or in the future (76–77). To help facilitate the swift acquisition of such strategic knowledge, Brewster and Palmer provide a table arranged in columns and rows. The first column attempts "to give some of the most important desires or tendencies," the second offers "suggestions of types of advertising that may be used as stimuli," and the third lists "examples of some of the products that may be advertised" in the tactical manner they outline. Companies, we are told, increasingly adopt such schematic approaches to the field when deciding how to market items, thus relying on information that is methodically gathered—often via laboratory tests—by scientifically oriented psychologists. Recently collected data indicate that the personality traits most worth taking into consideration include the "instinct of imitation," since "the desire to be like others" is a "great buying force" (86). Typically strong impulses are the desire to receive "approval, praise"; to be esteemed by others (90); alongside the common urge "to 'get ahead' in the world, the desire for pleasure and comfort, the desire to make money and to accumulate wealth" (101). Lastly, in a subsection titled "Getting into the Subconscious," the authors discuss the importance of "the frequent repetition of a name, trade-mark, slogan, or selling point" as an essential technique, one grounded in the idea that people not only involuntarily retain what they have seen and heard but also, correlatively, are more inclined when the need arises to purchase merchandise that they either remember or recognize in a store display (92).

While Brewster and Palmer do not note their sources for what have become commonplaces today, it is reasonable to assume they consulted Hugo Munsterberg's *Psychology and Industrial Efficiency* (1913), the third part of which ("The Best Possible Effect") was a pioneering attempt to bring the rationalizing methods of scientific experimentation to bear on "feelings, demands, and satisfactions" as these pertain to the economic sphere.[23] In chapter 20, "Experiments on the Effects of Advertising," Munsterberg, having already pointed out that advertisements "must attract the passer-by or impress the reader or stimulate his impulse to buy" (256), notes that they can most efficiently reach these ends by striking the memory vividly so as to force the contents of the ad into the mind. And it is through psychological laboratory experiments, he claims, that one secures the knowledge necessary to accomplish this task. "The color, the type, the choice of words, every element, allows an experimental analysis, especially by means of time-measurement" (261). Notably, from this perspective, the subject is treated as an automaton, as an entity whose future actions are predictable and programmable by external influences. The psychologist in this instance searches for the laws of the mind in order to guide the advertising industry in its efforts to control persons, to make them behave in an involuntary manner. Psychotechnology legitimates its project on the grounds that when the goal is to secure "with the greatest possible certainty the greatest possible mental effect in the service of economic purpose," "systematic construction" is far superior to the "mere chance arrangements founded on personal taste" (279). Chapter 23, "Buying and Selling" turns from the impact of "inanimate objects, posters or displays [. . .] labels or packings" to the living agents in commercial transactions: the salesmen. Here too the explicit crux of the matter is the manipulation of others; salesmen must figure out how "to enhance the impulse to buy and suppress the opposing ideas" (294). One must be taught to develop "the whole process through a series of stages so that the attention slowly becomes focused on one definite point," and once this narrow region is isolated, one should pursue inhibitory tactics, striving to "eliminate everything which distracts and scatters the attention." The skilled salesman should base his tactical moves on his estimation of "the psyche of the individual with whom he is dealing." Is this someone who can be persuaded through logical argumentation, or will suggestion work better? The salesman must decide "how far he may calculate on the pleasure instincts, on the excitement of emotions, on the impulse to imitate, on the natural vanity, on the desire for saving, and on the longing for luxury" (295) and then proceed accordingly.

Crucially, without methodological study, such verbal exchanges will involve "a tremendous waste of energy" (296); the commercial transaction "dissolves into a flood of talk, because no one has taken the trouble to examine scientifically the psychotechnics of selling and to put it on a firm psychological foundation" (297).

Despite their shared heritage in scientific rationalization, neither Eisenstein's nor Dos Passos's cultural undertakings should be conflated with the economic enterprise. The methods of modern advertising may overlap with those of modernist art, but the social ambitions of these two men were obviously incompatible with the goals underlying contemporaneous advertising practices. Endorsing commodities is hardly the same as promoting revolutionary convictions or radical antipathies. The significance of the montage of attractions technique, then, is that it treated affect as the site of social struggle. Rather than cede the terrain of emotional intensity to the opponent, Dos Passos in *Manhattan Transfer* sought to actively intervene in an ideological battle waged at the time at the level of intense feelings. Significantly, this project led him (as well as Eisenstein) to experiment with Joyce's trademark contribution to modernist aesthetics.

Late in the novel we see a jobless and about-to-be divorced Jimmy Herf wandering aimlessly through the streets in a feverish state of mind. Unable to decide what to do with his life, Jimmy also has difficulty warding off the coercive stimuli that ceaselessly circulate through his linguistically saturated metropolitan milieu. To convey the subjective impact of predominantly verbal materials on the overwrought character as he walks "through the city of scrambled alphabets, through the city of gilt letter signs" (298), Dos Passos utilizes the stream of consciousness or interior monologue technique—a formal device the writer relies on intermittently throughout the text to register states of emotional intensity.

Notably, it is overheard sales pitches for assorted commodities that saturate the psyche and shape its mood: "Spring rich in gluten . . . Chockful of golden richness, delight in every bite, THE DADDY OF THEM ALL, spring rich in gluten. Nobody can buy better bread than PRINCE ALBERT. Wrought steel, money, copper, nickel, wrought iron. *All the world loves natural beauty.* LOVE'S BARGAIN that suit at Gumpel's best value in town. Keep that schoolgirl complexion . . . JOE KISS, starting, lightning, ignition and generators" (298; emphasis in the original). As he stops to eat lunch, Jimmy's "thoughts" continue to run "wild," and when he leaves Dos Passos again gives us access to the character's unruly mental processes. A proliferation of slogans, jingles, brand names, and catchphrases, all designed to entice people into buying bread products, cosmetics, menswear, automobile parts, and tobacco, swirl in his mind. "*Express service meets the demands of spring.* O God to meet the demands of spring. Not tins, no sir, but there's rich quality in every mellow pipeful . . . SOCONY. One taste tells more than a million words, than a million words" (299; emphasis in the original).

The discursive barrage leads Jimmy to reflect on a recent ill-fated robbery (the story of which he must have seen in the newspaper), the association no doubt triggered by the idea that the youthful bandits were driven to engage in criminal activity by their desperation to obtain the luxury items (jewelry in particular) they couldn't otherwise afford. Filled with the vapid and vaporous verbiage he has involuntarily inhaled, Jimmy can only envision performing isolated acts of anarchic resistance, imagining himself in confused succession as a Peeping Tom, a demonic graffiti artist, and a prankster running amok in the commercial marketplace: "With every deep breath Herf breathed in rumble and grind and painted phrases until he began to swell, felt himself stumbling big and vague, staggering like a pillar of smoke above the April streets, looking into the windows of machineshops, buttonfactories . . . felt . . . the smooth whir of lathes, wrote cusswords on typewriters between the stenographer's fingers, mixed up the pricetags in department stores" (299). He then begins to hallucinate, imagining himself as multiple selves on trial in a court of law (his uncle the judge) for having squandered his "twenties." Though held under various indictments, the unnamed crime each one of them is secretly charged with is having failed to reconcile himself to the frenzied excesses of capitalist modernity in an era of unprecedented expansion. Found guilty, they will soon be deported as "undesirable aliens." Once he calms down, quieting the rather bizarre call of his conscience, Jimmy thinks to himself "print itches like a rash inside me. I sit here pockmarked with print" (301). The trope figures the irritating effects of journalism and advertising: the two verbal forces have ruined his cerebral surface, leaving him with nothing except the need to scratch his distressingly textured brain.

When Franco Moretti takes up the topic of the stream of consciousness in the second half of his book *Modern Epic*, his initial concern is to examine the complicity in Joyce's *Ulysses* between the literary method and advertising procedures. Whereas advertising functions in the text as "the inexhaustible transmitter of the capitalist metropolis," stream of consciousness "captures and organizes fluctuating stimuli" (135). But if the latter performs the traditional modernist task of bringing a semblance of order to chaos, it also enacts a relatively salutary capitulation to the sensory flux of everyday life in the city. In the case of Leopold Bloom in *Ulysses*, for example, it signals the character's complacent acceptance of the myriad impressions his urban environment yields as sufficiently enjoyable in themselves. Advertising and a modernist style are barely discernible here in their shared endorsement of a "fantasizing possibilism," which puts the character "at ease in the world of commodities, because it allows him to pick up hundreds and hundreds of stimuli, and play freely with them" (140). Bloom enriches himself by casually looking at the multifarious world that is accessible to his gaze as he roams through the city, much as advertising displays—in Moretti's assessment—solicit department store shoppers to derive fleeting pleasures by visually embracing images rather than seeking to possess the items themselves (130–31).

In both situations the relaxed subject perceives broadly, looking in an unfocused superficial fashion that merely "slide[s] over things," and this relaxed accommodation to "the absence of meaning" "helps Bloom to live [. . .] *in the metropolis*" (156; emphasis in the original). The character's tranquilized tolerance for whatever his environment brings to mind illustrates how best to survive "in the big city" (167).[24] It is no doubt evident, given my account of *Manhattan Transfer*, that I do not find Moretti's thesis to be entirely applicable to the novel, for it eliminates any impulse to resist the ideologically coercive thrust of advertising practices. Clearly, in contrast, Dos Passos wished to maintain the tension between contemporaneous marketing techniques and experimental writing, a tension that is canceled by treating them as two sides of the same coin. From my perspective the critical significance of his cultural intervention is that he wages war against his opponent *without abandoning the realm of affectivity*. Subjectivity for Dos Passos was a battleground on which competing discursive practices fought, each deploying whatever persuasive tactics they could devise to coax people to feel and do what the persuader wanted. Since the avowedly commercial enterprise encouraged the belief that gratification comes from obtaining the objects one demands, the modernist writer committed himself to an act of dissuasion, his aim to conquer what he viewed as the socially and politically pernicious appeal of advertising by making the degraded, dissatisfying experience of the subject of urban-industrial modernity as palpable as he could.[25]

Returning to the aesthetic strategy of a montage of attractions, it is now feasible to propose that stream of consciousness amounts to an internalized, subjective correlative of the approach Eisenstein theorized. In stream of consciousness it is simply the mind that is put on display, made into a spectacle.[26] Dos Passos utilized the formal method he learned partly from Joyce to exhibit his character's "interiority," to organize psychic materials on the page in an affectively charged fashion, in "a series of connecting shocks arranged in a certain sequence and directed at the audience" (Eisenstein, quoted in Wollen, *Signs and Meaning* 39).[27]

My discussion of montage in Dos Passos started out from the claim that the juxtaposition of images of external reality, of everyday life in the early twentieth-century city, was designed to arouse the reader to feel how repulsive the current state of the world had become. The bulk of the reading above has been devoted to demonstrating how the novelist's dynamic performance, his arrangement of episodic scenes, was calculated to disgust readers to the point where they would react to social conditions as intolerable and in desperate need of change. Such reactions are not exclusively emotional, for the subject must also be compelled to reflect intellectually on the historicity of the world he inhabits. As Deleuze puts it in *The Time-Image* in reference to Eisenstein: "the shock has an effect on the spirit, it forces it to think, to think the Whole" (*Cinema 2* 158). When the "artistic essence of the images is realized [. . . it produces] *a shock to thought, communicating vibrations to the cortex, touching the nervous and cerebral system directly*" (156; emphasis in the original). The combination of images generates an affective charge that then gets the mind working; if "the shock wave or the nervous vibration" leads beyond the impression that one sees and hears toward an "I FEEL, 'totally physiological sensation,'" this powerful feeling in turn acts "on the cortex," giving "rise to thought, the cinematographic I THINK: the whole as subject" (158).

Dos Passos's late aesthetic procedure exemplifies what Deleuze, still in the context of an analysis of Eisenstein's cinematic theory and practice, calls the "second moment which goes from the concept to the affect," which returns from thought to the image, in the process "giving 'emotional fullness' or 'passion' back to the intellectual process" (158). This second moment, which is properly inseparable from the first, helps account for the description of Jimmy's mental state as he roams the streets of Manhattan in a daze. This is the pathic or sensory complement to the intellectual appeal, the "highest form of consciousness" thus inextricably linked to "the deepest form of the subconscious" (159) as coexisting moments in the overall procedure. Too distressed to grasp the causal forces determining the conditions of existence he experiences (the "highest form of consciousness"), the confused character is rendered subject to the random flow of sensory impressions, to mixed-up calls to buy manufactured goods. The concept of capitalism as a product of historical change escapes him while one of the economic mode of production's constitutive elements—the discursive practice of advertising—infiltrates and takes over his psyche. Indeed, the "whole is no longer the logos which unifies the parts," no longer an idea that can make sense of everything, but is instead "the drunkenness, the pathos which bathes them and spreads out in them" (Deleuze is still commenting on Eisenstein, *The General Line* in particular): "From this point of view images constitute a malleable mass, a descriptive material loaded with visual and sound features of expression [. . .] This is a primitive language or thought, or rather an *internal monologue*, a drunken monologue, working through figures, metonymies, synecdoches, metaphors, inversions, attractions" (159; emphasis in the original). Indeed, at this late stage of *Manhattan Transfer*, we observe Jimmy staggering around in a kind of hypnotic trance, if not actually intoxicated. Utterly immersed in his surroundings, whatever he sees or hears functions as shocking stimuli that trigger in turn a series of cognitively aberrant tropes. "Everything made him bubble with repressed giggles[. . . .] Life was upside down, he was a fly walking on the ceiling of a topsy-turvy city" (298). Initially figuring himself as an insect crawling inside an inverted architectural construct, the latter serving as a synecdoche for his spatial milieu, he feels shortly thereafter as if he has become gaseous ("staggering like a pillar of smoke") only to then undergo a liquefaction: "Inside he fizzed like sodawater into sweet April syrups [. . .] cherry vanilla dripping foam" (299). Next he becomes an Alice in an urban wonderland: "He shrank until he was the smallness of dust, picking his way over crags and bowlders [*sic*] in the roaring gutter, climbing straws, skirting motoroil lakes" (260).

The stream-of-consciousness technique functions in *Manhattan Transfer*, then, as a means of staging the degraded condition of the emotionally overexcited, schizoid subject of capitalist modernity, as a way to register the debased state of mind of the intoxicated consumer. And this is precisely what the montage of attractions, as the underlying principle of the organization of the novel as a whole, is designed to counteract: the aim of the modernist text's juxtapositional method is to make the reader feel disgust not just at the commercially circumscribed desires of the masses but also at the capacity of advertising to atomize individuals, to break them up into mere molecules, into particles of dust or bubbles of water caught up in an impersonal flow of sensory intensities. The prerequisite for sociopolitical solidarity is a literary presentation of its spectacularly repulsive antithesis.

Although the emergence of a literary variant of slapstick modernism was on the horizon in the mid-1920s, I am not proposing that *Manhattan Transfer* be classified in accordance with this term. Rather my claim is that we can appreciate the significance of Dos Passos's novel, retrospectively, as having paved the way for the imminent development of slapstick modernism. His ideologically motivated reorientation of the novel away from passive representation toward a more active, if not activist approach, and his correlative focus on the reader's psyche as the target of his verbal performance were indispensable preconditions for the spectacular autobiographical interventions of Céline and Miller in the next decade and Kerouac's in the 1950s;[28] and the idea underlying Dos Passos's montage strategy anticipates the conviction that is fundamental to Burroughs's work after World War II: that "certain word combinations produce certain effects on the human nervous system" (Odier 28). What differentiates Dos Passos from his predecessors is that the latter proved willing to assimilate the comic energies of slapstick film into their formally innovative literary projects. If from the point of view of the present inquiry such a turn toward the cinematic enterprise constitutes a major step forward, then Dos Passos's next cultural venture amounts to a retreat of sorts. In the spring of 1927 he participated with four others in the formation of the New Playwrights Theatre, an ostensibly revolutionary undertaking that fell well short of its primary goal to establish an artistic practice that would, in contrast to the "bourgeois" drama, "justify the ways of politics (mass action) to the individual-in-the-mass" (Dos Passos, "Did the New Playwright's Theatre Fail?" 119).

The point, of course, is not to reproach Dos Passos for not being prepared to learn from silent screen comedy. Rather his reserved position vis-à-vis the film genre helps define the 1920s as a particular phase in the prehistory of slapstick modernism, one when certain modernist writers inclined toward and then withdrew from the influence of cinematic clownishness.[29] A decision that poet Wallace Stevens made early in the decade to excise a couple of allusions to Harold Lloyd from the poem "The Comedian as the Letter C" supports this contention.

"Approaching Carolina," the third section of "From the Journal of Crispin," contained thirty-one lines that Wallace Stevens chose not to include in the revised version of his famous long poem, first published in *Harmonium* in 1923:[30]

> A short way off the city starts to climb,
> At first in alleys which the lilacs line,
> Abruptly, then, to the cobbled merchant streets,
> The shops of chandlers, tailors, bakers, cooks,
> The Coca Cola-bars, the barber poles,
> The Strand and Harold Lloyd, the lawyers' row,
> The Citizens' Bank, two tea rooms, and a church.

Crispin is happy in this metropole.
If the lilacs give the alleys a young air
Of sentiment, the alleys in exchange
Make gifts of no less worthy ironies.
If poems are transmutations of plain shops,
By aid of starlight, distance, wind, war, death,
Are not these doldrums poems in themselves,
These trophies of wind and war? At just what point
Do barber-poles become burlesque or cease
To be? Are bakers what the poets will,
Supernal artisans or muffin men,
Or do they have, on poets' minds, more influence
Than poets know? Are they one moment flour,
Another pearl? The Citizens' Bank becomes
Palladian and then the Citizens' Bank
Again. The flimsiest tea room fluctuates
Through crystal changes. Even Harold Lloyd
Proposes antic Harlequin.

(991–92)

The significance of the passage in the context of the foolish hero's overall aesthetic education is of minimal consequence here. Whether or not we should take Crispin's emerging faith in the "essential prose" of realism as risible or seriously is less pertinent than the speaker's uncertain evaluation of Lloyd's physical gags. Are these worth being considered the equal of the improvisations of the capering buffoon of the commedia dell'arte? The question is itself inscribed in a more encompassing one: is the subject responsible for the beauty he perceives around him, or does the mundane world surreptitiously shape his visionary outlook? Is the re-enchantment of urban modernity something that sensitive individuals produce, or is such a transformation the illusory effect of an objective process beyond the control of the poet? No answers are forthcoming, but what is clear is that Stevens rejected the minor proposal. By eliminating the reference to Lloyd from the final version of his poem, Stevens dismisses the speculative notion that clownish performers in the carnivalized arena of motion pictures merit the faithful "researches" of "the marvelous sophomore" (55). Removed from the (semiautobiographical) romantic protagonist's "wide / curriculum," film comedians are by implication repudiated as viable role models for even the most comically oriented of modernist poets.[31]

Notably, Stevens's turn away from the slapstick film star coincides—in the passage, in the poem as a whole, and (with only a few exceptions) in his oeuvre in its entirety—with the problems associated with his mundane life in urban modernity. The seemingly insignificant cut speaks volumes about the status of nature and "bourgeois interiority" in his lyric poetry "as a motivated negation of New York," to which he was exposed on a regular basis from 1900 to 1916 (Lentricchia 133). For Frank Lentricchia, Stevens's existential and artistic predicament, which persisted into the late stages of his career, long after he had left Manhattan, was a spiritual exhaustion, an emotional lethargy borne of an "endless need for the new which alone can break us out of the grooves of boredom" (162). As Stevens himself put it: "What I want more than anything else in music, painting, and poetry, in life and in belief is the thrill that I experienced once in all the things that no longer thrill me at all" (quoted in Lentricchia 162). One wonders whether a partial solution to the poet's increasingly enervated state of mind lay in the pleasurably exhilarating, daringly athletic performances on screen of the popular slapstick comedian Stevens had rejected at a pivotal stage in his career.

3

The Politics and Poetics of Attraction II

Harold Lloyd's "Thrill" Films

> The generalisations to be drawn from these simple experiments are, if we do not expect too much, encouraging. Some light upon obscure processes, such as empathy, and upon the intervention of muscular imagery and tendencies to action into the apprehension of shapes and of sequences of sounds which had been supposed to be apprehended by visual or auditory apparatus alone [. . . .] These and similar results have been well worth the trouble expended.
>
> —I. A. Richards, *The Principles of Literary Criticism*

Harold Lloyd's athletic performances, his comic yet exhilarating acrobatics in dangerous situations, were designed to invigorate the spectating masses. His humorous physical escapades constituted an effort to help facilitate his prospective audience's acquisition of the bodily and mental skills necessary to survive everyday life in the modern metropolis. A social purposefulness thus underlay his kinetically accelerated movements on screen. This thesis requires speculation on the filmic text as a formative force, as motivated by the desire to perform an assimilative or acclimatizing task in the world. Here the screen emerges as a virtual space, which spectators are encouraged to imagine their way into in order to secure the neurological and physiological training they need to inhabit their historically new surroundings. Borrowing from the title of his most famous film, we might say that Lloyd's recurrent willingness to put "safety last" was intended to serve as a way to train people to master the threats that daily life in the city consistently posed to them. The depiction of risky behavior was envisioned as a means whereby members of society might prepare themselves to avoid suffering bodily harm in their actual environment.

Given Eisenstein's critical strictures against corporeal stunts or tricks ("Montage of Attractions" 30), to comprehend Lloyd's cinematic achievement from the point of view of the theory of attractions, it is necessary to rely on the contemporaneous statements of Eisenstein's theatrical associate Sergei Tretyakov. The latter's "The Theatre of Attractions" (1924) helps excavate the "utilitarian" aims that were operative in the silent comedian's daring maneuvers, for Tretyakov shared with Eisenstein the conviction that art should be assigned a "socially useful job," that it must confront directly "the day's urgent problems" (21–22). For both, the attraction was the most effective means of seizing "the audience's attention," compressing "its emotion," and discharging it (24). Commitment to such a goal entails that one seek to estimate "habitual viewer psychology" correctly. Figuring out what will startle them is the precondition for devising a construct that will "work on the nerves to produce a moment of alarm" (24). Also like Eisenstein, Tretyakov points to "the music hall, the variety show, and the circus program" as sources for the artistic strategies he has in mind, with the caveat that such forms of entertainment tend not to mobilize the affects they generate toward the forceful resolution of sociopolitical predicaments. Tretyakov's approach differs from Eisenstein's in that only the former considers "acrobatic demonstrations" to be a potentially valuable type of attraction insofar as they have the capacity to "provoke audience reflexes [. . .] that are connected to motor structures that are difficult and unfamiliar for the spectator" (25). Observing someone else perform enthralling bodily feats initiates the process whereby the observer begins to obtain this same skill set. The first step is to regret one's shortcomings, as audience members do when they say, "'What a shame that I can't control my movements like that, If only I could do cartwheels'" (25). Yet such confessions should lead beyond "platonic sighs over physical ineptitude" (25), and beyond admiration for the corporeal virtuosity of others, toward the self's acquisition of such amazing agility.[1]

A few years later, in "Our Cinema" (1928), Tretyakov restated his faith in postrevolutionary cultural practice as an activist or agitational intervention in everyday life. Now, however, it is motion pictures that he defends. If some in the world are still "naïve enough to believe [. . . that] the movie screen is a window into the enchanted realm of souls," directors in the Soviet Union have realized the importance of learning how to "stimulate people, to rouse their moods in connection with a certain task" (29, 35).[2] No longer is it sufficient to try to divert the masses from the "defects" of real life. The purpose of film has ceased to be a compensatory one in which people, in contrast to their "daily routine," "experience more adventures in an hour and a half than could ever fit into an actual lifetime" (29). Rather than provide spectators who are "starved for strength, beauty, happiness, and success" with "their daily ration of illusion," politicized filmmakers must strive "to distribute the shocks," must learn "how to structure a stimulating neural massage" (35). In sum, "we have to transform the one-and-a-half-hour movie screening into the ten minutes of morning exercise that puts an athlete in a cheerful and energetic state" (35).

Here we again encounter the less frequently emphasized meaning of "mimesis," the one in which the "image prompts its analogue" (Rancière, "Eisenstein's Madness" 23). Tracing both "forms of mimesis" back to Aristotle's *Physics*, Philippe Lacoue-Labarthe distinguishes between the two as, on the one hand, "a restricted form, which is the reproduction, the copy, the reduplication of what is given"; on the other hand, "there is a general mimesis, which reproduces nothing [. . .] but which *supplements* a certain deficiency in nature, its incapacity to do everything, organize everything, make everything its work—*produce* everything." The latter is a "productive" as opposed to a reflective mimesis, and it "accomplishes, carries out, *finishes* natural production as such" ("Diderot" 255–56; emphasis in the original). From the point of view of a productive mimesis, the power of art resides in its (prosthetic) capacity to make up for the limitations of human nature. My contention is that Lloyd's artificially contrived, technologically facilitated comic actions aimed to serve such a supplementary function. The (structural) social aspiration informing his exhilarating escapades on screen was to aid the members of his audience who were having difficulty adjusting (physically or psychically) to the kinds of stress that are endemic to everyday life in urban modernity. Viewer identification with the mobile image on screen was to establish an affective bond that would trigger in turn a dynamic relay: spectators would obtain from a gifted actor the desirable degree of dexterity they lacked.

High and Dizzy (1920) and *Never Weaken* (1921), two "thrill" films Lloyd made on the threshold of becoming a box-office sensation, illustrate the athletic aspects of the filmmaker's enterprise while also introducing his tendency to reflexively figure his cultural intervention in medical terms. Gerald Mast refers to these two films as having "mysteriously" combined "doctor gags and high-rise thrills" (157). It is this enigma that the present chapter addresses, for guided by Hal Roach (who directed *High and Dizzy*), Lloyd sought to legitimate his cinematic endeavor as an effort to heal the sick. Motion picture fun was worth the price of the ticket, because the technical media supplied a remedy for contemporary ailments.

Cinematic Remedies

> In those days we used to go to art movies to see silent pictures, because I had my culture [. . .] but you, poor thing, didn't understand anything at all about that yellow and convulsed shrieking which had all taken place before you were born, that grooved emulsion in which dead people ran about. But suddenly Harold Lloyd would go by and then you would shake off the water of your dream and would finally be convinced that all was well.
>
> —Julio Cortazar, *Hopscotch*

In a 1936 essay titled "Why 'Thrillers' Thrive," Alfred Hitchcock explained the appeal of motion pictures in terms of the excitement they supply. If we go "to the pictures [. . . to] see life reflected on the screen," it is a "kind of life" that we don't customarily "experience ourselves," the difference consisting of the "emotional disturbances, which, for convenience, we call 'thrills'" (109). We need these thrills to keep ourselves energized, for our "nature is such that we must have these 'shake-ups,' or we grow sluggish and jellified" (109). Because unmediated encounters with the threat of death are no longer a constitutive aspect of existence, we turn to the cinema for artificial versions of these: "our civilization has so screened and sheltered us that it isn't practicable to experience sufficient thrills firsthand." Rather than "sit by as spectators," the audience must be made "to participate" in the suspenseful actions, and the combined technical ingenuity of the director, cameraman, and editor accomplishes this task. According to Hitchcock, a scene in *Hell's Angels* (1930; dir. Howard Hughes) is exemplary in this regard. First we see a close-up of a British pilot's face—"grim, tense, even horror-stricken"—as the plane swoops toward its rendezvous with an enemy zeppelin. Then "we are transferred to the pilot's seat, and it is we who are hurtling to death at ninety miles an hour; and at the moment of impact—and blackout—a palpable shuddering runs through the audience" (110). Similarly, Cecil B. DeMille's *The Crusades* (1935) produces a salutary "shock" when it depicts the violent clash of opposing horsemen. Such exhilarating scenes (which Hitchcock distinguishes sharply from those created within the horror genre, which "supply the desired emotional jolt" by exploiting public fascinations with "sadism, perversion, bestiality, and deformity" [111]) revitalize the masses physiologically. They "set the blood pounding through the veins, [and] are highly beneficial for indigestion, gout, rheumatism, sciatica, and premature middle age. The audience thrives on thrills, the cinema thrives on the audience, the director thrives on the cinema, and everybody is happy." The suspenseful films of Harold Lloyd, Hitchcock's slapstick predecessor in the field of "thrill" production, rest on a cognate premise in that they too endorse the notion that image-based relays between spectators and actors are a collectively beneficial, symbiotic arrangement.[3]

The opening scenes of *High and Dizzy* evoke the therapeutic bond that Lloyd proposes to establish between himself and his viewers. In setting the stage for the story to come, the introductory intertitle suggests that the main character and the actor are alike in that both are prepared to take explosive measures to cure collective illnesses: "The Boy has rushed into the nerve racking whirlpool of professional practice. Graduated from medical college as an M.D., Ph.D. and T.N.T." Unfortunately, at this time the would-be caregiver has no patients and therefore has nothing to do but lounge around smoking and playing cards, biding his time until someone shows up. At last a couple arrives and sits down in the waiting room. Harold then goes to extreme lengths to convince his potential patients that he is the right person for the job, donning a series of disguises to give the impression that business is booming. The first time, he staggers out of the office through the main entrance pretending to be a feeble old man with a cast on his wrist; before leaving he hammers on the cast with his cane, indicating that after only "two treatments" the joint has become impervious to pain. He then returns wearing a blindfold, implying that he suffers from eye trouble. The third time, Harold weirdly appears as a ridiculously tall man, a false impression he creates by placing a bust on his head and wrapping an overcoat around his upper body. Read self-consciously, the scene indicates Lloyd's enduring ambition as an actor to widen his appeal, to become a huge success in the movies, and to help people in return for attracting their attention. As previous commentators have pointed out, no one worked more conscientiously than Harold Lloyd to find a commercially viable persona, trying out in the roughly one hundred short films he made at the start of his career such pre-glasses "characters" as Willie Work and Lonesome Luke, an obvious Chaplin rip-off in which Lloyd wore tight-fitting rather than baggy clothes in the vain hope of setting himself apart from the original.[4]

To return to *High and Dizzy*, when Harold finally makes time for the pair, an older man and a young woman, he mistakenly assumes it is the former who is unwell. It is of course "the Girl" (played by Mildred Davis, Lloyd's future wife) who is unwell. She is a somnambulist, and her father wants Harold to cure her involuntary behavior. Sparks fly when the doctor and the patient meet, their gazes (shown in successive close-ups) locked on each other. Even when he becomes intoxicated after drinking a batch of home-brewed beer with a buddy, Harold remains a likable klutz with the capacity to make girls laugh. More important, when he ventures (still drunk) onto the ledge of a tall building to rescue Mildred, whom he has spied sleepwalking out there, Harold, now high in two senses, clumsily exhibits his semi-heroism. Stumbling around in a state of panicky desperation, barely able to maintain his balance after discovering his spatial whereabouts, the terrified lad (his hair literally stands on end) is willing to risk life and limb to save the girl. This proves unnecessary when she climbs back inside herself (leaving him stranded on the other side of a locked window). But he is still rewarded for his bravery; after he saves himself, the two agree to marry.

Released in 1921, *Never Weaken* (dir. Fred Newmeyer) is another self-referential film that better illuminates the link between acrobatic comedy and medicinal matters in Lloyd's oeuvre. Playing a young stockbroker, Harold is engaged to a girl (Mildred Davis) who works in the office next door for an osteopath. The doctor is about to lay her off because he has no patients, but Harold comes up with a bright idea to solve her problem. Previously, while walking over to visit her, he had passed by a room in which a circus performer (Mark Jones) was practicing his tumbling routines. Thinking the man had injured himself, Harold rushed in to help. But the man flipped forward and backward to demonstrate that he was not hurt. Recalling this incident, Harold's plan is to drum up business by hiring the tumbler to go out in public, pretend to trip, and then allow Harold to fix him up in front of a crowd. After he recovers, any impressed observers in need of treatment will be directed to Harold's fiancée's boss.

The trick works perfectly. In the street the acrobat fakes a fall, whereupon Harold rushes over and twists the apparently injured man around in a wildly exaggerated manner. At first Harold resembles a wrestler applying a brutal hold, his aggressive manipulation of the purportedly wounded man's body initially unsettling, but he draws cheers from the onlookers when the man leaps to his feet, miraculously healed. The man pounds his chest to indicate his restored health, thanks Harold, and departs. The amazed members of the crowd then eagerly accept the business cards Harold passes out, and as the scene ends we see a man in a wheelchair and one on crutches hurrying off to secure an appointment, thoroughly persuaded that their damaged bodies can be quickly repaired by some violent physical therapy.

Shortly thereafter, to produce even more patients, Harold purchases a bag of soap flakes and mischievously spreads them on an intersection recently moistened by a street cleaner. As a policeman tries to chase Harold away, the cop—as well as pedestrians everywhere—repeatedly slips to the ground.

When Harold arrives back at the office, he is pleased to see the place filled with infirm persons, confirming that he was on the right track, at least as far as financial success is concerned.

The allegorical connotations of the earlier scene are unmistakable. The gesture of handing out business cards resembles the act of selling tickets, and what the customers are paying for is both an entertaining show in which spectacular stunts will be performed and the promise of reinvigoration. The second reel of the film confirms this reflexive interpretation when Lloyd's character unexpectedly confronts a situation in which he must accomplish several marvelous feats while suspended high in the air. Due to a visual mix-up, Harold believes his lover has forsaken him for another, and he has decided to commit suicide. After a series of amusingly inept attempts to end his own life, a runaway girder lifts the heartbroken character (his eyes closed) out of his building onto the scaffolding of a skyscraper under construction next door. Once he becomes an unwilling daredevil, it is possible to recognize the crowd gathered on the street in the first reel as our surrogates. As have the spectators earlier in the story, we now watch in amazement as a physically well-trained individual contorts his body; correlatively, the film itself undertakes a task analogous to the one Harold had performed in the previous scene: to heal broken bodies (and hurt minds).

Both situations are triangular. In the first scene the tumbler fakes an injury, Harold pretends to heal him, and the gullible crowd is inspired to visit the osteopath. In the second scene Harold as actor pretends to be in danger of falling to his death, the film starring Harold is the agent of the cure for the fear of heights, and the viewer of the film is someone who is inspired to go (back) to the cinema for treatment. Is the therapeutic project in question thus undertaken cynically as opposed to sincerely? Is the film star as cultural physician a scam to make some cash? Or is he engaged in a noble attempt to use the medium to aid the sick? The interpretive ambiguity reflects the contradictions that are inherent to commercially oriented cultural practices in a capitalist (as opposed to a socialist) milieu.

In any event, the terrifying act requires the performer to exhibit his balancing skills and to display a significant amount of mental and physical strength, for, once Harold realizes where he is, he must struggle to maintain control over his fear of falling. Moreover, as he scrambles around trying desperately to preserve his life, the subjectivized filming technique facilitates the spectator's corporeal identification with the actor. Two startling point-of-view shots create the viscerally exhilarating sensation that we too are suspended precariously in space. The first of these shots angles straight down at the street below, while the second is a shaky aerial pan; both bring into view what Harold presumably sees from his elevated location. By miming the vision of the panicking character, the camera work produces the vertiginous feeling that we are about to drop to our deaths. The laughter would be nervous in this case, for it is difficult to shake the impression that we are in grave physical danger. Indeed, as in a non-comic action film, we remain scared as much for our own sake as for the character until the latter finds his way back down to the ground.

Lloyd's third feature film, *Dr. Jack* (1922), justifies itself (and by extension Lloyd's overall cinematic enterprise) as a viable cure for ailing people more explicitly than did the two shorts discussed above. Logically enough, in positing slapstick film as a worthwhile means of rejuvenating weary individuals, *Dr. Jack* isolates Lloyd as the remedy's active ingredient, as the key element in the pharmaceutical substance manufactured to help treat the fatigued. In this instance his performance proves an effective way to facilitate the recovery of wealthy young women suffering from a nervous disorder.[5]

Throughout the opening credits there is an "Rx" in the upper left-hand corner of the screen, a symbol that, in conjunction with the verbal declaration that the motion picture has been "prescribed" (rather than produced) by Hal Roach, indicates the filmmakers' decision to identify their product as a legal drug, one designed to make those who take it high and dizzy in a pleasurably recreational sense. The purpose of the film as chemical compound is to revitalize its ailing audience. The listing of the cast under the heading of "In Consultation" extends the therapeutic metaphor, suggesting that the actors agreed with the diagnosis and are willing to help with the treatment. The dosage is not specified, but presumably one should consume as many comic films of this brand as one can afford.

Set at the mansion where a "Sick-Little-Well-Girl" (Mildred Davis) dwells, the opening scene of *Dr. Jack* depicts her in the foreground draped in a shawl and sitting in a room, while in the background we can see through a window a number of youths her age having a great time outside energetically running around, playfully chasing after each other, holding hands, and so on. A nurse enters and yanks down the curtain, cutting off visual access to events in the garden, because, according to the orders of the girl's primary caregiver, Dr. Ludwig von Saulsbourg, she must not be exposed to sunlight. Given that the window was the only brightly lit area of the gloomy chamber, and that she has been forbidden to look at the activity it frames, it is evident that in truth what she is not permitted to do is watch motion pictures, especially those that feature bodies moving around quickly. An intertitle confirms that von Saulsbourg's concern is to remain on the household payroll rather than to improve his patient's mental condition. Capitulating "to the disorder's demands," von Saulsbourg's version of the "rest cure" ensures that the girl will not get better. Worse, the sinister physician's ultimate goal is get her kind yet overprotective father to agree to have her placed in the private sanitarium he runs. That Mildred, immobilized in her chair, wonders between sobs why she can't be like other girls, free "of dark rooms and shadows," might seem to place the blame for her malady not simply on the vast array of medications her nurses regularly spoon feed her but on the cinema as well. Yet, as the narrative unfolds, it becomes glaringly apparent that the sort of affectively charged, chaotic fun that slapstick comedy supplies its viewers possesses the power to rejuvenate the young neurasthenic.

When the film introduces Dr. Jack (Lloyd), it is evident he cares less about making money than contributing to the general well-being of those who live in the small town where he works. Constantly in a hurry (on duty from "7 A.M. to 7 A.M."), he races to his first emergency in a dramatically energetic manner, even stealing a motorcycle cop's vehicle and then a young boy's chainless bicycle to arrive in time. His dying patient, however, turns out to be a child's doll that has fallen to the bottom of a well. After rescuing the toy and comforting its sorrowful owner, he goes inside her house to examine another child, Sonny, who is showing signs of having pneumonia. Here again the condition is more mental than physical, the boy's symptoms a result of his not wanting to go to school. Solving this problem is equally simple: all Jack has to do is trick the boy into believing he won't have to attend class and he starts leaping exuberantly around his bedroom. Duplicity plays a role in Jack's next case as well. Perceiving that an elderly woman's failing health is a result of her loneliness, Jack lies to her son so that he will come to visit his mother. Social interaction with loved ones proves to be the best antidepressant available. His next patient is a musician with a bandaged foot, who only needs to be encouraged to play his instrument to forget his pain. Lastly, Jack boxes with an old man, rough-housing all the latter needs to stay healthy. The point is that in all of these allegorical scenarios what Dr. Jack does in the narrative for those he treats is precisely what *Dr. Jack* is meant to do for those watching it in the theater.

Eventually, a concerned family friend, who has pled with the Sick-Little-Well-Girl's father to seek another professional opinion, manages to get Jack brought in as an eminent specialist. The friend advises Jack before his first visit to stick to his own methods and ignore von Saulsbourg's ideas. Entering her room, Jack glances at the array of bottled medicines on a table and correctly surmises that Mildred's main problem is those supervising her care. He immediately seeks to open the curtains of her room, only to be stopped by von Saulsbourg, who insists that Jack examine the "pupillary reflex" of her eyes to bright light. As the two youthful characters make eye contact, the girl involuntarily reaches out to hold Jack's hand, confirming an attraction that is clearly mutual. Unfortunately, while scrutinizing her eyes more closely, Jack stumbles and accidentally kisses the girl, an act witnessed by her father, who promptly fires Jack.

Though off the case, he is allowed to stay the evening. Later that night the girl, though having been prohibited from seeing him again, sneaks downstairs to say good-bye to him in private. Suddenly a couple of prison guards appear, informing the couple that a dangerous lunatic has escaped and may be on the premises. The girl's unexpected response to the report of danger is "Oh! Isn't it thrilling? My heart is going bumpety-bump," which leads Jack to realize that this is "the only medicine she ever needed," that her fragile condition stems from the fact that she "has never known excitement." Von Saulsbourg, of course, instructs her to go to bed immediately on the grounds that a "shock might cause a relapse," though Jack knows better and devises a plan to demonstrate to her father that "excitement is just what she needs." He then dresses up as the aforementioned escapee and proceeds to scare the entire household, hopping about madly, performing somersaults and cartwheels like a whirling dervish. The servants want to flee, while the girl, evidently in good spirits and feeling courageous, eagerly participates in the effort to capture the apparent intruder.

As a zany chase ensues, it becomes evident that dramatic actions of this sort are good for Mildred. An artificially contrived situation, in which Jack successfully clowns crazily, energizes the girl, so much so that she willingly joins in the fun. After observing by way of a wall mirror that Jack has been masquerading as the intruder, Mildred understands that Jack has staged the sequence of events for her benefit, that, as she subsequently explains to her father, the doctor has been doing it all for her sake. She then surreptitiously dons the disguise he has discarded in an effort to ensure that von Saulsbourg, who has admitted his nerves are unstrung, will leave the mansion. Becoming an actor seems to be the next stage in the girl's progress toward a full recovery, though this process may just as effectively occur for the actual spectators in an imaginary fashion via an act of identification with the figures on the screen. Either way, the indirectly articulated message of the film is that corporeally invigorating and emotionally exciting modes of kinetic play are an indispensable good for everyone.[6]

Lloyd's cinematic achievement thus reveals the blind spot of E. E. Cummings's celebratory affirmation of both the circus and modernist art as "curative institution[s]" on the basis of their shared penchant for an aesthetic of "mobility."[7] For in his 1925 article "The Adult, the Artist, and the Circus," published in *Vanity Fair*, he forcibly denied that the newer medium should be grouped conceptually together with those cultural practices he deemed capable of presenting onlookers with "unbelievably skillful and inexorably beautiful dangerous things." Whereas for him the "circus-show entirely belongs" to the set that includes "certain authentic 'works of art'" on the grounds that both furnish "thrilling experiences of a life-or-death order," "going to the movies" is "most emphatically" not a member of this set (254–55).[8]

The Work of Art in the Age of Mechanical Reproduction (reprise): *Speedy*

> There are also, of course, movies that teach you how to drive automobiles.
>
> —Hollis Frampton, "The Invention without a Future"

In "To the Planetarium," the final section of *One-Way Street* (1928), Walter Benjamin articulated one of his earliest speculations on the way in which modern technology was organizing "a *physis*" through which humanity would relate to its surroundings "in a new and different form": "One need recall only the experiences of velocities by virtue of which mankind is now preparing to embark on incalculable journeys into the interior of time, to encounter there rhythms from which the sick shall draw strength as they did earlier on high mountains or on the shores of southern seas. The 'Lunaparks' are a prefiguration of sanatoria" (487). Though empirically unverifiable, Benjamin's hypothesis—that mechanized amusement parks can be conceptualized as a kind of second nature where visitors might receive up-to-date treatment for the diseases of modernity—parallels the notion I am pursuing by way of Lloyd's feature-length films. My argument is that he too sought to furnish the subjects of urban-industrial modernity with the energy they needed to maintain (or recover) a state of mental and physical well-being. That Lloyd's on-camera stunts actually enhanced the muscular power, manual dexterity, and neurological quickness of those who watched (and identified with) him is unlikely. However, the notion that he wanted to provide his age with the accelerated images that it required for its health supplies a viable context for hermeneutic understanding, for this ambition governed his cinematic venture during its most commercially successful and culturally ambitious phase. Below I seek to develop this claim by proposing (counterintuitively) that Lloyd's film encourages its spectators to relate to its cinematic imagery in a way that anticipates the use of simulated environments in the realm of virtual reality for training purposes.

The protagonist's memorable ascent in *Safety Last!* (1923), Lloyd's fourth and most famous feature film, has its origins in the actor's fascinated observation of a human fly agilely climbing a skyscraper. Lloyd's stated ambition was to furnish his audience with a vicarious version of this spectacular experience, one combining "thrill and dread" and therefore "heir to the strong sensations and visceral emotions evoked in the early silent era's 'cinema of attractions.'"[9] In so doing, the film helps illustrate, albeit in a comically hyperbolic manner, one of Benjamin's more intriguing theses in "The Work of Art" essay. In section 18 of the essay, Benjamin defends entertainment received in a state of distraction on the grounds that it can enable the masses to habituate themselves to their environment. He finds the collective response to architecture instructive in this respect, with the *tactile* appropriation of buildings through use demonstrating an exemplary accomplishment toward which contemporary cultural practices should strive. "Since [. . .] individuals are tempted to evade such tasks, art will tackle the most difficult and most important tasks whenever it is able to mobilize the masses. It does so currently in film" ("Work of Art," 2nd version 120). From this vantage point, *Safety Last!* would be not simply an optical experience that represents for its audience how ordinary people, when challenged, may acclimate themselves to their material milieu. Rather, insofar as film reception functions according to Benjamin's model as a "*true training ground*" (120; emphasis in the original), the spectators would be corporeally engaged, whether they realize it or not, in the process of acquiring the neurophysiological skills needed for self-preservation. Identifying with the comedian as he desperately clings to the sides and ledges of the architectural construct, the audience, without concentrating, would be undergoing the process of gradually mastering their built surroundings via the work of art (120).[10]

Lloyd's vertical acrobatics in *Safety Last!* are legendary, whereas few people recall his equally remarkable penchant in this film and elsewhere for involving himself in high-speed movements on the horizontal plane. I am thinking in this regard of the scene in which, fearing he will be fired if he arrives late for work, Lloyd, playing "The Boy," successfully fakes an injury to secure a ride in an ambulance. The vehicle then races away with Lloyd lying on a stretcher inside. Two different shots work together to convey the impression that the automobile is traveling very quickly indeed through densely populated sections of town. The first, an overhead shot angled down toward the street, is commonplace; the other, however, photographed from within the ambulance, is unusual. Though incongruously matched to Lloyd's perspective as he repeatedly peeks out the back and side windows, the shot evidently derives from a camera mounted on the dashboard and thus aimed through the front windshield. Accompanied by the use of a fast-motion technique, this point-of-view shot creates the marvelously effective illusion that we are either passengers in or operators of the careening rescue vehicle—one that, while heading to its destination, narrowly avoids smashing into other cars and only barely manages not to run over defenseless pedestrians by swerving erratically at the last minute.

The significance of *Speedy* (1928), Lloyd's final silent feature, is that in the process of integrating such subjectively oriented "traveling" shots into the narrative, thus providing a stronger thematic motivation for the formal procedure, the motion picture also supplies the necessary key to comprehending the functional aspirations governing Lloyd's aesthetic preoccupation with kinetic exhilaration.[11] That many of his films feature breathtaking traversals of urban space can be understood as an attempt to enable embodied audiences to adapt in a non-subservient fashion to their historical circumstances. Slapstick cinema from this perspective was intended to function as a training ground for the inhabitants of urban modernity, as a machine people might utilize to acclimate themselves apperceptively to demanding situations. By offering vivid impressions of traveling at comically excessive velocities, his proto-action films sought to help facilitate the acquisition of the sensorimotor skills individuals require to operate mechanized vehicles under conditions of extreme stress. His highly entertaining films were designed on some level to teach people how to drive really fast.

A montage of establishing shots—using stock footage—locate New York City as the film's setting. After views (from the far side of the East River) of the Brooklyn Bridge and the Lower Manhattan skyline, we catch a glimpse of tugboats gliding across the water and then progress to a heavily congested Times Square with an elevated train platform standing out on the right side of the frame, the sequence ending at another hectic thoroughfare. An intertitle then places us in a neighborhood where life moves more slowly than in the busy areas of town we have just seen. We have arrived at an "old fashioned corner" that has not yet "acquired the pace of the rest of New York." Elements of the plot are hinted at when a tour guide with a bullhorn draws the attention of a group of sightseers to a "vehicle that has defied the rush of civilizashun [*sic*]—the last horse car in New York." Owned and operated by Pop Dillon (Bert Woodruff), this remnant of an earlier system of transportation is the only obstacle to a planned expansion of the Inter-City Railroad Company. An agent for the latter has offered to purchase the old man's rights to the track (which he retains as long as he runs once every twenty-four hours), but Pop has refused to sell until the agent agrees to offer what Pop believes his small franchise is worth. An exasperated company executive then threatens to push the old man out of business.

Ultimately it is the task of the character Lloyd plays (Harold Swift, aka "Speedy") to make sure that this does not happen. Engaged to Pop's granddaughter, he needs to protect the traditional mode of transportation only until the forces of capitalist modernity are willing to pay a fair price. Yet when we first encounter him he seems an unlikely candidate to resolve this financial matter. Though he displays considerable manual dexterity as a soda jerk, his compulsive interest in a professional sport is a constant distraction that eventually costs him his job. A devoted Yankees fan, his focus on the score of a baseball game prevents him from completing an assignment to deliver a bouquet of flowers in a timely manner. Having failed, he goes home, realizing that he will be fired anyway.

To forget about his troubles in the vocational realm, Harold takes his girlfriend, Jane (Ann Christy), on a date to Coney Island. What distinguishes *Speedy* from the other motion pictures released in 1928 that also feature a trip to this amusement site is that only the slapstick film proposes that fairground forms of fun may enable individuals to adjust in an empowering fashion to the anxiety-inducing conditions of existence that are characteristic of urban modernity. Although the couples in King Vidor's *The Crowd* (1928) and Paul Fejos's *Lonesome* (1928) enjoy many of the same Luna and Steeplechase Park rides that Harold and Jane do, play comparable games, and eat at similar concession stands, the experience of the lovers in the non-comic films are not presented as being profoundly related to what is expected of them as members of the American workforce. The same goes for a previous Lloyd film, the two-reel comic romance *Number, Please* (1920). Set entirely at the boardwalk of a smaller amusement park, the short film has some exhilarating footage shot from the rider's point of view on a rollercoaster—as does Walter Ruttman's *Berlin: Symphony of a Great City* (1922) and René Clair's avant-garde classic, *Entr'acte* (1924)—but makes no effort to correlate the frenetic events of this day of leisure with the kinds of tasks people can anticipate having to perform as laborers.

In contrast, *Speedy* suggests that the exhilarating corporeal experiences and correlative mental commotion that carnival rides generate may serve as a valuable way to get ready for the challenging jobs one might secure in the metropolis. What flying through the air in a miniature airplane suspended from wires, steering a bumper car along an undulating and presumably magnetized surface, plunging down a water slide into an artificial pond (Shoot-the-Chutes), trying to stay on one's feet while walking through a revolving drum (Barrel of Love), or struggling to remain at the center of a spinning disc (Human Whirlpool) have in common is that such activities produce vertiginous states of sensory disorientation. The use in the film of a spiraling line as a dissolve between the scenes showing the characters on various attractions reinforces the idea that their basic appeal is a result of their capacity to cause individuals to lose their balance and consequently their mental equilibrium.[12] That the perceptual confusion Harold has enjoyed during his recreational visit to Coney Island has served not simply as a restorative respite from his ordinary responsibilities but also as excellent preparation for them is soon apparent. The training he has received in the realm of entertainment proves indispensable when he is hired the next day as a taxicab driver. Having learned to accustom himself to an onslaught of external stimuli, Harold has improved his chances of safely navigating his way through traffic-filled streets, his peripheral vision sufficiently developed so that he can react quickly and steer clear of the obstacles that come at him from all angles. *Speedy* thus demonstrates that pleasurable (and perhaps painful) jostling has the capacity to enable people to achieve a degree of control over the physiologically and psychologically demanding aspects of everyday life in the big city.

More important are the three driving sequences that follow immediately after the trip to the amusement park, for together these propose cinematic experience as a sufficient way for people to equip themselves to handle the mechanized elements of their milieu. Harold starts off his workday in a rather clumsy manner, failing due to a series of mishaps, such as forgetting to release the taxi's hand brake, to get any fares. Yet when a couple of police detectives hop into the cab and instruct him to "step on it," he performs admirably, swiftly taking them to Pennsylvania Station. Four shots are edited together in this initial trip across town. The first is taken from a vehicle following the taxi; the second from a vehicle ahead of the taxi; whereas a third, similarly aimed shot comes from the taxi itself and shows a motorcycle cop who has joined the chase trailing behind. In the latter two shots the camera tilts and swivels to convey the rapidity of the movement, while the illusion of depth is generated in both by a vanishing point that extends far down the avenue, thus providing the viewer with a measure of stability. The final (and lengthiest) shot, deriving from a stationary camera set up just off the sidewalk and that captures Harold's auto passing by, serves intermittently to keep the spectator at a comfortable remove from the chaotic action depicted on screen.

The second sequence is more revealing in that it begins to close the spatial gap between the viewer and the viewed, eliminating in the process the optical distance that the laws of perspective enforce. While waiting, as he has been instructed to by the detectives who have left to hunt down their suspect, Harold receives a ticket from the motorcycle cop who doesn't listen when the character tries to explain the situation. A subsequent mix-up leads Harold to mistakenly believe that the detectives are back in the cab and that he has been authorized to drive again as fast as he can. In this next pursuit, roughly the same set of shots are combined with a few others, one taken from the side showing Harold at the wheel and the other looking into the cab at the startled passenger, an older man unable to stop himself from bouncing up and down as the machine rockets forward. Taken together, the acceleration of the imagery via a superfast-motion technique, the jolting rapidity of the cuts, the exaggerated use of an off-kilter camera to create the impression of erratic swerves, and the closer proximity of Harold's taxi to the camera (in the shots taken from an unseen vehicle in front of the character's car) greatly intensify the feeling that we too are traveling at an extremely high rate of speed. When the taxi arrives at his destination, the enraged police officer stomps up to the car window and barks at Harold, "Say, you crazy nut, where did you learn to drive like that?" Utterly pleased with himself, Harold replies that he didn't, that "it's a gift." Yet the film has already suggested that his skills are not innate, that the character has developed them (however unknowingly due to his state of distraction) by indulging at the amusement park in technologically mediated forms of play.

Aspects of the third sequence are even more remarkable, largely due to the intermittent employment of a still astonishing, relatively atypical shot. Frustrated by the fact that he has now been given two speeding tickets, Harold decides to take a break from work and hurries off to see Babe Ruth, who is signing autographs at a local orphan asylum. Realizing he is on the verge of being late for a game, the baseball star requests a ride to Yankee Stadium from Harold, who is delighted to oblige his idol. The race against time is one of the primary motifs that Lloyd and his stable of directors repeatedly relied on to structure his feature films. In the exciting finales of both *Girl Shy* (1924) and *Heaven Can Wait* (1926), for instance, Lloyd must overcome myriad obstacles, in the process making use of a series of different modes of transportation: in the first film he must get to church before his girlfriend marries another man; in the second he must arrive before his own wedding is called off. Similarly, the two-reel film *Get Out and Get Under* (1920) is almost entirely devoted to Lloyd's strenuous efforts to get to a local play in his beloved automobile before the show starts, and the feature *Hot Water* (1924) contains near its beginning a disastrous drive around town, during which Lloyd manages to wreck the brand-new car he has just bought for his wife.[13] The climax of *Speedy* is similarly organized around the urgent need to get from one place to another before it is too late, yet the taxicab ride with Ruth stands out from all of these because of its exceptionally fast-motion projection of images originally photographed by a camera mounted on the front of the moving vehicle (in these tracking frontal shots one can see the hood ornament at the bottom center of the screen). Though shot from a point external to the cab's interior, the spectator has the illusory impression that he or she is positioned inside and thus looking out through the windshield as the car travels at an impossibly swift pace through Manhattan.[14] Recalling (by way of its inversion) one of the primal scenes of early cinema, the ostensibly terrifying sight of a locomotive bearing down on the audience, this portion of *Speedy* retains the capacity to make the intensely involved viewer (credulous or not) cringe, to involuntarily recoil at the prospect of either plowing into a crowd of pedestrians or crashing into another vehicle. Braced for impact, the corporeally engaged masses in the theater are aligned with the semi-hysterical passenger in the film, who can barely keep his eyes open because he is so scared that a head-on collision is about to occur. Propelled forward and then thrown side to side as if on a carnival ride, yet deprived of the reassurance that everything is under control as it would be at an amusement park, the ball player, nervously wiping his brow, declares in reference to Harold's chaotically swerving style of driving, "I don't miss 'em half as close as you do." Effectively immersed in the action by virtue of an unusually hyper-kinesthetic filming technique, the thrilled spectators are similarly compelled to feel as if they narrowly avoided being involved in a disastrously awful automobile accident.

That it is a famous athlete who evinces a fear of getting hurt is significant in that one logically credits the great home-run hitter with possessing outstanding hand-eye coordination skills. Yet Ruth's ability to make contact with a fastball (or a curve) pales in comparison to Harold's extraordinary capacity to correctly manipulate the automobile's steering wheel while barely paying attention to the road. (Later we see a clip of Ruth hitting a home run in an actual game.) Urged to watch where he is going, Harold is so eager to carry on the conversation with his prestigious passenger that he repeatedly turns around to face Ruth, relying on what seem to be super-reflexes to avoid a crash. Ultimately the experience proves infantilizing for the Babe, who is nearly reduced to tears as he begs Harold to concentrate on what he is doing. Leaving the cab after the ride is complete, Ruth whines, "If I ever want to commit suicide, I'll call you." Having outshone the widely admired sports star in the realm of transportation, Harold's neurological responsiveness and corporeal daring have perhaps earned him considerable respect from those observing him. Who would not want to attain such a splendid degree of muscular and mental mastery over a modern machine? Excelling as the baseball hero does at a pastoral pastime is impressive, but the more crucial task at hand is to learn how best to survive the perils of everyday life in a hectic urban environment. Hence the claim of two contemporaneous sociologists that "speed of movement is one of the criteria by which the city selects its inhabitants; the human organisms which become adjusted to its demands, or that survive best, are those capable of responding in some organized fashion to the increase in rapidity and intensity of stimuli" (Anderson and Lindeman 205).[15]

Correlatively, ten years later two psychologists begin an essay titled "A Theoretical Field-Analysis of Automobile-Driving" by claiming, "Of all the skills demanded by contemporary civilization, the one of driving an automobile is certainly the most important to the individual in the sense at least that a defect in it is the greatest threat to life." They then go on to propose that the "remedy" for inadequate and therefore dangerous driving practices "is not merely increased vigilance or tension in the driver, but the development by learning of semi-automatic perceptual habits and motor habits" (Gibson and Crooks 453, 458).[16] My argument is that *Speedy* proclaims itself to be a viable solution—one on a continuum with amusement park rides—to this more or less existential task; as the spectators enjoy watching the slapstick comedian's amusing performance on screen, the film proposes, they are simultaneously being taught (due to involuntary acts of muscular and mental imitation) how to operate vehicles in the real world. In a sense, Lloyd had "realized" something analogous to what, according to Vachel Lindsay in *The Progress and Poetry of the Movies* (1925), few others at the time had: "how closely akin is the moving picture to the all-conquering Ford car. The most inert soul in the world when learning to drive a car, even a Ford, is swept relentlessly past his own resolutions and convictions. The motion picture does the same thing to the human mind. To the inevitable speeding-up process of the motion picture quite recently has been added the speeding up of all other things in America" (quoted in North, *Camera Works* 125).

In his introduction to *Autopia: Cars and Culture*, Peter Wollen provides a particularly apt explication of the psychoanalyst Michael Balint's distinction between "philobats" and "ocnophiles" as this might pertain to operating an automobile. The ocnophile customarily fears high-speed movement and therefore has "difficulty in acquiring the minimal skills required to enjoy the 'thrill' that driving might otherwise offer." In contrast, philobats confidently "assume complete control of equipment" in their "pursuit of excitement" and possess the capacity to transform "the reality of traffic 'into a kind of fairy land where things happen as if desired,' as if automatically." Aspiring "to a kind of 'effortless accomplishment,'" the "philobat becomes a kind of hero," one who, because of a highly developed ability to handle "'the sudden emergence of a hazardous object that has to be negotiated'" in his visual field, "lives in the illusion that it is within his power to overcome any obstacle, that 'he can certainly cope with any situation.'" He therefore tends "towards an undue optimism and confidence." This is as a good a description as one is going to find of the admirable *type* Lloyd portrayed on screen, arguably for the benefit of the less bold members of his mass audience (Wollen, "Introduction" 14–16).[17]

On the basis of its comic driving sequences, *Speedy* may be considered a genealogical successor to a previous cinematic phenomenon: Hale's Tours. Named after its entrepreneurial promoter, George Hale, an ex-fireman, this "Illusion railroad ride" (Rabinovitz 46) made its commercial debut at the 1904 St. Louis Exposition and quickly became a "popular craze, as many as 500 installations in operation a year later" (Musser, "Moving toward Fictional Narratives" 93).[18] Designed to replicate the sensation of travel, the experience of viewing motion pictures in this manner "relate[s] more to the attractions of the fairground than to the legitimate theatre" (Gunning, "Cinema of Attractions" 58), and it is therefore logical that they were for a few years consistently among the biggest moneymaking concessions at assorted amusement parks across the country (Rabinovitz 47). Seated in an artificial railway car (though variants included subways and trolleys) that swayed from side to side, the audience would watch images previously photographed from the cowcatcher of a locomotive while listening to a recording of the clattering sounds of wheels on rails. However, once the novelty of the exhibition mode wore off, the Hale's Tours began to fade away, the decline beginning around 1909.[19] What Lloyd's reckless driving exploits share with this obsolescent novelty is the ambition to eliminate the distance between the spectator and the spectacle, a procedure that entails a shift in accent away from a purely optical toward a haptic model of perception.[20]

Although it is legitimate to consider the driving portions in *Speedy* as a humorously inflected continuation of previous cinematic undertakings, this point of view misses something essential. The turn backward to the past in this case tends to reinforce the notion that Lloyd's primary goal as a filmmaker was to bring "pleasure and fear" together in order to furnish sensational thrills, to "produce both a physical and emotional frenzy" (Rabinovitz 48) by convincing his audience that they were hurtling dynamically through an urban milieu in a potentially catastrophic manner. What such a historically informed perspective overlooks is what the retroactive and "inter-medial" style of thinking that Benjamin pioneered brings into focus: the functional aspirations structuring such aesthetic procedures. It is only in retrospect, and from the point of view of future events that occurred beyond the realm of film, that we catch a glimpse of the social purposefulness of the synthetic experiences Lloyd fabricated.

What I have in mind is the rise of virtual reality (VR). VR offers a touchstone for us not as a means of measuring Lloyd's practical contribution to the contemporary pursuit of perceptually persuasive electronic mirages, but as a way to discern, after the fact, the degree to which slapstick film strained aftereffects that could "be more easily achieved with a changed technical standard—that is to say in a new art form" (Benjamin, "Work of Art," 2nd version 119).[21] It is from the vantage point of cyberspace that we may realize that "'computer programming is really a branch of moviemaking'" (quoted in Rheingold 76). In other words, "one of the primary tasks" of silent comedy was "to create a demand" for full-body immersion in artificial worlds, the full satisfaction of which would have to wait for the new millennium. Support for this assertion can be found in Howard Rheingold's *Virtual Reality*, an account of the quest throughout the latter half of the twentieth century to interact in three-dimensional space and real time with digital versions of the world we inhabit. While acknowledging that the achievement of such a goal would become genuinely feasible only in the wake of advances in computer science and graphics as well as electronic miniaturization (the discovery of integrated circuits, transistors, microprocessors, and so forth), Rheingold nevertheless profiles visionaries working in more archaic entertainment media as figures of considerable relevance to the story he wishes to tell. Rheingold's discussion in his book's second chapter, "The Experience Theatre and the Art of Binocular Illusion," of Morton Heilig, inventor of the Sensorama Simulator, is a pivotal case in point. Visiting Heilig at his West LA home in 1990, Rheingold feels privileged to have the opportunity to play around with what he refers to as a "3D multisensory cinema packed into an arcade device": "I sat down, put my hands and eyes and ears in the right places, and peered through the eyes of a motorcycle passenger at the streets of a city as they appeared decades ago" (50). Since the system for conveying odors was down, Rheingold had to "settle for the stereophonic audio-visual-tactile version of the Sensorama experience" (52). During the conversation that follows, Rheingold learns that Heilig, who had already "got hooked on film-making as a young man" (53), had his most profound revelations while attending Cinerama and 3D film showings in the early 1950s. As he explains it, his appreciation of such innovations began while watching TV or when in a movie theater, for while "sitting in one reality" he found himself "looking at another reality through an imaginary transparent wall." Enlarging that window sufficiently had given him "a visceral sense of personal involvement. You *feel* the experience, you don't just *see* it. I felt as if I had stepped through that window and was riding the roller coaster myself instead of watching someone else. I felt vertigo." This experience led him to contemplate "where the technology might go in the future," ultimately convincing him "that the future of cinema will mean the creation of films that create the total illusion of reality" without frames (55; emphasis in the original)

Equally pertinent are Heilig's remarks on the historical link between such cinematic endeavors and the construction of flight simulators, for it is on the basis of this connection that the functional ambitions these two phenomena shared become apparent. Cinerama was invented, he explains, by Fred Waller, whose initial experiments in the field were made possible when the military gave him a contract to build motion picture displays for the first flight simulators (54).[22] Only after World War II did a Hollywood producer (Mike Todd) agree to fund Waller's efforts to develop a widescreen process that would encompass peripheral areas of vision. It is almost certainly with this in mind that Rheingold asserts at the beginning of his book that if he "had to choose one old-fashioned word to describe the general category of what this new thing might be, 'simulator" would be my candidate. VR technology resembles, and is partially derived from, the flight simulators that the Air Force and commercial airlines use to train pilots" (16–17). The crucial point in the present context is that it is on the grounds of a shared sense of social purposefulness that the disparate media may be most profitably aligned. As Heilig's 1962 patent application demonstrates, the Sensorama Simulator was designed to do something more than provide enjoyment to its users: it was also a mode of rehearsing difficult operations in conditions of relative safety:

> The present invention, generally, relates to simulator apparatus and, more particularly, to apparatus to stimulate the senses of an individual to simulate an actual experience realistically.
>
> *There are increasing demands today for ways and means to teach and train individuals without actually subjecting the individuals to the hazards of particular simulations* [*sic*]" (49; emphasis in the original).[23]

I place Lloyd in this cultural lineage in order to draw out an otherwise hidden motivation that structures his cinematic undertaking. The images of driving in particular and mechanized movement in general, which most of his films contain, may be understood as having been designed to help facilitate the development of the skills necessary for the completion of a potentially hazardous task: the operation of a moving vehicle. The audience was encouraged to project itself into the illusory realm depicted on screen in the hope that upon their return to reality they would have improved their hand- and mental-eye coordination and sharpened their reflexes, in the process adjusting physiologically and neurologically to a relatively new technology.[24] In this sense, Lloyd, more than most, gave "the age" what it "demanded," "an image of its accelerated grimace" (Pound, "Hugh Selwyn Mauberley" 186).

In 1923, while working on *Girl Shy*, Lloyd expressed his hopes for the future of cinema in a *Los Angeles Times* interview: "I believe that the man who invents a means of producing a perfect stereo motion picture will have accomplished the greatest achievement since the first motion picture." He added: "Today, the motion pictures projected on the most perfect screen are lacking in solidity and relief. If the characters could only be made to stand out as they do in stereopticon pictures, and still retain the action of motion pictures of today, I think the ultimate would be reached by the cinema." Three decades later, after his career in the movies was over, he revisited the topic while being interviewed at Columbia University, articulating his regret that the film industry had not fully committed itself to making the switch to the alternative technology: "I think if they'd handled [the transition to] sound as horribly as they did three-dimension, we wouldn't have sound today." Remaining convinced throughout the rest of his life that the promise of cinema lay in 3D, Lloyd enthusiastically devoted much of his time to the field of stereoscopic photography, becoming the inaugural president of the Hollywood Stereoscopic Society and shooting more than 200,000 slides, only a small portion of which have been published in book form.[25] Lloyd's enduring fascination with 3D technology and stereoscopic photography may not prove the argument this chapter has pursued, but it suits the contention that he was an especially forward-looking filmmaker in the 1920s, one who wished to move beyond the representational constraints of the medium.

Following chapter 5, in a "Theoretical Interlude," I revisit (with additional support from Benjamin) the implications of Lloyd's cultural practice for an understanding of the functional aspirations of slapstick modernism as an attempt to help facilitate adjustments on a collective scale to the conditions of existence in urban-industrial modernity. Derived to an extent from his encounter with silent screen comedy (and later Disney animation), Benjamin maintained that projected images had the potential to contribute to the social formation of an invigorated or "innervated" mass body, one with the power to master the forces of an otherwise enfeebling machine technology. Before pursuing this topic, however, I would like to begin conceptualizing (by way of Gilles Deleuze and Félix Guattari's study of Franz Kafka) the process of becoming-child. The irreverent affirmation of immaturity and correlative rejection of adult behavioral standards is one of the strongest links between silent screen comedy and the counterculture of the 1950s and '60s. The bizarrely babyish performance style of Harry Langdon, the all but forgotten fourth star in the constellation of major silent screen comedians, supplies an excellent point of access to this motif, one that presupposes a relative openness to the task of environmental adaptation.

4

Becoming-Child

Harry Langdon

> Actually the great comedians are representing or portraying children or the things that children do.
>
> —Hal Roach, *Living with Laughter*

A great deal of critical commentary on slapstick film has addressed the significance of the childish traits that performers in the field tended to exhibit. In *Time and Western Man* (1927), Wyndham Lewis isolated the "child factor" as the secret of Chaplin's public success as a "revolutionary propagandist," a role the writer did not approve of on the grounds that this "child-man" and the "infant cult" he epitomizes appeal to the masses at the expense of their respect of figures of heroic greatness (67–68). In an essay composed during World War II, Sergei Eisenstein proposed to examine Chaplin's "strange cast of mind"—more exactly, to ascertain the distinctive way of "looking at life" that gave rise to the film star's "unique and inimitable" conception of humor ("Charlie: The Kid" 243). The title of the piece, "Charlie: The Kid," indicates the path Eisenstein intended to follow. Possessed of a remarkable capacity to retain "'a child's eye view'" when perceiving the world, Chaplin manages "to see the funny side" of things, such as the cruelty of existence, which makes "other people's flesh crawl" (244). Eisenstein declares that this trait, when found in adults, "is called 'infantilism,'" and "the comedy of Chaplin's constructions" are customarily based on this "device" (244). Eisenstein presumes that the actor utilizes the motif of infantilism as a means of liberating himself from the pressure to conform to the norms of American society, as a way to evade the rationalized insistence that all people behave in accordance with established modes of conduct: "In a particularly ordered and regimented society, this [desire to] escape to freedom from the fetters of 'a once and forever strict regime' must be especially strong" (245). "The short hop into infantilism serves [. . .] Chaplin himself as a psychological escape beyond the bounds of the measured, planned and calculated world of activity that surrounds him" (251). Due to "the subtleties of the method," which contains "an infantile 'prescription' for imitation," Chaplin infects the spectator with the impulse to break away from "the conventions and necessities of everyday life" (251). There is thus a collective purposefulness underlying the fact that his plots are frequently organized around the conflict between an innocent, childlike attitude toward life and the stern, adult reproofs such an outlook inevitably engenders. The collision of these two antithetical dispositions may cause laughter, but the burden of the artistic design is to encourage audiences to repudiate what they have been instructed to respect: the world of ethical maturity and moral responsibility.[1]

In "Chaplin Times Two," a piece composed in the early 1960s as a tribute to Chaplin on the occasion of his seventy-fifth birthday, Theodor Adorno characterized the cinematic icon as a cryptic figure whose secrets are destined to remain inaccessible to adult thought, whether these are carried out in the name of philosophical profundity, psychoanalytic insight, or aesthetic judgment. Those who have grown up inevitably fall silent when confronted with the comedian's image, "in whom fleeing Nature bids a shocked adieu," and their efforts at interpretation will only "inflict more injury the higher they elevate him" (270). Only to the very young does the truth of the performer reveal itself; therefore "more information about the clown is to be found among children who, as mysteriously as they do with animals, communicate with his image and with the meaning of his activity, which in fact negates meaning. Only one [who is] capable in the language common to the clown and to children, a language distanced from sense, would understand the clown himself" (269–70).

Among the more recent investigations of this topic, two stand out. Drawing on Adorno, Benjamin, and Deleuze to explore the significance of "the composite image of child-clown" in several of Chaplin's motion pictures, Laleen Jayamanne argues that by disorganizing habitual sensorimotor actions, Chaplin's childishly spontaneous gestures open up new relationships to things in the world, his improvisational playfulness converting ritual objects deserving of respect into touchable, toy-like curiosities (186–91, 197–98). And Karen Beckman, under the heading "Eternal Children," has delineated the problematic aspects of previous speculations on the meaning of Laurel and Hardy's enduring immaturity, diagnosing their comic aesthetic as masochistic (86–104).[2]

Here I explore the critical productivity of approaching Harry Langdon's relatively neglected body of work from a perspective that is roughly analogous to those articulated above. My point of departure is Deleuze and Guattari's idea of "becoming-child," a concept they formulate in, among other places, *Kafka: Toward a Minor Literature*. Notably, Deleuze and Guattari neither adhere, as Eisenstein does, to the notion that maturity is the ultimate goal of the artist, nor do they identify artistic recourse to childishness as evidence of a regressive tendency, as a symptomatic yearning to return to a lost paradise, to "the golden age of infantilism" (Eisenstein, "Charlie: The Kid" 251). Instead, the two thinkers posit the child as immanent within the adult, thus grasping the adoption of mannerisms associated with the former state as part of an attempt to reactivate blocked desires so that they may function as a disruptive force in the world.

Determined to break the hold that tragic as well as psychoanalytic paradigms have long exerted over understandings of modernist writing, a key component of Deleuze and Guattari's philosophical intervention into the field of literary modernism is the notion that interpretive approaches that are reliant on such paradigms inevitably obscure the humorous repercussions of experimental procedures. To privilege Oedipal coordinates when analyzing Kafka's body of work is to miss the fact that he frequently subjects familial themes to comic amplification. His primary concern, they insist, was to exaggerate and enlarge paternalistic principles (and the neuroses they inflict) to such a degree that serious matters like this begin to look ludicrous (though admittedly these principles, at least in the stories, often reassert themselves, sealing off the escape routes the rhetorical tactic [of hyperbole] had temporarily opened up) (*Kafka* 9–15). Those who treat Kafka as an author of weakness and solitude, as a tormented individual who desperately sought to withdraw from the world, neglect everything vital in his oeuvre. Readings that are preoccupied with guilt and misfortune, and that stress Kafka's need to find refuge from life in art, are a result of the "trap" he set with his "clownish declarations" (41). The truth is that "he is a political author, prophet of the future world" in the sense that he "plugs into socialism, anarchism, and social movements" in order to anticipate the "diabolical powers" of "fascism, Stalinism, and Americanism," which he heard knocking at the door of the present before everyone else. Uniting his enunciations with desire, he devoted his exploratory literary energies to an interrogation of the totalitarian, bureaucratic, and capitalist regimes or assemblages he was able to foresee before their full historical development. With this in mind, Deleuze and Guattari declare, "Never has there been a more comic and joyous author," one for whom "everything leads to laughter" (42).

At the end of "Blocks, Series, Intensities," the penultimate chapter of *Kafka*, Deleuze and Guattari describe the two poles that together constitute the writer's "schizo-buffoonery." In Kafka's output, "childhood blocks" do not function, they argue, like Oedipal memories, serving primarily as a means of stopping the flows of desire, of neutralizing proliferating connections in order to reterritorialize everything back onto the parents (78); rather, Kafka's blocks operate as charged forces of deterritorialization, which in the exemplary figure of "the Orphan" facilitate shifts in time that may "reanimate the adult as one animates a puppet [. . .] giving the adult living connections" (78–79). Kafka's compositional method of "injecting the child into the adult" results in a "strange mannerism" that should not be conflated with attempts on the part of adults to imitate or act like children. On the contrary, his creative procedure aims to produce a metamorphic (as opposed to mimetic) process of "becoming-child." This process is facilitated by the grafting of affective intensity or state of desire of the child—its relations of movements and rest, speed, and slowness—onto the adult in order to furnish the latter with a *real* (as opposed to imaginary) way out of confining situations.[3] Kafka's art establishes a zone of proximity between grown-ups and kids, rendering the difference between the two indiscernible in the hope of eluding socially manufactured constraints. The mannerism of childhood coexists in Kafka alongside a more worldly mannerism of politeness, "a too studied salute, an overly insistent submission" (80) designed to halt the encroachment of authorities. Here, an excessively rigid adherence to conventional codes of behavior, to good manners, is a way to keep threatening people at a distance. Hypothesizing that Kafka made use of both methods in his life as well as his literary activities, Deleuze and Guattari conclude that Kafka's literature (and mode of existence) demonstrate the virtues of what they intriguingly term a "machinic art of the marionette" (80).

Having started his on-screen career in 1924 as part of Mack Sennett's troupe of comic actors, Harry Langdon had emerged by the end of the decade as a star in his own right on the basis of three well-received, feature-length films—*Tramp, Tramp, Tramp* (1926), *The Strong Man* (1926), and *Soldier Man* (1926)—all of which were made at First National in close collaboration with the director Frank Capra. Virtually all commentary on Langdon has grappled with the strange way his on-screen persona unsettles conventional corollaries between the biological and behavioral; yet in remarking upon the weirdness of a forty-year-old man who refuses to act his age, critics have not sufficiently formulated the profound implications of the character's comic mannerisms.[4] James Agee describes the effect of Langdon's outfits as making it appear as if he was "an outsized baby wearing diapers under his pants" and that his "walk was that of a child which has just gotten sure on its feet" ("Comedy's Greatest Era" 12). But Agee also seeks refuge in the rhetorical category of metaphor from the peculiarity he perceives. If Langdon "wandered into areas of strangeness which were beyond the other comedians," he did so through an "instinct for bringing his actual adulthood and *figurative* babyishness into frictions" (13; emphasis mine). His risible infantilism is simply a tropological detour away from the proper maturity of the real man, which therefore serves as the ultimately stable ground of his outlandish appearance. In reference to Langdon's trademark mental and physical hesitations, Kerr instructs us just to "look at him. His motor responses, and to some degree his cerebral responses, are approximately those of a five-year-old. Call him and he doesn't know whether to come or not. Children are uncertain about how to respond properly; they have difficulty in reading the social message that is being imparted" (267).[5] While acknowledging the paradoxically composite nature of Langdon's indeterminate being—"A five-year-old and not a five-year-old. A twelve-year-old and not a twelve-year-old. A full-grown functioning male and not a full-grown functioning male" (268)—Kerr, too, takes recourse to a linguistic model to mitigate the bizarreness of what he admires. Langdon's last picture with Capra, *Long Pants* (1927), is thus said to reduce the indefinable ambiguity of his previous performances by "yielding to literalness." As the critic sees it, to this point Langdon's artistry has hinged upon his status as a (visual) figure of speech, as an amusingly unreal entity giving shape to a biological impossibility.[6]

Saturday Afternoon (1926), one of the last of the short films Langdon made for Mack Sennett, provides an opportunity to analyze the forceful affects of the comedian's childish mannerisms that such semanticizing points of view overlook. The film's opening scenes firmly establish that the conflict structuring his existence is a consequence of Harry Higgins's (Langdon) boyish incorrigibility in relation to his spouse's (Alice Ward) rigid household rules. The misogynistic cliché—wife as mother and thus figure of parental prohibition—serves as the basis for the motion picture's comic assault on familial and financial systems of constraint. The first intertitle's allusion to Lincoln's Emancipation Proclamation situates the male character in a position of enslavement with respect to his domineering mate, who justifies (to a neighboring widow) her rigid treatment of him as a necessary means of maintaining ownership over an object of private property ("The first step in losing any man is letting him have his way"). She also controls the distribution of funds in the home, as evidenced by her exasperation when her child-husband spends the nickel she has allocated him on tobacco instead of on popcorn as he had promised her he would. Although Harry is old enough to hold a job at the local steel plant, he incongruously remains a kid. When he misses the streetcar at his lunch break, he, like a schoolboy who has missed his bus, immediately calls home to apologize for his tardiness. Later, upon being bawled out for trying unsuccessfully to hide some loose change under the living room rug, Harry furiously rebels (but only when he believes he is alone and therefore unobserved). Stamping his feet, lashing out verbally, and presumably laying down the law to his mommy-spouse, Langdon thus presents the audience with the perplexing impression of a grown man playing a boy, who is in turn pretending to be an adult and demands in immature fashion that he be allowed to keep the money he has earned at work.

The treatment of sexuality in Langdon's films customarily follows along similar lines. Although he is married in *Saturday Afternoon*, erotic contact has remained mysteriously fascinating to him. Holding hands sends him into a paroxysm of joy, as if he has never touched another human being in this way. When his pal flirts with a young woman, Harry watches attentively—and receives a jolt each time their lips make contact. As if to satisfy Harry's curiosity, the kissing couple are momentarily frozen in place, which enables the surprised character to scrutinize them more closely. More telling is a remarkable scene in the feature-length film *The Strong Man*, in which seduction serves as a means to convey the childish core of adult sexuality. To avoid arrest, a thief's girlfriend has put a bundle of stolen loot in the naïve protagonist's pocket, and in order to recover it she fools him into believing she is the girl he loves yet has never met. (He has only a photograph of his pen pal Mary Brown, with whom he corresponded by mail during the war.) Initially, Harry is quite pleased with the cuddling that has taken place on the ride to the woman's apartment, but when, behind closed doors, she begins to put the moves on him, he starts to panic, desire shading into terror. An overhead shot shows the frightened protagonist writhing on the bed, the unusual camera angle communicating his emotional disorientation. The prospect of going too far, of engaging in intercourse, obviously throws him into a state of extreme anxiety, yet the implication of the scene is not simply that he is a particularly inexperienced, virginal individual. The critical thrust of the hilarious display of male hysteria implies that manly confidence is merely a façade, the haunting specter of copulation inducing a degree of emotional agitation that individuals must successfully stifle to engage in the act itself. Under the threat of a puncture wound, Harry yields, allowing the woman to surreptitiously remove the wad of money from his trousers. She then falls back dramatically, as if fully satisfied. Stunned by the unexpectedly quick conclusion to the encounter he had anticipated with horror, Harry seems to derive a small amount of pride at the outcome. But he nevertheless rushes away, only to enter a sculptor's studio, where the sight of a fully exposed nude model confronts him. The shock of exposed genitalia knocks him head-over-heels backward and down a flight of stairs. Again, we are not dealing here with a specifically traumatized adult plagued by memories of past experiences, real or fantasized. Rather, Langdon's intense overreactions to such manifestations of female desire function as revelations of the terrifying aspects of sexuality that the posture of virility strives to defend itself against.

Instead of marking the failure of a would-be adult to conform or measure up to a socially agreed upon ideal of adult manliness, the becoming-child of the adult forcefully tears the mask off of maturity in general. The climax of *The Strong Man* clearly illustrates this point. Captured during the Great War, Paul Bergot (Langdon) has been brought to the United States after the armistice to serve as the stagehand in his ex-captor's ("The Great Zandow") traveling show. The two émigrés eventually find themselves in Cloverdale, a formerly idyllic small town that a gang of bootleggers has transformed into a den of modern iniquity. Because Zandow has drunk himself into a stupor and cannot perform, Paul must take his place on stage. Wearing an absurd costume several sizes too big for him, he fakes a few feats of strength to keep the crowd happy but then becomes angry at the rowdy mass of criminals when they announce their intention to defile the girl of his dreams (a blind girl named Mary Brown, daughter of the crusading local parson). Having revealed this visibly weak, un-muscular boy to be the titular protagonist, the film then demonstrates his prowess as a social reformer. First, he swings wildly above the fray on a trapeze, hurling bottles at the heads of his many attackers. Then, in a formal reprise of the film's opening sequence, Paul aims the stage show's central prop—a cannon—at the audience. Tugging on the rope of the device like a child playing with a toy, he blasts the music hall apart, whereupon the fleeing patrons are run out of town by the followers of the impassioned clergyman. (Meanwhile, Paul, all tuckered out, curls up on stage and takes a nap.) The last scene clinches the film's mildly subversive investment in immaturity, for Paul now appears as an amusingly boyish embodiment of "the majesty of the law"; dressed as always in an ill-fitting outfit, his silly appearance in conjunction with his job as police officer evokes the dubious qualifications of established legal authorities.

In this way, Langdon's on-screen performances unsettle the fixity of the terms we customarily rely on to chart the growth and development of individuals. Rather than privilege one side of the child-adult opposition over the other, the actor's method of ceaselessly switching back and forth between the two poles opens up an awareness of the conceptual instability of the related categories. Rather than imitate or identify with specific children, Langdon establishes a zone of proximity within which an indeterminate child and an adult coexist in an incomprehensibly close symbiosis. His ongoing engagement in the process of becoming-child suggests that to be an adult is to hold desire in check and thus to keep the self in a state of diminished emotional intensity. Langdon's affective and kinetic performances propose, then, that the principal function of acquiring the status of an adult is to stop libidinal energies from circulating erratically.

Crucially, Langdon is not to be taken as an evolutionary accident, as an oddity put on display to reassure the (adult) spectators of their own mature normalcy. On the contrary, in the realm that his silent comedies constitute, non-regressive "involutions" spark a critical awareness of the defensive strategies the purported grown-ups who seek to belittle him have adopted. In *Saturday Afternoon*, for example, the wife of his character Harry Higgins can be perceived as a little girl maintaining a false front, as someone desperately clinging to the role society has granted her. Correlatively, those around him tend to get swept into the same antic process of becoming in which he perpetually engages. In this same film, this occurs when Harry and a buddy get involved in an argument on a street corner with two unattached women (possibly prostitutes). Obviously overexcited due to his temporary liberation from the bonds of marriage, Harry overreacts to a flirtatious slap from one of the women by wildly flinging a brick into a jewelry store window. The foursome scatters in the aftermath of the shattering glass, all of them briefly caught up in the risky pleasures of irresponsible vandalism. Later, while on an arranged date with two "nice" girls, Harry gets beaten up in a fistfight with a couple of male bullies. He crawls off in a daze to sleep, only to wake up shortly thereafter and find he is unsafely perched on the running boards of two automobiles moving in unison. He predictably ends up wrapped around a telephone pole, whereupon his wife rescues him and drives the repentant boy-man home. The fun may be over, but not before the film has demonstrated the degree to which the urban landscape may be comically transformed into a playground, into the site of violent and erotic encounters. Such encounters can be judged as reprehensible only in accordance with the standards of the adult world that the film refutes as a precariously regulatory one.

To the degree that its purpose is to shake grown-ups loose from the repressive paradigms to which they are expected to adhere, *Saturday Afternoon* enacts the process of becoming-child. While it would be premature to seek to generalize this assessment and claim its applicability to slapstick film as a whole (though it may certainly be considered a minor cinematic genre in Deleuze and Guattari's sense of the term), it holds convincingly for a considerable portion of Langdon's work in the field. This is especially true of *Tramp, Tramp, Tramp,* in which Langdon's trademark comic procedure again serves to reveal the childishness embedded in typically adult behaviors and activities.

In the film Langdon plays Harry Logan, the son of a crippled shoemaker whose business is about to go under due to the increasingly competitive nature of an economic marketplace dominated by large manufacturers. The fact that Harry's father cannot pay the rent to his arrogant landlord, Nick Kargas, makes it evident that the small business won't survive much longer. Kargas is also a famous athlete preparing to participate in a race across the continental United States, sponsored by the Burton Shoe Company as part of a national advertising campaign. Hoping to make some money, Harry signs on as Kargas's manservant, but the two have a falling out on their way to the race's starting point. Harry arrives just as the announcer introduces his ex-employer, "The Champion Walker of the World," and the starstruck crowd frantically rushes to embrace their idol. Yet what seems at the outset to be an ordinary case of mistaken identity will turn out to have been an accurate prediction. By the end, Harry will have defeated the burly, medal-wearing Kargas, in the process thoroughly demolishing the status of the stereotypically brawny male athlete.

Despite the obvious disparities between the two contestants at the level of physique and competitive experience, Harry repeatedly gets the best of his opponent. Late in the film, Kargas stands out impressively against a barren landscape, striding vigorously along. Harry appears out of nowhere, clumsily scrambling to catch up. His baggy pants are dragging on the ground; his floppy sweater sleeves extend well beyond his wrists; his feet are wrapped in rags. To make matters worse, he is lugging a heavy ball that he does not realize is no longer attached by a chain to his ankle (having been arrested for stealing fruit and sentenced to hard labor breaking rocks in the sun, he has managed to escape). However, while interrogating Harry, Kargas, in exasperation, gets tangled up with the ball and chain and winds up sliding off-screen down a hillside. This displacement anticipates the more decisive demolition of the heroic ideal that occurs near the conclusion of the cross-country trek. Having reached the West Coast, the two are trapped together in a barber shop when a cyclone hits Sand City, the town where the leader and expected victor had spent the night. Harry has donned a frock (made from a shower curtain), since the wind has blown his clothes away while he was disrobing; his vaguely womanly appearance is simply the precondition for Kargas's becoming-child. Scared out of his wits by the twister, the latter falls to his knees and clings to his Harry-mommy's skirts, crying, "Save me." To call this a mere role reversal is inadequate, for the overall effect of the scene is to blow the cover off athletic masculinity. Harry is in a sense analogous to the disastrously swirling force of nature that, after causing the walls of the shelter to tilt wildly, obliterates the man-made structure, leaving only ruins behind: like the storm, the misleadingly diminutive actor possesses the capacity to rip gendered constructs off the material bodies such constructs are meant to shape into bordered territorialities.[7]

The film's peculiar conclusion self-consciously acknowledges Langdon's ongoing commitment as a comic actor to the process of becoming-child. Having beaten the twister back into the desert by hurling bricks at it, Harry rescues his love interest, the daughter of the shoe company's owner (played by a young Joan Crawford), and later that day dashes across the finish line just ahead of his rival. Presumably he then marries Crawford, for the next time we see the two characters they are gazing together through a window at a rather massive crib containing their newborn son. When the baby pops his head up, however, it is Harry; he then goes through a series of infantile mannerisms: nuzzling his teddy bear, sneezing, trying to suck milk from a bottle, and so on. In this decidedly non-Wordsworthian scenario, the man plays the child he has fathered.

If the paradoxical entity Langdon portrays is based on the impossible coexistence in a single entity of mutually exclusive ages, then his acting style vividly manifests silent comedy's general refutation of representational imperatives. In this regard, Langdon's oeuvre furnishes a solid point of entry into the nonimitative elements of slapstick film practice: its repeated willingness to disregard the constraints of verisimilitude that governed most contemporaneous uses of the cinematic medium. Such repetitious breakings of the realist contract are precisely what offended Walter Kerr when he looked back later in life at what he judged to be the "formally vulgar" and artistically unethical output of Keystone Studios. Although the "public's thirst for the real, and the camera's capacity for satisfying it, were known quantities to Sennett, [. . .] the gifts bestowed by the camera did not stir in Sennett any sense of reciprocal obligation." Instead he self-indulgently reveled in excessively fantastic actions, in "transparent frauds," which interfered with the technological apparatus' "promise of authenticity, violating the integrity of the instrument" (64–65).

This "anti-institutional" approach to representation is indeed operative in the exuberant shorts Langdon made early his film career after signing with Sennett.[8] The first of these, *Picking Peaches* (1924), is especially notable in that its deployment of various film "tricks" takes place in an erotically charged atmosphere. Langdon plays a shoe clerk, once again named Harry, who derives considerable pleasure from the opportunity his job supplies him to fondle women's feet. Though married, he decides to take the latter half of the day off to go to the beach with a sexy customer. As the two of them entertain themselves by watching a bathing beauty contest, the subjectivized camera mimics the look of the highly stimulated character, narrowing its focus to the bodies on display on the stage. Such a technique amounts to a self-conscious acknowledgment on the part of the filmmakers that they are perpetuating exhibitionist tendencies dating back to the turn of the century—Edwin S. Porter's *The Gay Shoe Clerk* (1903) the most pertinent point of historical reference. The commitment to presenting simultaneously amusing and arousing views justifies an understanding of a motion picture like *Picking Peaches* as a prolongation beyond its period of dominance (lasting roughly up until 1906–1907) of what Tom Gunning has influentially dubbed "the cinema of attractions." That the film gleefully ignores the demand for referential veracity is evident here in the way one of the contestants (Harry's wife wearing a mask) defies gravity in performing a double backflip during the diving portion of the show. No attempt is made by the filmmakers to hide the fact that what we see is the (rather crude) result of a camera trick: as she leaps off a pier and then hangs suspended in the air before completing her somersaults, it is obvious that we are watching a cinematically determined stunt.[9] *Picking Peaches* further shatters realist illusionism by amalgamating animated images with live-action footage. At one point a hand-drawn devil dances around on Harry's shoulder, whispering bad advice into his ear and then hopping to the ground and vanishing in a burst of flame. Later, a question mark appears above the head of a puzzled man who is on the verge of discovering Harry hiding in his bed, and when the latter is caught, a series of cartoon daggers shoot from the other's eyes into those of the cowering protagonist. Similarly, in *Smile Please* (1924) scratches on the filmstrip serve to graphically render the flow of an electric current. Due to a set of mishaps primarily caused by the shenanigans of an obstreperous little boy, Langdon's character, Otto Focus, who is a studio photographer struggling to take a portrait of his wife and her family, gets his father-in-law caught in a closed circuit. As the charge passes through and shocks the body of the latter (who is holding a lightbulb), sparks fly everywhere. It is as if the traditional status of the image as an accurate copy of persons and things, emblematized here by the still-photography camera, must yield to the motion picture's humorous demolition of this convention.

Combined with the sped-up imagery of silent comedy at the point of projection, such typical effects indicate the resistance of slapstick filmmakers to replicating the preexisting world for any other sake than as a means to generate laughter. Rather than work to facilitate the implementation of realist paradigms, slapstick movies' predilection for playing with the machinery of film frequently resulted in the appearance of cracks in the dominant system of representation. To return to Deleuze and Guattari's assessment of Kafka, we might say that in silent comedy the image is opened to an intensive utilization that makes it take flight along creative lines of escape, in the process releasing it from the burden of major cinemas of mirroring things as they are (*Kafka* 26). In sum, slapstick filmmakers commonly treated the cinematic apparatus as a pleasurable toy rather than a tool of accurate cognition.

Technology as Toy; or, Harry Joins the Infantry

> In my opinion the weakness of the world we live in is to consider childishness a sphere apart [. . . .] Yet we are all childish—totally, unreservedly, and we should even add, in the most surprising way.
>
> —George Bataille, *Literature and Evil*

In "Toys and Play"(1928), a review of Karl Gröber's *Children's Toys from Olden Times: A History of Toys*, Walter Benjamin reflected upon the mistakes previous commentators had made when seeking to comprehend the role of toys in the lives of children. Benjamin's first thesis was that toys are the site of conflict between adults and children. All too often the former seek to impose man-made objects on the latter for pedagogical purposes. Toys function in such instances as instruments that are mobilized to educate kids in a domineering fashion; they are the means through which grown-ups attempt to exert power over children. Crafting toys for the purpose of controlling young people is consistent with a misguided view of playful activity as an effort to imitate one's elders ("Toys and Play" 118–19). Similarly, Benjamin had asserted the year before, in a section of *One-Way Street* (1926) titled "Construction Site," that "Children [. . .] produce their own small world of things within the greater one. The norms of this small world must be kept in mind if one wishes to create things especially for children, rather than let one's adult activity, through its requisites and instruments, find its own way to them"

(448–49). For Benjamin, then, child's play is more properly understood as a self-directed mode of learning whereby one acquires the skills necessary to inhabit the world; and it is therefore not surprising that in "Toys and Play" he argues that residing over this developmental procedure and governing its "rules and rhythms" is the "law of repetition" (120). The reason, he asserts, perhaps with Freud's *Beyond the Pleasure Principle* in mind, that children give in to the urge to do the same thing again and again is because such behavior helps diminish emotional distress. Reenactment helps alleviate traumatic pain by numbing the youthful subject. Repetitious play is a "way to master frightening experiences—by deadening one's own response, by arbitrarily conjuring up experiences, or through parody" (120). Conversely, play has the potential to enable people to recover the happiness they felt in the past when they dominated someone or something. Considered as a "means of enjoying one's victories and triumphs over and over again, with total intensity" (120), play serves as a way to reinforce a fleeting sense of superiority. Benjamin's evaluation of the aesthetic effects of corporeal play, then, is grounded in his conviction that repetitious behaviors are socially purposive and are the indispensable condition of an anguished subject's successful adaptation to his or her external environment: "The transformation of a shattering experience into habit—that is the essence of play"; play is "the mother of every habit," which thus "enters life as a game" (120).

Comparable assertions appear in another Benjamin essay composed in 1928. "Old Toys" examines the compulsion of parents to fool around with the toys that belong to their children. Adults do this, he proposes, because of their need to defend against the fear their otherwise intolerable surroundings induce in them. By playing, subjects do not retreat in escapist fashion from their daily conditions of existence; on the contrary, play is a way to beneficially modify an otherwise constrained relation to the forces of everyday life, to attain a degree of freedom in one's milieu. "When the urge to play overcomes an adult, this is not simply a regression to childhood." Rather it is a potentially liberating resurgence of active responsiveness to a set of circumstances one wishes to master. "Surrounded by a world of giants, children use play to create a world appropriate to their size. But the adult, who finds himself threatened by the real world and can find no escape, removes its sting by playing with its image in reduced form." And for Benjamin, such an impulse, the "desire to make light of an unbearable life[,] has been a major factor in the growing interest in children's games and children's books since the end of the war" (100).

Two Langdon films, *All Night Long* (1924) and *Soldier Man* (1926), both produced by Mack Sennett, are of interest in this context, since both mimic the mental mechanisms of war veterans struggling to come to terms with their previously shocking experiences on the battlefield. Both therefore address in comic fashion the emotional experiences Ernest Hemingway dealt with seriously at the same historical moment in *In Our Time* (1925).

In *All Night Long*, Harry Hall (Langdon) wakes up alone in a movie palace, evidently having fallen asleep during the picture. His wife has gone home, leaving behind a note. As Harry tries to exit the theater, he stumbles upon a robbery in process. Unfortunately, not only is the night watchman, Gale Wyndham (Vernon Dent), part of the gang, but also he recognizes Harry as someone he loathes. Though the two men served together in the Great War together, Wyndham is eager to exact revenge on the startled protagonist. Two flashbacks explain his anger to be a result of the fact that although he initially outranked Harry (a private), Wyndham (a sergeant) lost his girl, a local French girl named Nanette Burgundy (Natalie Kingston), to his rival. (The recollected incidents appear to burlesque a comparable sequence of events in King Vidor's *The Big Parade* [1925], although the similarity must be a coincidence given the release date of the latter.) While Harry's triumph is a contingent consequence of unintentional heroics, he had already infuriated Wyndham by involving him in a battlefield accident. Ordered to crawl across "No-Man's Land," Harry becomes ensnared in barbed wire. The enemy then tosses a hand grenade at him, which Harry uses to escape, pounding his way free. But when he casually flings the grenade aside, it detonates. After the smoke clears, we see Harry trapped in a pile of dirt. The position of what we assume are his legs, which are sticking up out of the mound too far forward to be still attached to his body, suggest the character has been cut in half at the torso. This is an illusion, however, for the legs turn out to belong to Wyndham, the blast having left him buried facedown in the ground. Hoping to get even, Wyndham sends Harry on a mission to the "Suicide Post." But an explosion sends Harry hurtling through the air, where he impossibly snags an American colonel. After the ensuing dash to safety, Harry is credited with having rescued the officer. He receives a medal, gets promoted, and wins Nanette. Back in the present, the police arrive and take the crooks to jail. Wyndham (who has not been arrested) tosses a cigarette aside, which lights the fuse to several sticks of dynamite still lying under a safe. The final, post-explosion scene begins with a shot from behind of Nanette flanked by three children as she pushes a stroller down the street. The next shot shows the two heavily bandaged men sitting next to each other in the vehicle, their wounds sufficiently serious to have infantilized them.

Purportedly set immediately after Armistice Day, *Soldier Man* depicts Harry as "The Soldier," seemingly the only serviceman still abroad. Apparently, he has failed to realize the conflict is over, because he believes he escaped from a POW camp. In fact, the drunken guards were celebrating the declaration of peace and simply let him go. On the loose in "Bosmania," he ultimately ends up impersonating the country's monarch, King Strudel the 13th, so as to put down a citizen rebellion a scheming minister has engineered. But at the end of the roughly half-hour picture we learn that everything we have seen was a dream and that in truth the Soldier had come back from the fighting with everyone else. We are thus retroactively alerted to the fact that the preceding sequences have all originated in the sleeping subject's psyche. The movie is thus structured formally as if the main character should be diagnosed as a neurotic individual having difficulty coming to terms with the stressful experiences he endured while a member of the armed forces abroad. In this sense, *Soldier Man* makes light of Harold Krebs's unsuccessful struggle in Hemingway's short story "Soldier's Home" to reconcile himself to his humdrum life as a civilian.

More pertinent for my purposes, however, are the opening scenes of *The Strong Man* (Langdon's second feature-length film). By depicting the conversion of a piece of heavy artillery from a means of killing people into an amusing toy, the film broaches the possibility of transforming military weaponry into a source of physically harmless fun. Set somewhere in Belgium near the end of World War I, the film starts with seemingly authentic combat footage. We observe soldiers far in the distance moving across a battlefield, airplanes high in the sky, and men amid ruins shooting at the latter with antiaircraft guns. A brief sequence of cuts leads us to "No-Man's Land," where Langdon (named Paul as mentioned earlier) is presumably located. Instead of the protagonist, however, we see next a series of unexplained explosions in the sand. An iris-in on a can of beans suggests that the blasts are occurring in the context of target practice. A close-up of a firing machine gun, with a barely visible hand at the edge of the frame repeatedly pulling the trigger, confirms this intuition while revealing that the previous shot had been from the point of view of the weapon's operator. The increasingly close range of the imagery combines with the subjective inflection of the camera's look to suggest that the camera has brought us nearer the truth of military conflicts. But what we are shown is mere fun and games, the implication perhaps that there is an infantilism that is inherent to those serving in the infantry. In any event, Langdon finally appears on screen as a bored soldier looking for ways to kill time (rather than people). Exasperated by his lousy aim with the machine gun, he pulls a slingshot out of his uniform pocket and succeeds in doing with the simply constructed toy what he could not with the technologically sophisticated weapon. The sudden emergence of an attacker out of a foxhole reinforces the already pervasive atmosphere of silliness. Rather than recoil in terror after a bullet grazes his shoulder, Paul delays his reaction and admonishes himself to be more careful; he has learned his lesson and will keep his head down next time. But he nonchalantly disregards the need to protect himself. His lackadaisical attitude and slow movements enable his opponent to wreck the machine gun. But Paul then resourcefully deploys his slingshot to counterattack with a barrage of crackers and onions that incites the German to run away.

Dogs of War (1923), a product of Hal Roach's studio featuring Our Gang (also known as the Little Rascals), nicely complements Langdon's adventures in comic militarism in that it features a sort of guerilla-style attack on a cinematic production by a group of insubordinate children.[10] The opening sequence of the film shows assorted kids engaging in a mock battle as if they were adults, the corporeal codes they observe and facial expressions they employ for the most part those that customarily belong to mature people.[11] Later going to a studio lot to watch one of their friends participate in the making of a run-of-the-mill melodrama, the members of the gang sneak onto the set during a break and mess around with the unattended equipment, shooting their own version of the "super feature" "Should Husbands Work?" The scenes of profilmic activity during which the kids "make pitchers" can be said in historical retrospect to prefigure the silliness of Taylor Mead and Jack Smith in Ron Rice's wonderful underground farce *The Queen of Sheba Meets the Atom Man* (1965–1967), with Alfalfa's lampshade skirt and flower-basket hat presaging the bizarre fashion sense the two performers will exhibit in the postwar era.[12] Shortly thereafter, the director (played by Harold Lloyd) of the film within a film eagerly sits down in the screening room with members of the cast to view the daily rushes, yet the print reveals that the kids' fun has ruined his past labor. First, ghostly superimpositions of the children cavorting appear over the original image. Next, a series of close-ups indicate that there has been some sort of nitrate damage and that the celluloid strip has been mutilated: due to the brutal treatment of the film stock, the head shots are either blotted out entirely by wavy lines, or the faces are severely distorted, stretching fluidly into unusual shapes. (Here, too, if only for a few seconds, the silent comedy augurs accomplishments in the postwar avant-garde cinema, for the material damage *Dogs of War* foregrounds anticipates Stan Brakhage's attentiveness to the materiality of the medium in his modernist masterpiece *Dog Star Man* [1961–1964]). The rotation of the image 90 degrees, which results in the prancing of the kids to take place along the vertical rather than the horizontal axis, is the last straw for the furious director, and he tears his hair out in exasperation. The boisterous children, however, remain suitably proud of their achievement and congratulate themselves for having mastered the apparatus to their great satisfaction.

Toying with a relatively new machine technology, the irrepressible kids are delighted to see that they have messed up the representational aspirations of the grown-ups to whom the equipment belongs. Given the interracial composition and working-class origins of the group of boys and girls who temporarily seize control of machinery in this fashion in the film, it is not entirely far-fetched to read their uninhibited indulgence in a mode of juvenile play, one that occurs at the expense of adult ambitions to turn a profit, as an intimation of the many uses the counterculture would discover in the 1960s when social conditions made it possible for previously disenfranchised social groups to "spring cinematic technology free from its industrial function" (D. E. James, *Allegories of Cinema* 18). Conversely, it is legitimate to consider such privileged instances in slapstick film as a partial realization, albeit in a different expressive medium, of the kind of empowering practice Benjamin had in mind when in the late 1920s he composed "Program for a Proletarian Children's Theatre."[13]

Setting to the side questions of moral influence, in this piece Benjamin calls for an educative theater, one aimed at those between the ages of four and fourteen, that will allow its participants to engage themselves entirely, that will provide a "defined space" where "the whole of life can appear [. . .] framed in all its plenitude" (202). Dedicated to the development of gestures, such a theater will decrease the emphasis that teachers customarily place on the final, completed performance; instead, undisciplined improvisation will be encouraged, since no "pedagogic wisdom can foresee how children will fuse the various gestures and skills into a theatrical totality," their "thousand unexpected variations" impossible to anticipate (204). Freeing its young performers of the burden of past experiences (the children will "carry no superfluous baggage around with them, in the form of overemotional [. . .] memories" [205]), the theater in question will allow childhood to fulfill itself "through play" in refreshingly unsentimental ways that adults will only be able to "wonder at" (205). Envisioned as a group undertaking ("the child, too, is [. . .] a collective" [203]) that "will unleash [. . .] the most powerful energies of the future" (202), Benjamin praises the sociopolitical "relevance of childlike forms and modes of conduct" as "unsurpassed" (203). According to him, the proletarian children's theater even has the potential to establish itself as a modern equivalent to ancient forms of popular festivity. Optimistically declaring that its performances will amount "in the realm of children

[to] what the carnival was in old cults," Benjamin extends the comparison in Bakhtinian fashion: "Everything was turned upside down; and just as in Rome the master served the slaves during Saturnalia, in the same way in a performance children stand on the stage and instruct and teach the attentive educators. New forces, new innervations appear—ones the director had no inkling of while working on the project. He learns about them only in the course of the wild liberation of the child's imagination" (205).

Toward a Slapstick Modernism

> In the beginning. A few puppets. Then I'll scatter them to the winds.
>
> —Samuel Beckett, *The Unnamable*

Three's a Crowd (1927) is the motion picture over which Langdon exerted the most creative control in his career—he directed it himself after breaking with Capra. However, the film marked the beginning of the end of his short time as a major star. A commercial catastrophe, the film has been evaluated by past commentators as an artistically confused effort to match the kind of pathos Chaplin achieved on screen in *The Kid*. Indeed, the unnamed character (the primary cast members are listed respectively as "One," "Two," and "Three" in the opening credits) Langdon plays is a pitiable figure: an impoverished and overworked youngster whose wish to get married and start a family is destined to remain unfulfilled. The Oedipal resonances of the plot are immediately evident. Having rescued a rag doll from a barrel of trash, Langdon tries to mimic his boss's interactions with his son, tossing the doll playfully in the air, only to be cruelly laughed at by his ostensible role model. We then learn that the latter is also Langdon's rival. The boss's wife lavishes maternal attention on Langdon, and when a pigeon deposits on the windowsill a love letter addressed to his "Sweetheart" (signed "lone-some Boy"), it becomes evident Harry has plans to win her heart. When his semi-incestuous passions are brought to light, Langdon must dash away to avoid punishment from the pistol-wielding paternal figure. Shortly thereafter he takes in a young pregnant woman who has left her irresponsible husband and, after she gives birth, begins to care for the child as his own. Here again Langdon's happiness is short-lived. A remarkable nightmare sequence pre-figures his loss to his new rival. After falling asleep in a makeshift crib while rocking the infant, he dreams that he is in a boxing ring preparing to fight for the hand of the young mother, who is the sole spectator. Before the bout begins, he faces her and indicates he is sure to win, for he has an enormous boxing glove on one of his hands; she gazes on this seemingly swollen body part with great delight, as if reassured that he possesses the necessary virility to win her. Before long, however, he is lying flat on his back on the canvas while his boss, appearing as the referee, viciously beats him on the head with an ax-shaped implement. Reality then confirms the boy's fantasized defeat and (symbolic) mutilation at the hands of his "father." The conjugal couple blissfully reconcile, leaving Langdon to suffer alone.

The set design and several of the film's gags suggest the actor should be viewed as a cinematic marionette. Located high in the air at the end of a marvelously angled staircase, the shed Langdon lives in contains an assortment of devices held together loosely with string. An improvised shower apparatus includes a watering bucket hanging from the ceiling as well as a tied-up phonograph horn. Surrounded by cords, Langdon looks just like a puppet when he exercises early in the morning on a homemade weight machine with a pulley system. A bit later he finds himself suspended in the air, clinging to a rug that has fallen through the apartment's trap door. The more he struggles to climb to safety, the less material there is to hold him up, until he finally falls. More significantly, after his boss notes the resemblance, the aforementioned doll serves as Langdon's metaphorical double rather than as his substitute child. Left outside to endure the harsh winter cold, and then ripped to shreds by a dog, the doll subsequently becomes part of a kite and ends up permanently caught in the telephone wires over the street. The object of several lingering shots, the broken toy's tragic fate mirrors the protagonist's: neither is able to ward off the abusive blows of the modern world.

However, lingering elements of humorous levity serve as a counterforce to *Three's a Crowd's* bleak portrayal of the character's apparently foreordained and seemingly interminable suffering. Thus in the final scene Langdon manages to exact a measure of revenge against Professor de Motte (a verbal condensation of "marionette"), the neighborhood palm reader who has previously assured the lad that he need not worry, that he is about to get what he has always wanted. Realizing that a charlatan has tricked him, Langdon contemplates hurling a brick through the fortune-teller's shop window. Although the character abandons his plan and tosses the brick away, in doing so he releases from the bed of a truck a huge canister, which promptly rolls through the window, shattering the building's façade. Although the character's inclination is to submit, to remain obedient to the law and accept the cruelties of existence, he nonetheless remains corporeally complicit with an act of comic aggression aimed at those who claim to know what the future will bring. A comparable tension structures the film as a whole. While the narrative enforces a melancholic view of life as necessarily and therefore predictably unsatisfying, the amusing routines, always based on the contingent outcome of arbitrarily linked events, maintain a joyfully vigorous optimism, encouraging spectators to laugh heartily at the unknowable.[14]

It was in response to a film like this one that the first glimmerings of the emergence of a slapstick modernism in the United States can be seen in the early autobiographical novels and literary criticism of the minor American writer Edward Dahlberg. In a 1929 critical essay titled "Ariel in Caliban," Dahlberg encouraged his literary peers to look for guidance in cinematic instances of puppetry in order to craft an approach to novelistic composition suited to machine-age circumstances. Dahlberg felt that the expressive task in the near future would be to disclose in lyric fashion the effects of inhabiting "a life and nature thoroughly mechanized" (3). Strongly endorsing anti-pastoral undertakings, Dahlberg credits Baudelaire with having understood the need to pursue such projects, as evidenced by his preference for artifice and the artificial, for "rouged women and metal trees. [. . .] Nothing has contributed so much to this aesthetic of diablerie as modern industrialism" (3). More recently, the productions of the German UFA cinema had begun to demonstrate how to convey adequately the psychic and corporeal impact of new "social and economic conditions." Thus the gestures of the maidservant in *Backstairs*—a 1921 expressionist film directed by Paul Leni—"suggest a puppet [. . .] bent and gnarled by suffering. Here tragedy, in its true Greek sense, has transmuted the face into a mask and the body, its twists and contortions, into a marionette (4). But it was American silent comedy, as epitomized by Harry Langdon, that constituted Dahlberg's most valuable point of reference for the use of such reifying techniques.

As he saw it, Langdon's mournful way of behaving in front of the camera had the potential to alert innovative writers to the aesthetic significance of depicting living beings as inanimate things. The actor "has without conscious design rivaled the marionettes of the Grand Guignol in the Tuileries.[15] His face, faunlike, his long swallow tail coat, his inelastic jerks and movements have bodied forth Bergson's theory of the comic. Too, there is another element upon which Bergson has not touched and that is the tragic suggested by the mechanical" (4). It is in the historical context of a situation in which the "metaphysics which arise from machinery and mechanism [. . . have] more aesthetic value" than "naïve phenomena" that slapstick film proves meaningful to literary modernism. Assuming that "philosophy and art, like all physical processes, are ever becoming, and must of necessity move toward a nature with mechanical and industrial encrustations" (8), Dahlberg posits a silent comedian as exemplary for those concerned to depict what happens to the human in a radically altered environment.[16]

In utilizing free indirect discourse throughout his first novel, *Bottom Dogs* (1929), to narrate the youthful years of his autobiographical protagonist, Lorry Lewis, Dahlberg develops a rhetorical method that in effect enacts the becoming-child of the author. But it is allusion to Langdon in Dahlberg's second fiction, *From Flushing to Calvary* (1932), which indicates the writer had modeled his surrogate self on what he took to be the quintessential marionette of modernity. Lorry confronts the truth about himself, his unfortunate lack of control over his destiny, in a late scene set in the milieu of mechanized systems of transportation. Having arrived at "Death Avenue," the sad-sack character first looks through a roundhouse window "at the squads of locomotives at a standstill inside" and then modifies his gaze to take in what "the shiny glass threw back." "Lorry stared like a lowbrow heavyfooted comedian out of work at his face. [. . .] His head and features were already a kind of phony halloween mask of hopelessness. As he gazed into the plateglass of the roundhouse, he responded to the silly helpless Harry Langdonesque image that gaped back at him: 'For God's sake, don't be so unlucky.' Then he walked away from his face as if he was moving away from destiny" (244). Dahlberg's fascination with puppetry as a mode of characterization, then, was a fascination with the possibility of bringing into focus the misery of the city's forlorn inhabitants. Perceiving the marionette as a mournful "cipher of the mechanical-commodified," as a coded message about the worthlessness of life conditioned by the inhuman forces of twentieth-century capitalism (H. Foster 126),[17] Dahlberg sought to invest the puppet figure with "socio-critical significance" as an expression of the victimized and alienated mode of existence of the melancholic subject of urban modernity (Benjamin, *Arcades* 694).

Although Dahlberg's criticism and fiction presage the appearance in this country of a slapstick modernism, the time when this by no means gloomy event would take place was still off in the distance. In the interim, however, three novelists working abroad made significant advances with regard to the cultural coalescence under investigation. Louis-Ferdinand Céline was undoubtedly the most directly influential of these on postwar American writers; his achievement in *Journey to the End of the Night* (1932) and *Death on the Installment Plan* (1936) was an inspiration and model for the most important of the Beat generation figures, not to mention black humorists like Kurt Vonnegut and Thomas Pynchon. Kerouac's declaration that "reading *Voyage au bout de la nuit* was to me like seeing the greatest French movie ever made" is merely one of several indications of the substantial debt he and his close associates owed to their notorious predecessor Céline, whose third novel was titled *Guignol's Band* (1944) (Kerouac, "On Céline" 90).[18] The second and third of the important precursors of the post–World War II rise of a slapstick modernism in the United States were Henry Miller and the Polish modernist Witold Gombrowicz, both of whom saw their early work banned in their respective homelands.[19] (One could add Nathanael West to this short list but probably not William Faulkner, given the difficulty of isolating the slapstick elements in the latter's comic modernism—a much broader category that in the 1930s encompasses the fiction of Djuna Barnes and the Flann O'Brien of *At Swim-Two-Birds* [1939].[20] However, O'Brien's *The Third Policeman*—published posthumously in 1966, though written in the Depression era—is a good candidate for inclusion in the category of slapstick modernism, as is much of Samuel Beckett's oeuvre.[21]) That I privilege Gombrowicz at the expense of Henry Miller in the next chapter may seem surprising given that, no doubt due to the non-translation of his *Ferdydurke* (1937), Gombrowicz had no discernible impact on American literature in the decade following the Second World War. (It was not until 1961 that an English-language translation of the novel appeared in print, the same year that a court case cleared *Tropic of Cancer* [1932] of charges of obscenity, finally making it legally available in the United States.) Nevertheless, *Ferdydurke* is an especially revealing exemplification of what happens when the process of becoming-child is located at the center of a novelistic endeavor; and taken together with Céline's Depression-era output, Gombrowicz and Miller demonstrate the astonishing effects of integrating the comic energies of slapstick cinema into formally daring literary projects.

PART II

1930s

5

The Emergence of Slapstick Modernism

I have described the nature of my own humor
[. . . as] chaplinesque in its violence. Why always *violence*?
[. . .] I have ofter asked that myself.

—Wyndham Lewis, *The Wild Body*

In "Modern Times against Western Man: Wyndham Lewis, Charlie Chaplin, and Cinema," Scott M. Klein proposes that there is "a genealogy of comic modernism that connects Chaplin to Lewis to Beckett" (139). However, Klein acknowledges that Lewis's relationship to the slapstick tradition was a vexed one, as evidenced by his denunciation in *Time and Western Man* (1927) of the film star's childishness and his disparaging allusions to the icon in *The Childermass* (1928) as a symptom of all that he loathed about industrialized culture (mechanization, copying, lack of genuineness (128).[1] The resonance of the silent comedian in Céline's prose style as this would manifest itself at the beginning of the next decade was much less equivocal, as Allen Ginsberg and Peter Orlovsky humorously recognized many years later in a public letter that was ostensibly addressed to the aging motion picture comedian: "Have you read Louis-Ferdinand Céline? He wrote the most Chaplinesque prose in Europe" (441). This was an opinion with which Fredric Jameson would concur in the 1990s in "Céline and Innocence," noting there that the author "has more affinities with Chaplin than with most novelists," and then adding that Céline's "capacity to write the collective" in a state of frenzy was a technical "achievement of the greatest significance for literary history" (49).[2] Gombrowicz's ability to reproduce conditions of slapstick lunacy in verbal form, as demonstrated in *Ferdydurke,* was a similarly impressive accomplishment. Taken together, the early fiction of the two writers furnishes us with an opportunity to examine slapstick modernism at the moment of its literary inception. The concept of becoming child remains applicable to the work of both thematically and at the level of linguistic style in Céline, whose project also provides an opportunity to speculate on the cathartic dimensions of the slapstick modernist's effort to use words in an electrifying manner.

The Power of Humor: Céline and Catharsis

> Positively, if any writer of this age had brought together in literary form—and in readable English—instead of upon the screen as has Sennett—the pie-throwers, soup-spillers, bomb-tossers, hot-stove stealers, and what not else of Mr. Sennett's grotesqueries—what a reputation! The respect! The acclaim!
>
> —Theodore Dreiser, "Best Motion Picture Interview Ever Written"

Just a few years after Dreiser imagined, in the context of an interview with Mack Sennett, the possible emergence of the cultural hybrid I have named slapstick modernism, his wish came true, albeit initially in readable French. Indeed, to the extent that reading Céline is analogous to the experience of watching an outrageously offensive silent comedy, one might describe his oeuvre as a marvelous actualization of what Dreiser proposed as a mere idea in the late 1920s. But what kind of social intervention did this literary project constitute? Were the elaborate verbal performances of the physician/writer as showman aimed at furnishing a cathartic cure for his potential readers?

An admittedly dubious notion, catharsis has never been satisfactorily defined, much less verified at the level of actual effect. Did Aristotle mean, for instance, "a medical or a lustratory metaphor, whether the genitive which follows *katharsis* is of the thing purged or of the object purified" (Wimsatt and Beardsley 352; emphasis in the original). Is it a term for a strictly physiological outlet, or does it designate a philosophical process of dialectical overcoming?[3] Is it a primarily affective force, or does it have cognitive dimensions as well?[4] Though Walter Benjamin's striking affirmation of silent screen comedy as a mode of social catharsis answers none of these questions satisfactorily, it does supply an intriguing frame for understanding certain cultural practices as oriented toward therapeutic tasks. Benjamin no doubt overestimates silent comedy as he remarks on the civic virtues of the cinematic phenomenon, yet his idea is worth rehearsing. Diagnosing the psychic toll that the rise of (what he has termed earlier in the essay a *first*) technology has taken on the subjects of modernity, he boldly proposes that the tendency of slapstick film (as a *second* technology) is to perform a prophylactic task at the site of reception: "*If one considers the dangerous tensions which technology and its consequences have engendered in the masses at large—tendencies which at critical stages take on a psychotic character—one also has to recognize that this same technologization has created the possibility of psychic immunization against such mass psychoses. It does so by means of certain films in which the forced development of sadistic fantasies or masochistic delusions can prevent their natural and dangerous maturation in the masses.*" For Benjamin, the "collective laughter" that silent comedies generate functions as a "preemptive and healing outbreak" of the mental illness that would otherwise take hold of persons in reality. That such films feature an array of "grotesque events" is a symptom "of the dangers threatening mankind," a "graphic indication" that "the repressions implicit in civilization" could have a disastrous outcome. The mediated consumption of such images of brutality in the form of "American slapstick comedies and Disney films" has the potential, however, to "trigger a therapeutic release of unconscious energies," and this is precisely "the context in which Chaplin takes on historical significance" ("Work of Art," 2nd version 118; emphasis in the original).

Could motion picture genres truly function in a preventive manner, as a vaccine for increasingly aggressive spectators, enabling them to temper their perverse drives and violent impulses before they developed into full-blown pathologies? Probably not, especially in light of the fact that the films were not quite as grotesque as Benjamin claims here. On the other hand, Céline's Depression-era narratives do put myriad "sadistic fantasies" and "masochistic delusions" on display. Could these books, then, in humorously enacting or staging more or less unconsciously structured scenarios of cruelty and suffering, keep individuals from acting them out in real life? Could literature protect the subjects of urban-industrial modernity from falling victim to aberrantly paranoid hallucinations? Could it enable them to overcome their deadly passions? Again, it is highly unlikely that the texts in question managed on an empirical level to remedy the sicknesses they exhibited. Nevertheless, Benjamin's theoretical speculations supply a valuable hypothesis in regard to the ethical motivations underlying Céline's astonishing cultural intervention (not to mention Burroughs's in *Naked Lunch* two decades later). The writer may not have achieved his ultimate goal, but the quasi-medical aspiration guiding his literary practice may well have been to heal the diseased psyches he detected everywhere around him.[5]

That his literary aesthetics derived a great deal of their emotional force from the example set by slapstick film performances is something Céline never claimed, yet there are numerous examples in his novels to support the contention that his style of writing benefited greatly from his exposure to the realm of silent comedy. For instance, *Death on the Installment Plan* presents a series of gruesomely hilarious episodes, many of them organized around the vomiting or excreting body. Ferdinand's family's awful experiences on board a ship that is taking them to England for a vacation is a case in point. So seasick are they that they can't keep from throwing up on the wife of another passenger, whose enraged husband savagely attacks the narrator's father. What follows is repulsive slapstick, albeit with bodily fluids replacing the pies and hot soups of the relatively non-scatological cinematic genre:

> The strong man jumps on him and starts hammering at his face . . . He bends down to finish him off . . . Papa was bleeding all over . . . The blood poured down into the vomit . . . He was slipping down the mast . . . In the end he collapsed . . . But the husband still wasn't satisfied . . . Taking advantage of a moment when the roll has sent me spinning he charged me . . . I skid . . . He flings me at the shithouse . . . like a battering ram . . . I smash into it . . . I bash the door in . . . I fall on the poor sagging bastards . . . I turn around . . . I'm wedged in the middle of them . . . They've all lost their pants . . . I pull the chain. We're half drowned in the flood. (125–26)

Even more extreme is the scene in which the narrator returns home in disgrace after having spent the money given to him for groceries on liquor instead. Rather than apologize, he attacks his father with extraordinary violence, brutally smashing him in the head with a typewriter, tearing the mustache off his face, biting him, and then choking a neighbor who tries to intervene (316–17). But the grotesque apotheosis of Céline's signature mixture of horror and humor takes place late in the novel shortly after Courtial des Pereires, a lovable reprobate, has committed suicide with a shotgun. Ferdinand and Pereires's widow, Clemence, have wrapped the corpse in the tattered remnants of his cherished balloon when a clearly insane clergyman arrives and insists on viewing the decaying corpse. At first he simply "sniffs full in the meat" of its "blasted face." Then he "starts howling," works himself into a frenzy, throwing "another fit" until his "whole body is shaking." He decides to "try to cover the head up again," but as he "pulls at the canvas" he goes "stark raving mad," his increasing paranoia convincing him that the corpse won't let him be covered up. In response, the clergyman "sticks his fingers into the wound," digging "into all the holes, tearing "away the soft edges":

> He pokes around . . . He gets stuck . . . His wrist is caught in the bones . . . Crack! . . . He tugs . . . He struggles like in a trap . . . Some kind of pouch bursts

> . . . The juice pours out . . . it gushes all over the place . . . all full of brains and blood . . . splashing . . . He manages to get his hand out . . . I get the sauce full in the face . . . I can't see a thing . . . I flail around. (560)

When a formally innovative writer puts on the page a grotesquely disgusting variant of the comic delirium that had formerly appeared only on the silver screen, the result is a slapstick modernism.

Céline's integration of motifs derived from the film genre into an experimental mode of writing is equally apparent in the novel's assorted scenes featuring decidedly eccentric inventors. Ferdinand, for example, fondly recalls his uncle Édouard as having been "crazy about inventions . . . any kind of mechanical idea . . . Those things really sent him" (284).The narrator's father finds his brother's penchant for "always getting a kick out of something nonsensical" to be irritatingly "idiotic, absolutely unbearable." A fictive incarnation of the type of character played by Buster Keaton, Snub Pollard, and Charley Bowers, among others,[6] Édouard "got on my father's nerves . . . with his mechanical gadgets, his jalopies, his three-wheelers, his funny-looking pumps" (285). The inventor, like his slapstick precursors, perseveres, constantly tinkering in the hopes of securing a patent for such ingenious contraptions as a shaving razor, "tricky and modern," that could be put "together in all directions even backwards," the only problem being that "it took an engineer to change the blade" (323). Eventually Édouard introduces the narrator to the indefatigable Ferdinand Roger-Martin Courtial des Pereires, whose screwball entrepreneurial schemes and zealous undertakings constitute the bulk of the subject matter of the hilarious second half of the novel.[7]

The author of popular handbooks like *Be Your Own Doctor*, *The Story of Polar Voyages from Maupertuis to Charcot*, *How to Make Ions*, and *Electricity without a Bulb*, as well as a study of the inseparability of muscles and mind titled "The Human Battery and Its Upkeep," Pereires is also the editor of *Genitron*, the favorite magazine of artisan-inventors in Paris because of its capacity to turn out "definitive, incontrovertible explanations and digests of the most preposterous, hairsplitting, farfetched, and nebulous hypotheses" (Céline, *Death* 330). Pereires is less successful in the practical realm: "The resistance of matter gave him an epileptic fit . . . The result was wreckage" (333). "Whenever he tried to do any tinkering with his own fingers, it ended in disaster" (334). In the past he had almost become famous "for his original and extremely daring studies on the 'All-Purpose Cottage,' the flexible, extensible dwelling, adaptable to families of every kind in all climates!" (360). Unfortunately, the amazing edifice was immediately obliterated upon exhibition at a stand at the 1898 World's Fair, the feverish mob "so avid that it combusted all the materials" (362). Determining whether or not Keaton's *One Week* (1920), with its multiple gags organized around a young groom's efforts to put together a do-it-yourself dwelling, served as a touchstone for Céline's account of his character's ill-fated project is less important than recognizing the affinity between the silent comedian and the modernist author.[8]

Pereires's most catastrophic failure is his attempt to wire fields of potatoes in order to raise a crop of "radio-telleric" vegetables, yet for the most part he maintains an adversarial relationship to industrial modernity. One of his fixed ideas is that there is not "a moment to be lost" in the fight against "the rising peril of mass production" (360). His "resolute belief in progress" notwithstanding, Pereires "always detested standardization" on the grounds that it signaled the "death of craftsmanship." As madcap a bricoleur as his many slapstick brethren, the character repeatedly seeks to put his design skills to use in order to amaze and impress, his marvelously bizarre contraptions clearly assembled in defiance of the disciplinary imperatives of economic rationalism.

Set in London and opening with a remarkable description of the city under military attack, Céline's comic novel *Guignol's Band* takes the violently frantic escapades of a gang of crooks as subject matter for an anarchically comic literary performance. Indeed, Céline devotes a considerable portion of his compositional energies here to the construction of slapstick scenes of riotous brawling. In one of the barroom battles in which the narrator gets caught up, two prostitutes engage in a whirlwind knife fight, hysterically shrieking, tearing and ripping off each other's clothes. The loser ends up being taken to the hospital to repair her severely wounded rear end. More extraordinary is the sequence of events late in the novel that result in the accidental death of the pawnbroker/fence Titus Van Claben. Thoroughly intoxicated, either from smoking suspicious cigarettes or polishing off a bottle of gin, Ferdinand, in a fit of paranoia, fears his friends are trying to coerce him into participating in an orgy. As the hallucinatory madness intensifies, Van Claben somehow gets his head split open. Another character, named Boro, then sets fire to the shop, trapping the narrator and a woman named Delphine, but they do manage to escape just before flames consume the building and the dead body abandoned inside. It is difficult to convey the affective intensity of scenes like this one and the others mentioned above, although anyone exposed to the slapstick films of the first quarter of the twentieth century will immediately recognize the cultural tradition within which Céline worked.

Given his seamless incorporation of key elements of silent screen comedy into his semi-autobiographical practice, it is fitting that Céline, in *Conversations with Professor Y*, a more critically oriented text published in 1955, implicitly praises his own inventive style of writing as having defeated the movies, as having rendered the adjacent form of entertainment obsolete: "'So the cinema [. . .] is done for! [. . .] outmoded, lost its glow, ruined'" (107). The writer's appalled interlocutor (the Colonel) protests that this is a preposterous, self-aggrandizing claim—"'Nonsense! . . . Nonsense!'" (107)—yet Céline refuses to yield the point, insisting that his spectacular literary accomplishment has left "nothing for the cinema! I've made off with all its effects." "I seized all the emotive stuff" (109).[9] Intriguingly, throughout *Conversations* Céline characterizes his exceptionally forceful writing method by way of analogies with a modern system of transportation. When asked how his idea of his "'so-called new style'" ever came to him, he replies: "'Through the metro!'" (73). "'I owe the revelation of my genius to the Pigalle station!'" (91). Modeling his unconventional aesthetic technique on the swiftness and power of underground trains, Céline proposes that the unstoppable energy of his art constitutes a way to handle the otherwise intolerable conditions of everyday existence in the city:

> "The Surface [the Place de la Concorde at rush hour, for instance] is hardly livable! . . . it's true! So I don't hesitate, not me! . . . my genius in action! no formalities! . . . I ship all my friends off on the metro, correction! I take everybody, willy-nilly, with me! . . . charge along! . . . the emotive subway, mine in a dream! No drawbacks, nor congestion! . . . never a stop, nowhere! . . . straight through! Destination! In emotion! . . . powered with emotion! Only the goal in sight: full emotion . . . start to finish!" (93)

Troping subjective impact in terms of objective physical movement, Céline makes extravagant claims for the feelings one experiences when reading his novels; reading is comparable to riding a thrilling rollercoaster. Like efficiently fashioned railway tracks, the lines of his novel carry his readers along as if they were riders traveling in a recreational simulation of a subway car, hence the tendency of his loopy text to take dangerous curves too swiftly: "'Thanks to my streamlined rails! My streamlined style!'" "'Streamlined on purpose! . . . special! The metro and its rails, I bend them! I do, I admit! Its rails so rigid! . . . I give them a helluva twist . . . all it takes!'" "'the violence also! . . . admittedly! . . . all the passengers enclosed, locked in, double-bolted! everybody in my emotive cars!'" (95). Urban modernity in its entirety is combined and carried away in his sensationally exciting mode of literary transport: "'And the whole Surface comes with me! you see! the whole Surface! on board! amalgamated on my metro! all the Surface ingredients! all the distractions of the Surface! by sheer force! I leave the Surface nothing! . . . I make off with it all!'" (95).

Rather than recoil (as had the observer in Pound's "In a Station of the Metro" decades earlier) in dismay at the threat the new system of rapid transit posed to the aesthetic sensibilities, Céline celebrates his assimilation of the distinguishing traits of the mechanized phenomenon—massive power and raw speed—into his literary technique. Comparing literature to Le Métro identifies the writer as the conductor of a verbal train that packs the referential world into its cars and takes it away: "'everything into my emotive metro! . . . houses, guys, bricks, broads, pastry cooks, bikes, cars, shopgirls, cops as well! Heaped up, "emotive cells"! . . . in my emotive metro! I leave nothing above ground! Everything, in my magic transport!'" (*Conversations* 95). Designing an electrifying aesthetic that shocks his audience neurophysiologically—"'the style to touch the very quick of the nerves!'" (95)—Céline puts words and things into motion: "'My metro stuffed, so stuffed . . . absolutely filled to overflowing! . . . plugged right into the nervous system . . . it charges right into the nervous system!'" (107).[10] And Céline (or the megalomaniacal speaker in *Conversations*) clearly regarded his pioneering literary method as an immensely valuable achievement, his aesthetic discovery more significant than major scientific breakthroughs: his "'metro-all-nerve-magic-rails-with-three-dot-ties' is more important than the atom!"[11] Implicitly denying his debt to a popular form of entertainment (silent comedy), Céline predicts—accurately enough—that the book industry will soon co-opt his "originality," rendering his seemingly singular investment in emotional intensity a commercial norm. As he endeavors to explain to his interlocutor, "The inventor of a new style is but the inventor of a technique!" The question is whether or not it will "prove worthwhile." The essence of the "little gimmick" on which the writer holds the patent "is emotion":

> Style with an emotive yield? Does it work? . . . I say it does! . . . a hundred writers have tried to copy it, still trying, to make a buck out of it, plagiarize it, fake it, pastiche it! . . . so much so, you'll see, by dint! . . . won't be long! . . . my gimmick will become pop literature itself! Yes, dear Professor! You'll see! Just watch! . . . as though I were there now . . . pop stuff!. . . . maybe thirty . . . forty years! (32–33).

Several of Céline's prominent commentators have correlated his invention of an affectively forceful style of writing to an evacuation of its semantic dimension, to a kind of cathartic elimination that takes place at the level of language rather than the body. Explicating further the novelist's reflexive figuration, Pierre Macherey argues, for instance, that Céline's rhetorical procedure wrecks the conventions structuring the discursive transmission of meaning: "Céline's sentences, with their jerky lines, their unexpected digressions and their sumptuous rises, but also their platitudes and their falls, accelerate and decelerate, swell and collapse as they move to an alternative, irregular and broken rhythm like that of the metro." The author thus "gradually perfects a machine for disrupting communication. He takes the natural functions of language to extremes and twists them until they break. The final product is a shattered, irrecuperable and indefensible language" (135, 139). Similarly, for Deleuze and Guattari, Céline's achievement was to push language beyond representation until it reached its limit or breaking point as impassioned shout or sheer exclamation. Tracing the evolution of his syntactic methods from *Journey* through *Death* to *Guignol's Band*, Deleuze and Guattari argue that the primary function of the "crazy creation" Céline finally assembled was to generate nothing but sonorous intensities, to speak "with a kind of 'minor music,'" and this is what establishes him as the progenitor of a "pop writing" (*Kafka* 26).[12]

Julia Kristeva has examined in greater detail Céline's stated ambition to "*resensitize language*, to have it *throb* more than *reason*" (quoted in Kristeva 190; emphasis in the original). Citing as well his determination to impart "to thought a certain melodious, melodic twist [. . .] a minor harmonic feat," Kristeva asserts that his "worship of emotion . . . slips into a glorification of sound" (190). Céline's innovative use of colloquial speech patterns and a nonstandard vocabulary (both of which are difficult for a nonnative speaker to register) add expressive force to his utterance, but they do so at the expense of sense. The verbal informalities that rhythmically punctuate his prose amount to a kind of assault and battery on his unprepared reader's sensibilities: "'Slang . . . knocks the reader out very nicely . . . annihilates him! Completely in your power!'" (quoted in Kristeva 191), and it is by delivering such verbal blows that he approaches the "emptiness of meaning" he desires (191). Drawing on Leo Spitzer's analysis of Célinian syntax, Kristeva goes on to describe Céline's "musical" procedures as involving what we may call the becoming-child of the writer. The surging intonations of his staccato speech derive from archaic structures and therefore recall the kinds of sentences children learn at the beginning of their initial entry into language as subjects. Yet the stylistic method does not amount to a simple regression to an early stage of impassioned speaking. Rather, his active investment in charging syntax with intense feeling takes place on the far side of linguistic competence. His childish mannerisms are an artificially contrived, skillful supplement to adult or mature modes of communicating: "The emotion so dear to Céline is not uttered in any other way except by a return of repressed enunciative strategies; added to normative syntax, they make up a complicated mental machine in which two programs are meshed (enunciation and statement), just as a piano performance results from conjoined playing by two hands" (Kristeva 197).

With this in mind, one of the narrator's happier recollections in *Guignol's Band* acquires the status of a reflexive allegory, one that articulates the joyously tactile elements of the novelist's past and present compositions. Hanging around with a set of low-life scoundrels, he remembers spending much of his time with a bomb-throwing ex-chemist named Borokrom, who "played the piano delightfully when he had nothing else to do." He then informs us that on occasion they performed together on the same keyboard. Much as the bodily distinction between the two characters blurs, the piano figuratively morphs into the mechanical device that is so indispensable to Céline's unique style of writing: the typewriter. He informs us that we should have heard their collaborative performances, their charming "'three-handed' numbers," in which the speaker "did the 'one-armed' bass, my octave run." He then declares that the "big secret" is that one "has to keep going," that one can "never slow up never stop," that "it's got to keep popping away like seconds, each with its little trick" to the point where it "perks you up with a trill . . . nicks you! . . . tinkles right into your worries . . . plays tricks with time, tickles your trouble, teases, pleases and tinkles your worries, and tum! tum! whirls you around! . . . carries you off . . . constant gallop! Notes and notes!" "When it came to the ivories," Borokrom was the more amazing of the performers, his "flighty rhythms," his vast "repertoire," his remarkable "memory," his improvisatory capacity ("variations ad infinitum"), demonstrating that his "mind was in his fingers." Though "rather uncouth by nature and really just a brute and pretty impossible with his mania for explosives," this obvious role model for the author clearly has another side to him, a penchant for artistic inventiveness that has enthralled and inspired the narrator (*Guignol's Band* 142).

The musical figuration evokes Céline's conviction that his affectively charged aural enterprise was a curative one. Here the "flighty rhythms" perk up the audience. The relentless onslaught of notes tickles their troubles away, converting their worried state of mind into a pleasurable one. Correlatively, he claims in *Conversations* that were the masses to receive the "emotive waves" of his orally based writing technique, there "wouldn't have been any more wars," would have been "no more butchery" (21). In turn, failure to appreciate his aesthetic accomplishment is one of the causes of the generalized "turn to hysteria! to savagery, pillaging, instant assassination" (23). "Man's path" will cease to be "strewn with blood and bone" (23) only when the overly aggressive subjects of modernity start taking the aesthetic remedy the author has prescribed for them.[13] Equating sickness with signification, Céline's theory and practice proposes that expelling or conquering the signified is one of the preconditions for collective health. If clinging to the illusion of meaning is a symptom of mass mental illness, then neuroses and psychoses may be alleviated through regular injections of high dosages of sheer sound.

A swift return to the beginning of Céline's *Journey to the End of the Night* confirms this diagnosis at the thematic level. While it reads like a literary version of Chaplin's film *Shoulder Arms*, the character Bardamu's account of his wartime experiences underscores how these exorcised the remnants of significance in propagandistic discourse: "patriotic, ethical, word-propelled considerations, ghosts that the mayor tried to hold fast, but they faded away" (37). Similarly, while his American girlfriend adheres to ideological models of self-sacrifice, since his "enlistment" the character has "grown phobically allergic to heroism, verbal or real. I was cured. Radically cured" (41). The semantic substance of such concepts cannot withstand the painful shock of his repeated encounters with "human viciousness" (18). Indeed, "before a thought can start up in the brain of a jughead, a lot of cruel things must happen to him" (20).

Of Profs and Pupils: Gombrowicz's *Ferdydurke*

> Ah, but I was so much older then.
> I'm younger than that now.
> —Bob Dylan, "My Back Pages"

Susan Sontag begins her foreword to the most recent English-language translation of *Ferdydurke* by noting how perfectly the title of Gombrowicz's first book, *Memoirs of a Time of Immaturity* (1933), would have suited his second. The compatibility of the two works is further supported by the fact that the author incorporated two stories from *Memoirs*—"The Child Runs Deep in Filidor" and "The Child Runs Deep in Filibert"—into *Ferdydurke*, where they function in part as a digressive means of impeding the progress of the narrative. Taken together these two selections (and their respective prefaces) disclose the novel's sustained investment in the process of becoming child as a mode of undermining both philosophical seriousness and artistic pretentiousness.

After discrediting in amusing fashion the commonplace assumption that artworks as a whole are more than the sum of their nonuniform parts, the speaker in the fourth chapter of *Ferdydurke*, "Preface to 'The Child Runs Deep in Filidor,'" wonders with mock sincerity if there will "ever be a sufficiently serious-minded genius who will look life's trivia in the eye without bursting into a dumb giggle" (71). He then contests the mistaken notion that artistic reception involves a one-to-one relationship between an individual and the work of art. To define listening to a musical performance, for instance, in such "utterly egocentric terms" is a sign of "how impure, murky, and immature is the artistic aspect of culture." The idea that we experience "art totally on our own [. . .] in hermetic isolation from your fellow man," mystifies the fact that "in real life we're dealing with a blend of many emotions, of many individuals who, acting on each other, create a collective experience" (78). It is an illusion to believe that when "pale with emotion, [we] applaud, scream, carry on, writhe in enthusiasm," we are not unwittingly conforming to the similarly ecstatic behavior of other members of the audience. We involuntarily imitate others even when reading—albeit in a more sociohistorically mediated manner—insofar as our judgment of quality, and the correlative prestige we attribute to one writer instead of another, is conditioned by previous assessments of the admired one's "greatness" (79).

At this point the primary target of the preface comes into focus: the writer as noble soul. It is the pomposity of artists who believe themselves to be "creatures of a higher order" that the critic wishes to contest. Those who are certain that their mission in the world is "to edify and enlighten someone else, to lead and raise someone else into the sublime, or to improve someone else's morals," must be challenged. The elevated, superior status such purportedly grown-up or adult persons grant themselves is baseless, and they therefore deserve to be interrogated: "Who gave you the patent on Maturity?" (81). What is required, then, is a writer with a different attitude altogether, one who writes with a lucid awareness "of his immaturity" and who "knows he is [. . .] in the process of becoming but has not become" (82). To formulate the problem graphically, the speaker encourages us to imagine the following scenario: an "adult and mature bard, leaning over a piece of paper, is in the process of creating [. . .] but on his back a youth has squarely settled himself," or some other "nondescript slouch," perhaps a "lowbrow ignorant creature" (82). The latter then "pounces" on the soul of the great author, dragging it down, constricting it, "kneading it with his paws, yet at the same time [. . .] soaking it up, sucking it in," thereby rejuvenating "it with his youth," seasoning "it with his immaturity" (82). Everyone can and should be knocked off their pedestal, for in truth they are perpetually in debt to those they presume to dominate from above: "Every being who is at a higher level of development, who is older and more mature, is dependent in a thousand ways on beings who are less well developed, and doesn't this dependence permeate us through and through, to our very core and to the extent that we can say: the elder is created by the younger?" (83). To fabricate a genuinely creative or "universal style," the writer must henceforth learn "to embrace lovingly those who are not quite developed" (84), must realize that one's "element is unending immaturity" (85) and always be ready to admit to "that portion of silliness which time will reveal" (85). The authentically "wise" writer would, in sum, be one who is capable of benefiting from the childishly unrefined and stupid (84). Writers possessed of such insight would, upon encountering such persons, not pat them on the back "condescendingly [. . .] like a preacher or a pedagogue," but would instead "wail and roar in holy trembling," perhaps even dropping to their knees before them (84).

In the ensuing madcap anecdote, "The Child Runs Deep in Filidor," Gombrowicz (or the narrator) clearly takes his own advice, drawing a tremendous amount of his compositional technique and creative energy from the delightfully idiotic realm of Keystone motion pictures. Customarily read as a burlesque treatment of the relative merits of synthesis and analysis in Kant's *Critique of Pure Reason*, the tale renders the philosophical treatise's conceptual dichotomy farcical, depicting it as a furiously wacky battle between Dr. Filidor, a Leyden University Professor of Synthetology, and his archenemy, an unnamed analyst specializing at a different institution in decomposition. The struggle between the two nemeses, Filidor and anti-Filidor, gets under way when they volley noodles back and forth at a restaurant. The latter then switches tactics, listing certain orifices and corporeal appendages, which causes Filidor's obese wife great agitation. The anti-Filidor then secures victory by doing a "spot analysis of her urine," sending her to the hospital due to her loss of control over her various body parts, which now move "autonomously" (Gombrowicz, *Ferdydurke* 90).

Having lost the verbal joust, Filidor declares that the only way to halt his wife's physical disintegration is to be slapped in the face by his opponent. His rival eventually delivers this blow, and the two then arrange a duel. As the rule-bound combat dissolves into a free-for-all fracas, it seems as if a production crew supervised by Sennett has taken command of the narrative, or rather as if Gombrowicz has looked for guidance to the legendary "wild man" the studio kept around in order to take advantage of his "totally uninhibited imagination" (Agee, "Comedy's Greatest Era" 7–8). The carnivalized zaniness begins when an aberrant shot from the Analyst's pistol knocks off the High Professor's wife's finger. Before long each is firing nonstop, their skillful shooting leaving this lady and her counterpart "shorn bare of all their natural appendages and protrusions" (Gombrowicz, *Ferdydurke* 99). The narrator suspects, their grievous injuries notwithstanding, that the women "were delighted—being exposed to such marksmanship" (99). The battle concludes when successive bullets pierce the apex of the two female spectators' lungs, the numerous male bystanders compelled to "give a shout of admiration" as the "torsos died and slid to the ground" (100). Perplexed over what to do next, the two opponents wander the world, taking aim at whatever presents itself to their eyes; they then regress further to the state of adolescent troublemakers. What the juvenile delinquents like best is "breaking windows," but "they also liked to stand on a balcony and spit upon the hats of passersby," to "extinguish a candle by throwing a box of matches at the flame," and "to hunt frogs with a BB gun" (100). In the end, however, their greatest delight is simply "to buy a child's balloon and run after it through fields and forests—hey, ho! and watch it burst with a bang as if shot with an invisible bullet" (100). When reproached for his foolish behavior, the once-reputable academic, "an old man gone childish," explains, "The child runs deep in everything!" (101).

The companion piece, "The Child Runs Deep in Filibert," is just as grotesquely ludicrous. Located closer to the end of the text, this story recounts the process whereby a public tennis match becomes a frenzied slapstick melee. Sitting in the crowd, a colonel of the Zouaves decides it would be amusing to show off his pistol skills and hit the ball in midair. "Deprived of their object," the players briefly continue to swing their rackets, recognize the pointlessness of their movements, and then pounce "on each other with their claws" (Gombrowicz, *Ferdydurke* 199). Meanwhile, continuing on its trajectory, the stray bullet has struck a man in the neck. As blood spurts from "a ruptured artery," the wounded man's wife, since she cannot reach the colonel, slaps her neighbor, "a latent epileptic" who goes "into a seizure," erupting "like a geyser in jerks and convulsions": "The hapless woman found herself between two men, one spurting blood, the other foam. A thunderous applause rose from the spectators. Whereupon, a gentleman sitting nearby suddenly panicked and jumped on the head of the lady seated below, she in turn took off and, carrying him on her back at full speed, bounded into the center of the court" (200).

Galvanized into action, everyone, including those in the more "sophisticated sector," excitedly mount their partners. Hoping to stop the madness, the Marquis de Filibert hurls his visiting cards into the crowd and asks coolly who dares to insult his wife. A momentary silence falls, then "no fewer than thirty-six gentlemen began riding up at a slow canter, bareback on their elegantly and ornately dressed women [. . .] to insult the marquise" (201). The latter, terrified, suffers a miscarriage, while the marquis, "so unexpectedly made aware of the child that ran deep in him," withdraws in shame. Having realized that "when he was acting singly and as a gentleman mature within himself, how sustained and replenished he had been by the child," he is "overcome with embarrassment" and goes home (201).

Slapstick delirium pervades the main narrative as well. In the first section, where the thirty-year-old protagonist, Joey, is abducted and sent back to school as a sixth grader, Gombrowicz's comic method serves as a means of disrupting the coercive forces of educational institutions. Unhappily ensconced in an atmosphere of academic intolerance, the protagonist participates against his will in a kind of battle royal between two opposing classmates, one the epitome of studious docility, the other an obstreperous reprobate. Agreeing after a spat to work out their differences in the form of a face-making duel, the two adolescents grimace furiously at each other until one of them, Kneadus, escalating the conflict, calls upon his friends to assault his opponent. Worse, as the match dissolves into a chaotic brawl (a "mass of bodies lay entangled on the floor" [66]), Kneadus manages not only to pummel but also to "rape" his adversary, Syphon, verbally. As Kneadus bends over him and whispers, Syphon "turned green, squealed like a stuck pig, and plopped like a fish out of water." Kneadus then presses "down on him," "in hot pursuit of Syphon's ears," chasing them with his mouth, first one ear then the other." Syphon rolls "his head from side to side to protect his ears, but, realizing that escape was impossible he started to roar, and he roared to deafen the murderous words that were tearing at his innocence" (66).

Gombrowicz's compositional investment throughout *Ferdydurke* in decidedly non-adult modes of existence bears comparison with the approach Dahlberg employed in his first novel, *Bottom Dogs* (1930), in that the latter author's heavy use of free indirect discourse firmly locates the narrative point of view in the subjectivity of his autobiographical protagonist as he endures group life in an orphanage. Similarly, in his highly regarded *Zero de Conduite* (1933), the director Jean Vigo overtly aligns himself with the rebellious boys at the French boarding school, compassionately depicting the youngsters' anarchic efforts to repudiate the behavioral codes their pedagogical masters harshly impose. (Significantly, the only kind instructor, Huguet, does a Chaplin impersonation while monitoring the boys during recess in the schoolyard.) Yet Gombrowicz's work is more provocative than that of either Dahlberg or Vigo, for Gombrowicz interrogates and ultimately destabilizes the distinction between being young and old entirely. This critical procedure, enacted throughout the novel, is most elaborately thematized in the first chapter of *Ferdydurke*.

Waking one morning, the narrator experiences what he calls "a sense of inner, intermolecular mockery and derision, an inbred superlaugh" running wild through his body and mind (2). But his laughter is accompanied by terror, for due to a kind of mimetic frenzy he has lost the certainty that he is a "mature human being" (2) as opposed to a "green youth" (3): "The thirty-year-old man I am today was aping and ridiculing the callow juvenile I once was, while he in turn was aping me and, by the same token, each of us was aping himself" (2). At "this turning point" in his life, he has fallen into a state of generational indeterminacy. If all he knows is that he "was neither this nor that," it is because he is no longer certain that he has finished the formative process of growing up: "When I cut my last teeth, my wisdom teeth, my development was supposed to be complete, and it was time for the inevitable kill, for the man to kill the inconsolable little boy" (3). His previous attempt to "enter the social life of adults and deliberate with them" had led to the composition of a novel (*Memoirs from the Time of Immaturity*), the publication of which had embarrassed him, because in it he refused "to dismiss, easily and glibly, the sniveling brat within me" (4). Laughing at his ineptitude when it comes to ascending to the status of "a public and social being," he reflects on the fact that "a life that does not evolve in unbroken continuity from one phase to another [. . .] must inevitably end in a schizophrenic split of the inner self" (5). Nevertheless, this is both his condition and the fate of mankind in general, "because our existence on this earth does not tolerate any well-defined and stable hierarchy, everything continually flows, spills over, moves on" (5).[14]

The narrator's existential predicament has literary and political implications as well. The problem posed to the aspiring writer is to choose whether or not to address "those who are mature and fully evolved" and who correlatively adhere "to a world of crystal-clear ideas." The risky alternative is to remain "constantly plagued by the specter of the rabble, of immaturity, of schoolboys and schoolgirls" (8); and for the narrator, presumably a member of the upper crust, the pull of the latter is irresistible: "Not for one moment could I forget the little not-quite world of the not-quite human, and yet, terrified and disgusted as I was and shuddering at the very thought of that swampy green, I could not tear myself away from it, mesmerized by it like a little birdie by a snake. As if some demon were tempting me with immaturity! As if I were favoring, against my very nature, the lower class and loving it—because it held me captive as a juvenile" (8). Resigning himself to the fact that he is a "juvenile, and [that] juvenility" is his "only cultural institution," the narrator recognizes the risks he must henceforth run, of the loathing he can expect to encounter in the future due to his imprisonment in his "own underdevelopment" (10): "For there is nothing that the Mature hate more, there is nothing that disgusts them more, than immaturity. They will tolerate the most rabid destructiveness as long as it happens within the confines of maturity; they are not threatened by the revolutionary who fights one mature ideal with another mature ideal" (10). The slightest sense of immaturity is sure to increase the aggressivity of the Mature, as if detecting traits of childishness outside themselves is so threatening that they must expunge the bearer of these traits from existence. Acts of violence serve to police the unstable line between generations, protecting the old from recognizing the endurance of the young within themselves: "let them as much as sniff immaturity, let them sniff a juvenile or a sniveling brat in someone and they will pounce on him and [. . .] they will kill him with sarcasm, derision, and mockery, they will not allow a foundling from the world they have renounced long ago to befoul their nest" (10).

However, it turns out that the decision to maintain contact with the child within is not up to the individual. After defending his previous efforts as a writer "to stimulate, titillate, and attract the immaturity of others with immaturity" (11), the narrator gets upset and declares his determination to change, "to create my own form! To turn outward! To express myself!" (14). He therefore sets to work as a writer, assuming that in the act of producing a respectable body of work he will conceive his "own shape"; rather than continue to shoulder the burden of pretending to be a grown-up, he plans to become an adult once and for all. Unfortunately, shortly thereafter one T. Pimko, "a cultured pedagogue" (14), arrives uninvited at the narrator's door and insists on reading what Joey has written so far. An externally enforced belittlement then occurs as the writer finds himself humiliated and diminished by the representative of pedagogical authority. The condescending attitude of his institutionally accredited evaluator causes the narrator's world to collapse and to be promptly reset "according to the rules of a conventional prof" (15). Worse, when interrogated by the pedant, the narrator experiences a strange shrinkage, becoming tiny under the gaze of his self-appointed judge: "I became small, my leg became a little leg, my hand a little hand, my persona a little persona, my being a little being." Meanwhile, in inverse proportion, the intimidating professor expands in size: "he grew larger and larger, sitting and glancing at me, and reading my manuscript forever" (16). Involuntarily transformed "into a schoolboy scowling childishly" (17), the narrator, before he quite realizes what is happening to him, is taken back to school against his will and assigned a seat for the foreseeable future at "a first-rate educational institution" (18).

Disgraced, he must now accept a socially subordinate position as one kid among many, all of whom remain subject to the inanities and trivialities of their dictatorial instructors.

The narrator experiences an equally oppressive form of enforced regression at his new lodgings. Arranging for the narrator to live in the Youngblood household, Pimko, now referred to as the "Great Belittler," seeks to use the daughter of the family as a means of imprisoning Joey permanently in a stage of youthfulness. Worse, to succumb to the charms of Zuta, who "disdained maturity" and for whom "youth was the only time befitting a human being" (137), is to capitulate to the conventions of a lifestyle structured in accordance with the governing principles of rationalization. Unsurprisingly, given that Mr. Youngblood, her father, is a construction design engineer who admires "scientifically organized work" and is even "given to telling scientific jokes" (139), Zuta is "absolutely modern in her modernity" (105). The narrator worries that if he falls in love with her, he will be inculcated with the ideals of a thoroughly "Americanized generation" (110), and this coercive process would in turn ensure that he "never again crept out of boyhood" (109). He will epitomize the socially approved model of the modern boy, embracing like everyone else in the postwar era "athletics and jazz bands" while repudiating "custom and tradition" (108).

To resist the undeniably attractive appeals of the girl, and of the kind of pseudo-rebellious behavior that ultimately signals one's conformity to dominant paradigms of youthfulness, Joey determines he must introduce into his well-ordered modernized surroundings "foreign and heterogeneous elements, scrambling everything up for all it was worth" (146). His first attempt to free himself from Zuta's spell is a necessarily "anti-culinary and counter-palatable activity" (148). Hoping to defile the remarkably clean and composed young girl, Joey adopts a disgustingly puerile practice; he begins peeping at her through the keyhole in the bathroom door.

After this vile burst of sexual deviance fails to unsettle her, he is temporarily at a loss, yet shortly thereafter he gains inspiration from an anecdote recounted, significantly enough, in Chaplin's memoirs, a copy of which he has discovered open on the bedside table of her parents' bedroom. Reading the page that describes H. G. Wells performing for the film star a bizarre dance of his own invention, the narrator decides to do the same. No matter how dreadful in appearance, he too will abandon himself to a "solo dance," for only in this unconstrained manner will his "thoughts acquire flesh and become action" (155). Gaining courage through his frenzied movements around the room, Joey prepares himself to ridicule "everything around me," to draw "out a foul taste" and "spoil" (155) entirely the modern environment into which he has been confined. He is now ready to defy the schoolgirl's power to dominate all "those aging Boys of the twentieth century who had been drilled and driven, egged on and flogged with a whip" (162). Realizing that each morning through her morning ablutions she reproduces the image that transfixes her myriad suitors ("In spite of myself I had to admire the discipline that was involved in the girl's good looks! With all swiftness, precision, and dexterity she managed to dodge that most difficult transition—between night and day" [170]), Joey is nevertheless determined to distinguish himself from those others who masochistically devote themselves to what is merely an efficiently manufactured vision of health and beauty.

So he plots to humiliate his principal rivals—another schoolboy named Kopyrda ("her modern brother") and Pimko (who is said to have a right to her insofar as he is an "educator," "a licensed pedagogue" [164]). Significantly, as his scheme takes effect the novel once again begins to resemble the denouement of any number of silent screen comedies. Having each received a letter of invitation (composed, of course, by the narrator) to a clandestine meeting in Zuta's bedroom at midnight, when her two confused suitors encounter each other upon arrival, they are then forced to hide in separate closets after the narrator screams, "Thieves," to bring her parents into the mix. After considerable shouting and multiple accusations, the domestic farce predictably devolves into a scene of chaotic violence. While Kopyrda is busy chewing on Mr. Youngblood's "left flank," Pimko backs away from "the swirling heap" only to do "something exceedingly strange": "he voluntarily lay down on his back in a corner and raised his four paws in a gesture of complete helplessness" (189). Jumping "up and down [. . .] as if she were a referee at a boxing match," the sobbing girl pleads with her parents to stop fighting with her youthful lover, yet she too is soon swept into the action: "looking for a handhold, [her father] unwittingly grabbed her leg above the ankle. She fell. The four of them rolled on the ground quietly. [. . .] At one point I saw the mother biting her daughter, Kopyrda pulling Mrs. Youngblood, the engineer pushing Kopyrda, then Miss Youngblood's calf flashed on top of her mother's head" (189). Free to make his escape from the family and the school, the narrator bolts, suggesting that, for Gombrowicz, precipitating slapstick-infused acts of immoderate childishness has the potential to function as a means of eluding both the clutches of ideologically manipulative state institutions (the school and the home) and the model of (modernized) youthfulness they have a vested interest in perpetuating.

Gombrowicz's curious novel may be considered a kind of missing link in the evolutionary development of slapstick modernism. Despite its lack of American progeny, *Ferdydurke* merits recognition as a literary forerunner or Depression-era ancestor to Beat generation writers and black humorists alike. Part of the value of slapstick modernism as a critical category, then, is that it enables the cultural historian to appreciate in retrospect the taxonomical significance and value of artistic mutations (like *Ferdydurke*) previously thought to be unclassifiable.

At the same historical moment that this transformation in cultural practice was occurring, key components of a theory that would be able to do interpretive justice to it were being assembled (in Paris) in the Depression-era essays of Walter Benjamin. The burden of the following interlude is to describe the main parts of the theoretical apparatus he was in the process of putting together before his untimely demise in 1940.

Theoretical Interlude

Benjamin and the Question Concerning Second Technology

Lookout honey, 'cause I'm using technology
Ain't got no time to make no apology
—The Stooges, "Search and Destroy"

Walter Benjamin's Depression-era reflections on the collective functions of modernist poetry and slapstick film, on the ways they both struggled to negotiate the psychosomatic impact of capitalist modernity, provide a strong model for grasping the utopian impulses structuring the phenomenon I have termed "slapstick modernism." The strain of his thought that is most valuable in this regard is the one tending in the direction of an anthropological materialism. Particularly promising is the constellation of concepts that he was still in the process of elaborating at the end of his life: innervation, (corporeal) mimesis, second technology, and play. Holding these concepts together is the idea that affectively charged cultural practices may play a crucial role in fashioning an antifascist social body, one capable of adjusting to its technologically mediated environment. For Benjamin, literary modernism and silent comedy participated in the same general project: the historical mission or task they assigned themselves was to contribute to the construction of a collective agent that would be capable of determining its own future. If, as Miriam Hansen argues, Benjamin's investment in film was not the result of a "futurist or constructivist enthusiasm for the machine-age," but arose from his hope that the medium "might yet counter the devastating effects of humanity's 'bungled reception of technology,' which had come to a head with World War I" (*Cinema and Experience* 79), something analogous can be said about his attitude toward late nineteenth and early twentieth-century modernist writing.

In the second version of his "Work of Art" essay, Benjamin links the concept of second technology to the elements of play that drive artistic production; correlatively, he sets it in contrast to first technology, which he associates with modes of work.[1] First technology, which emerges out of ritual, is motivated by the need to dominate the external environment; what it seeks is permanent or eternal "'mastery over nature" and it is willing to sacrifice human beings to achieve this end (107). Presumably the development of the first technology has led to the current mode of organizing the work process, which is in turn responsible for the widespread oppression of mankind in present-day social circumstances. The origins of second technology, in contrast, lie "at the point where, by an unconscious ruse, human beings began to distance themselves from nature. It lies, in other words, in play." The results of this latter technology "are wholly provisional," for "it operates by means of experiments and endlessly varied test procedures," and its ultimate aspirations are toward establishing a more benign relationship between nature and humanity. Benjamin then proposes that this is the historical task that film—considered to be a manifestation of second technology—must now carry out: "The primary social function of art today is to rehearse that interplay [between nature and humanity[2]]." This thesis is particularly applicable to film insofar as its designated function "*is to train human beings in the apperceptions and reactions needed to deal with a vast apparatus whose role in their lives is expanding almost daily*" (108; emphasis in the original). It is at the movies that the inhabitants of urban-industrial modernity will learn that technology in the future may "release them from their enslavement to the powers of the apparatus," but this will only take place "when humanity's whole constitution has adapted itself to the new productive forces which the second technology has set free" (108). Motion pictures appear here as a utopian solution to the problematic impact of the forces of large-scale capitalism on its subjects. The (progressive) social function Benjamin attributes to the technical medium (with admittedly little basis in empirical fact) is to facilitate humanity's adjustment to its surroundings, which will help bring the tyranny of mechanization to an end and in so doing meet one of the preconditions for mass emancipation. If "the majority of citydwellers, throughout the workday in offices and factories, have to relinquish their humanity in the face of the apparatus," in "the evening these same masses fill the cinemas, to witness the film actor taking revenge on their behalf not only by asserting *his* humanity (or what appears to them as such) against the apparatus, but by placing that apparatus in the service of his triumph" (111; emphasis in the original).

A footnote in "Work of Art" establishes that Benjamin's affirmation of second technology as a (cinematic) mode of mimetic play is grounded in a theoretical understanding of the medium as a force that does more than record or reveal the truth of objective reality. In antiquity, he writes, mimesis was seen as "the primal phenomenon of all artistic activity" and was felt to possess two opposing aspects. "The mime presents his subject as a semblance. One could also say that he plays his subject. Thus we encounter the polarity [between semblance and play] informing mimesis" (127). Semblance, which can be aligned with the first technology, has been central to the tradition of aesthetic cognition, and its canonical formulation is no doubt the Hegelian or phenomenological notion of beauty as the sensuous manifestation of the idea, as the unveiling of an otherwise hidden essence. In contrast, art as "play is the inexhaustible reservoir of all the experimenting procedures of the second [technology]" (127).[3] Thus "the withering of semblance and the decay of aura in works of art is matched by a huge gain in the scope for play. This space for play is widest in film. In film the element of semblance has been entirely displaced by the element of play" (127). Moreover, in "The Significance of Beautiful Semblance" (1935/1936), a paragraph-long fragment within "Work of Art," Benjamin again defends play as a constitutive but historically overlooked element in traditional definitions of art, adding that it is only with the dimension of play in mind that one can comprehend art adequately as "a suggested improvement on nature; an imitation that conceals within it a demonstration [of what the original should be]. In other words, art is a perfecting mimesis" (137).[4]

A different footnote in "Work of Art" further elucidates Benjamin's view of film as an evolutionary force that enables humanity's "whole constitution" to adapt to "the new productive forces" (108). The "aim of revolutions," he asserts, "is to accelerate" adaptation to the new productive forces, a task accomplished by "innervations of the collective." Insofar as these forces are bringing into existence a "new, historically unique" biomechanical entity, a mass body "which has its organs in the new technology," there is the possibility that human beings will be liberated "from drudgery." This is what second technology aims at, and in so doing it enlarges the "scope for play" of individuals, immeasurably expanding their "field of action." They may not yet have fully mastered the power now available to them, but "the more keenly individuals belonging to the collectivity feel how little they have received of what was due them under the dominion of the first technology," the more intensely will they demand what is rightfully theirs (124): the capacity to bring about improvements in the way the collective as a whole inhabits its surroundings. The emancipatory promise of film, as a second technology, then rests on its ability to help mankind take possession of the machinery that plagues it, to incorporate technology directly into a developing social body. The historically unique purpose of the movies, then, is to balance out corporeally the relation of the masses to their environment, an achievement that occurs as humanity begins to experience or assimilate the apparatus as a satisfying attachment to or prosthetic extension of itself.[5] Mimesis from this perspective is not a symptom of what Mark Seltzer has termed the "body-machine complex" (4) and considers the cause of anxiety; rather, it is the means of establishing a productive liaison between the organic and the technological.

Utilized in the passage cited above, "innervation" is a somewhat baffling notion that one finds scattered throughout Benjamin's essays in the 1920s and '30s. Partly electrical and partly dialectical, partly figurative and partly literal, Benjamin often deploys the obscure term (borrowed from Freud) in a singularly collectivized manner in order to articulate the socially empowering dimensions of cultural practice.[6] The final paragraph of "Surrealism: The Last Snapshot of the European Intelligentsia" (1929) is a case in point. Forecasting mass upheaval, he uses the concept of innervation to designate a neurophysiological process whereby environmental flows of energy pass into and galvanize an otherwise wearied body politic, thus transforming it into a agent of social revolution. Asserting that the "collective is a body," he states as well that "the *physis* that is being organized for it in technology can, through all its political and factual reality, be produced only in that image space to which profane illumination initiates us." The political task the surrealists sought to carry out mainly with words is one that film in turn will strive to accomplish in its own realm: the interpenetration of "body and image space" such "that all revolutionary tension becomes bodily collective innervation." When this happens, and it can only occur through the good graces of modern technology, then "the bodily innervations of the collective" will "become revolutionary discharge" and reality will have "transcended itself to the extent demanded by the *Communist Manifesto* (217–18).[7]

Images—especially when they depict body/machine integrations—startle and thereby excite the nervous system; in so doing they tend to have an invigorating effect on the masses, transforming them into a positively charged corporeal entity with the potential to engage in socially disruptive actions.[8] In converting the forces released by the dominant mode of economic production into a source of collective power, psychosomatic relays of this sort both facilitate humanity's adjustment to its urban-industrial environment and pave the way for a revolutionary transformation of the milieu. Benjamin thus affirms avant-garde practice as a prelude to political praxis on the grounds that the former helps facilitate contact between machine technology and the social body and in so doing contributes to the affective bindings and motor responses that will bring widespread enslavement to the apparatus to an end. Here the evocation of collective emancipation from the drudgery of modernized labor appeals to a model that foregoes the traditional emphasis within historical materialist doctrine on achieving self-consciousness, the goal of attaining a working-class or proletarian identity replaced by a call for somatic modification on a mass scale.[9]

The conceptual opposition between first and second technology therefore corresponds to the critical distinction between progressive incorporations of machine technology and alienating capitulations to the disciplinary imperatives of capitalist modernity. But what accounts for the difference between, on the one hand, mechanized activities that subordinate people to the demands of economic rationalism (as, for Benjamin, amusement park attractions like "dodgem cars" did ["On Some Motifs" 329]) and, on the other hand, procedures that augur liberation from the burdens of deskilled wage labor? Assuming the aim and orientation of film as a second technology "*is to establish equilibrium between human beings and the apparatus*," how exactly does it accomplish this task? ("Work of Art," 2nd version 117; emphasis in the original). The next section turns briefly to "On Some Motifs in Baudelaire" (1939) to develop an understanding of corporeal mimesis as the means whereby this technologically mediated process of becoming empowered might take place and to underscore the kind of retroactive thinking that informed Benjamin's critical engagement with this topic, an interpretive approach that led him to locate the origins of the social project of slapstick film in Baudelairean modernism.

Baudelaire avec Chaplin

> Chaplin holds in his hands a genuine key to the interpretation of Kafka.
> —Walter Benjamin, *Walter Benjamin's Archive*[10]

The epigraph above indicates that Benjamin felt that filtering one's reading of modernist literature through the lens of slapstick film had the potential to render the former more comprehensible than it might otherwise be. This intuition, at which the notebook entry above hints, was most elaborately unfolded, albeit surreptitiously, in "On Some Motifs in Baudelaire."[11] For

Benjamin, Baudelaire's mission was to engage the forces of capitalist modernity in (dialectical) combat in the hopes of mastering them. Though the (hidden figure of the) crowd is characterized in several sections of the essay as the writer's antagonist, his ulterior aim was nevertheless to serve as a kind of individual conduit for his readers, circulating back to them at tolerable levels of intensity the otherwise unbearable amount of energy contained in the city and at the workplace.

We may begin with one of the canonical essay's most frequently quoted passages. Before addressing the degree to which traffic signals have subjected the sensoria of the environment's inhabitants to a new kind of disciplinary training, Benjamin takes note of the threat of bodily injury the car-filled streets of the big city present on a daily basis. The widespread need to keep alert, to remain in a state of readiness so as to ward off trauma, is precisely what the formal innovations of modernist poetry and then the formal principle (montage) of cinema as such were designed to satisfy. The task of literature, picked up subsequently by film, was to generate preparatory experiences, to reproduce the disorienting conditions of sensory existence in urban-industrial modernity before they devastated people. If negotiating traffic in the city "involves the individual in a series of shocks and collisions," "dangerous crossings" causing "nervous impulses" to flow through pedestrians [. . .] like the energy from a battery," it is the duty of the poet to try to generate on the page comparably intense sensations so that the subjects of urban modernity will be better prepared for the demands their environment makes on them. The need "to keep abreast of traffic signals" is an indication of the "complex kind of training" to which people must submit under the aegis of a first technology. The historical mission of Baudelaire's rudimentary because literary version of a second technology was to draw on "this reservoir of electrical energy" in the hope of attuning the sensorium of his readers to the demands of their surroundings in a non-submissive fashion. The rise of the nonverbal media made available a more effective means of fulfilling this same mission: "There came a day when a new and urgent need for stimuli was met by the film. In a film, perception in the form of shocks was established as a formal principle. That which determines the rhythm of production on a conveyor belt is the basis of the rhythm of reception in the film" ("On Some Motifs" 328).

What Benjamin has in mind is a dynamic, neurophysiological relay, a chiasmus on the level of corporeal and psychic reality between the authorial subject and the liquid body of the masses. Physical contact with other people serves here, then, as a kind of hydroelectric means of producing high voltages via the conversion of flowing water into mechanical energy. Moving through the crowded city, the poet is analogous to a turbine or metal shaft capable of generating mental and somatic excitation; correlatively, the lines that, when connected to a generator at a plant, transport power to those who need it are comparable to the lines of Baudelaire's poetry, which according to the trope supply readers with the charge they require to get things done in the world. In this striking way, words (and later cinematic images) are at the center of Benjamin's "mature theory of experience," of his model of technological becoming in which "the relationship between embodied human beings and their ever changing material domain" is constantly evolving (M. Hansen, *Embodying Technesis* 232, 246). For Benjamin, the French poet was someone who embraced language as a means of enabling others to adapt sensuously to their life world. The poet may have "literally *forced himself* to experience the inhuman rhythm of the modern industrial mechanosphere"; and by "sacrificing his own internal subjective rhythm, Baudelaire" may have "inaugurated [. . . a] corporeal form of mimetic agency" (246; emphasis in the original); but the suffering writer, having endured the pain of repeated environmental shocks, tried to verbally convey this anguishing experience in order to put others in position to reconcile themselves to their alienating conditions of existence. From this critical perspective, *Les Fleurs du Mal* is a record of the poet's heroic attempt to demonstrate how the forces flowing through his surroundings could be harnessed in a manner that could transform passive entities into creatively active agents. Whether or not Baudelaire's aesthetic experimentation really facilitated such existential conversions at the practical level of his actual readers is impossible to determine empirically, but his theoretical commitment (as elucidated by Benjamin) to this ambitious project is worth underscoring.

The primary point of interest for my purposes is the degree to which the image of Chaplin haunts Benjamin's discussion of the poet's social motivations. The ghostly presence of the film performer is strongest in the essay's eighth section. Faint impressions of Chaplin arise in Benjamin's analysis of historically new hand gestures such as the lighting of a match or the rolling of dice. The first recalls one of the comedian's trademark gags; the inert body of an unaware person frequently serves as the surface against which the character gets a flame started; the second evokes the memorable scene on board the ship in *The Immigrant* (1917), where Chaplin gets involved in a game of craps and goes through an elaborate baseball pitcher's warm-up before completing his toss. Benjamin's underscoring of Baudelaire's "jerky gait" also gives rise to the specter of Chaplin, as does the critic's emphasis on the poet's combative, feisty attitude toward others, both traits he shared with the Tramp.[12] Lastly, the final sentence of the passage from which I have quoted above ("That which determines the rhythm of production on a conveyor belt is the basis of the rhythm of reception in the film") derives from a fragment, written in 1935, that Benjamin ends with some reflections on the contribution that Chaplin's oddly jerky way of moving has made to our ability to perceive the discontinuities underlying the smooth flow of filmic appearance. At the time, Benjamin's fascination was with what rendered such staccato gestures amusing ("Now, what is it about this behavior that is distinctively comic?" ["Formula in which the Dialectical Structure of Film Finds Expression" 89][13]), but by the time he had completed "On Some Motifs," the more pressing question was whether such dissections of the "expressive movements of human beings into a series of minute innervations" might not perform a social task, helping the mass of spectators to acclimate themselves to their mechanized environment.

At any rate, once we notice that Chaplin is lurking in the wings of the essay, that his figure is hidden just off stage, it becomes apparent that Benjamin's exposure to Chaplin conditioned his (retroactive) assessment of the modernist writer.[14] This is not to say the critic simply conflated the two. Rather, Benjamin's impression of the complementary nature of their respective practices fit into his never fully articulated genealogy of socially purposeful cultural enterprises. Bringing the image of the Tramp out of the shadows of Benjamin's essay thus discloses the latter's faith in the notion that early modernist poetry found its historical successor in the form of silent comedy (as well as Disney animation). It is less film in general than a particular genre that had inherited Baudelaire's commitment to an innervating shock aesthetic. For Benjamin, the progressive mission of the modernist writer—to enable the masses to adapt to their present circumstances in non-traumatic ways—was not only prolonged in Chaplin's cinematic venture but also came closer to being genuinely realized due to the collective mode of reception that was more readily available to the latter. Chaplin was the true exemplar of a corporeal mimesis and the fate of the masses was therefore in his hands.[15]

If Benjamin's views of Chaplin mediated his idiosyncratic theory of modernism, furnishing him with a stronger sense of the functional imperatives structuring Baudelaire's formal innovations, such an outlook suspends the distinction between elite and popular practices in favor of a critically anthropological exploration of the instances in which art and mass entertainment collaborated on an ongoing social project. For Benjamin, slapstick film was well suited to take over the cultural task the poet assigned himself: the facilitation of collective adaptations to urban-industrial modernity. A passage from the first version of the "Work of Art" essay is revealing in this light. After prophetically declaring that it "has always been one of the primary tasks of art to create a demand whose hour of full satisfaction has not yet come," Benjamin states that the "history of every art form has critical periods in which the particular form strains after effects which can be easily achieved only with a changed technical standard—that is to say, in a new art form." He then asserts that in "its most progressive works, *above all in Chaplin*, film united" the effect of physical and moral shocks "on a new level" (38–40; emphasis mine).[16]

At the end of this study I extend this thesis, proposing, with Benjamin's outlook in mind, that in the latter half of the twentieth century the use of amplified instrumentation enabled forms of popular music to respond to this same demand for viscerally forceful effects. Did the states of emotional and corporeal intensity that the sonically intense performances of certain rock bands produced in the late 1960s and '70s enable the masses to acclimate themselves to their technologically saturated milieu? Tracking the rise of a slapstick modernism through the 1950s and early '60s will put us in position to grasp this difficult-to-answer question as the essential one to ask about cultural practice in the historical era under investigation.

PART III

1950s–1960s

6

The Rise of Slapstick Modernism; or, the Birth of the Uncool

> I just make up these little skits, that's all. [. . .]
> I just make a little slapstick.
>
> —William Burroughs, *With William Burroughs*

There were only a few scattered signs during the 1940s that the rise of a slapstick modernism was on the cultural horizon. Two great Eudora Welty stories—"Why I Live at the P.O." and "June Recital," collected respectively in *A Curtain of Green* (1941) and *Golden Apples* (1949)—almost perfectly bookend the decade, but little of importance happened in between them. In 1941 Louis Zukofsky wrote (but did not publish at the time) a short story titled "A Keystone Comedy" about a day in the life of a family of cocaine dealers; a slight effort, the story is nevertheless indicative of an intermedial inclination whose cultural significance would be disclosed in a little more than a decade's time.[1] The poet and filmmaker James Broughton's Chaplinesque acting style in his avant-garde film *Mother's Day* (1948) (paralleled a few years later by Kermit Sheets's performance in Broughton's *Loony Tom: The Happy Lover* [1951]) suggested a growing affinity within the realm of independent cinema for slapstick shenanigans,[2] as does his sometime collaborator Sidney Peterson's 1949 film, *The Lead Shoes*, which at one point engages in a surrealist distortion (with help of an anamorphic lens) of Buster Keaton's memorable antics in a diving suit in *The Navigator* (1924). Yet the only other cultural enterprise in the decade worth taking note of was a truncated one: James Agee's composition soon after the Second World War of a screenplay in which he posits the Little Tramp as the possible savior of a postapocalypse civilization. In the script, only recently unearthed from a library archive, the utopian community who has gathered around the legendary comic figure after a nuclear holocaust is the last hope for a humanely compassionate mode of existing in the world, the soul-destroying enterprises of the cruelly rationalist scientists, harbingers of an awful future. Unfortunately, although he sent the screenplay to Chaplin, Agee was unable to get the aging star interested in the project and it fell by the wayside.[3] To demonstrate his artistic and ideological devotion to the tradition of silent screen comedy, the modernist author of *Let Us Now Praise Famous Men* (1942) could only produce his well-received summary assessment of the film genre's past glories. His article "Comedy's Greatest Era" appeared in *Life* in September 1949 and garnered "one of the greatest responses in the magazine's history" (2).[4]

In the first half of the 1950s, evidence began to accumulate that a shift in the cultural sensibility or artistic disposition of American writers was starting to take place. Flannery O'Connor's first novel, the violent yet humorous *Wise Blood,* came out in 1952.[5] In the same year, the narrator of Ralph Ellison's *Invisible Man* disclosed that he had an image of the Tramp stored in his memory, for when he meets a vagrant pushing a cart in the streets of Chicago, he refers to him as "old Chaplin-pants" (177).[6] In 1953 Eudora Welty published a viciously comic novella, *Ponder Heart,* in serial form in the *New Yorker*. But it was two years later (as mentioned in the introduction) that significant new work by Heller and Kerouac first saw the light of day, indicating that a generalized shift in compositional priorities was occurring. As Heller recalled a quarter century later: "Without being aware of it, I was part of a near-movement in fiction. While I was writing *Catch-22,* J. P. Donleavy was writing *The Ginger Man,* Jack Kerouac was writing *On the Road,* Ken Kesey was writing *One Flew Over the Cuckoo's Nest,* Thomas Pynchon was writing *V.,* Kurt Vonnegut was writing *Cat's Cradle.* [. . .] Whatever forces were at work shaping a trend in art were affecting not just me, but all of us" ("Reeling in *Catch-22*" 214).

Let's begin with Kerouac. The customary way to locate the Beat writer in literary history is to correlate his career-long autobiographical endeavor with that of his favorite "lost generation" predecessor, Thomas Wolfe, who in 1929 initiated his own, similarly mammoth and modernist enterprise with *Look Homeward Angel* (a book avowedly inspired by James Joyce's *A Portrait of the Artist as a Young Man*). Both authors, in striving to capture in lyric prose the wealth of their past experiences, modified the generic conventions of the novel (as did Céline and Miller) to encompass more material from their actual lives than had been customary in the past. But here, in order to get what amounts to a critical survey of postwar Americans variants of slapstick modernism under way, I want to stress the determining impact on Kerouac's imagination of a trio of cinematic idiots whose initial appearances were contemporaneous with Wolfe's Depression-era output: the Three Stooges.

Composed in the early 1950s, *Visions of Cody* did not appear in print until the early '70s, yet it circulated through more or less underground channels well before its posthumous publication. *Visions of Cody* is the result of not only a commitment to formally experimental rhetorical procedures but also a profound (if intermittent) attraction to a decidedly violent brand of motion picture comedy. It is therefore telling that when making reference in *Visions'* preface to Proust's *Remembrance of Things Past*, Kerouac describes the latter as "one enormous comedy." In sum, Kerouac's text (which deals with roughly the same subject matter as *On the Road*, albeit in much more compositionally daring manner) is a testament to the ethical and aesthetic benefits of drawing upon the dual legacies of modernist innovation and slapstick film.

The key passage for my purposes occurs roughly three-quarters of the way into *Visions* in the form of an admittedly nostalgic meditation on the unrecognized worth of the Three Stooges. The reverie appears in a section of the loosely organized text called "Joan Rawshanks in the Fog." The title refers to a scene in a Joan Crawford vehicle, the film noir *Sudden Fear*, which the narrator, aimlessly wandering through San Francisco one night, observed being shot by a film crew on location. The narrator's critical disgust for Hollywood artifice is palpable throughout his description of the production process. Especially prescient is his assessment of the compatibility between the "decadent" movie business's ambition to exert control over the ultimately abashed members of the excited crowd and military ventures:

> The area of grass where I'd originally stood to witness my first kicks of the debacle spectacle was finally and suddenly used [...] and the whole crowd had to move over into a limited area (as though that's what the directors wanted not for kicks but in serious fascistic interest in the movement of crowds) which was also cut off from the street by floodlights on restricted ground [...] so nobody could go home in these fascistic intervals; there was no backway out, the audience, the crowd had been finally surrounded and looped in and forted in by this invading enemy. (279–80)

Whereas the director and producers, the "generals," confer in the darkness behind the "wet flapshroud" of their tent, the overexposed civilian spectators look on in awe as "the great drama [... unfolds] in the area of the blazing lights that were so bright and white[....] I thought they were being used by a new civil defense organization crew that makes tests to see how bright lights have to be for bomber planes to catch them on fogging frisco nights" (287). Clearly, in this account of a kind of "osmosis between industrialized warfare and cinema" (Virilio, *War and Cinema* 58), it is not simply the actor-soldiers who have roles to play in the operation, for the spectating masses find themselves arrested by the unnervingly disciplinary gaze of the film industry, which eventually takes on the status of a God-like Other: "in this brightness, so bright that it embarrasses, I myself and all the crowd were finally delivered up judged and damned to them, because we couldn't leave except through that restricted zone and because of that they put the light on the alley of exit, for Hollywood wants to see more than anyone of us, than we do, than anything, we all had to cross that catwalk of lights and felt ourselves melt into identity as we crossed from the fingerprint rack to the blue desk" (Kerouac, *Visions of Cody* 287). The end result of the crowd's desire to watch the making of a crime film from behind the scenes is that its members are surveyed and controlled by the agents of mass entertainment. This experience leads Kerouac (or the autobiographical narrator) to feel as if he is being compressed into an externally shaped mass entity, one that is vulnerable to legal interrogation and possible imprisonment by hidden forces of authority.

The speaker's reflection on the meaningfulness of the Three Stooges follows shortly after this distressing, panicky nighttime observation. Though they are part of the same system of mass entertainment he has just criticized as a technologically sophisticated cause of constraint and anxiety in the world, the narrator praises the physically aggressive comic trio as a potential source of liberation. His valorization of the film clowns stems from his dawning realization that recollecting their on-screen antics proves genuinely useful to those who are forced to endure an otherwise intolerable status quo in the present. This is the lesson the narrator gleans from the eccentric behavior of his idol and hero of the book, Cody Pomeray (alter-ego of Kerouac's friend Neal Cassady).

(It should be apparent by now that what is at stake in this chapter is not the impressions of charismatic coolness that linger in our memory of the Beats; rather it is the less frequently remembered images of deranged nuttiness that must be recalled. Kerouac himself drew the pertinent critical distinction, arguing that by 1948 "beatsters" were "divided into cool and hot," the latter being "the crazy talkative shining eyed (often innocent and openhearted) nut who runs from bar to bar, pad to pad looking for everybody, shouting, restless" ["Origin of the Beat Generation" 148; parentheses in the original]. I am thus tempted to call my topic, with the 1957 release of Miles Davis's *Birth of the Cool* in mind, the Birth of the Uncool).[7]

As the two buddies stroll along "the sidewalks of workaday San Francisco," Cody decides to show Jack "what and how the Three Stooges are like when they go staggering and knocking each other down the street" (*Visions of Cody* 300). The spontaneous demonstration sparks an epiphany, alerting the narrator to the emancipatory promise embedded in a relatively outdated, though not entirely obsolete, film genre. Guided by his friend, Jack realizes the intense pleasures that are attendant upon a decidedly irresponsible mode of existence organized around play as opposed to work. Though the ostensible purpose of the trip is for Cody to secure a job with the railroad so as to be able to support his family, his priorities are obviously elsewhere. Just before they reach the train station, "a great white temple of commercial travel in America," it comes "into Cody's head to imitate the stagger of the Stooges, and he did it wild, crazy, yelling in the sidewalk right there by the arches and by hurrying executives" (303). Cody's surprising act of corporeal mimesis discloses his irreverent attitude toward organized labor, revealing in turn that his emotional disposition is out of synch with the burdens of work and familial responsibilities. "I had a vision of him which at first (manifold it is!) was swamped by the idea that this was one hell of a wild unexpected twist in my suppositions about how he might now in his later years feel [. . .] about his employers and their temple and conventions" (303–304).

Astonished by his friend's enthusiastic imitation of the members of the comedy team, the narrator speculates on their ontological status: "Supposing the Three Stooges were real? (and so I saw them spring into being at the side of Cody in the street right there in front of the Station, Curly, Moe and Larry[. . . .] Moe the leader [. . .] making the others quake; whacking Curly on the iron pate, backhanding Larry [. . .] picking up a sledgehammer, honk, and ramming it down nozzle first on the flatpan of Curly's skull" (304). At stake in the hypothesis of the Stooges' reality is the possibility that remembered images can have a beneficially formative impact—via an act of identification—on individuals in the world. Recalling figures from the past enables one to imaginatively fashion an alternative or rebellious self in the actual present. Indeed, Cody displays a degree of factual independence after aligning himself with these fictive others. Copying the physical gestures of the unruly buffoons serves as the means whereby Cody fabricates his disorderly ego, in the process joining himself to a small yet powerful antiauthoritarian collectivity. "Then I saw the Three Stooges materialize on the sidewalk, their hair blowing in the wind of things, and Cody was with them, laughing and staggering in savage mimicry of them and himself staggering and gooped" (305). Dwelling in "an underground hell of their own invention" (304), the screen characters are brought back from the dead when the subject adopts them as role models. This is the secret source of Cody's exhilarating capacity to avoid the pressures of everyday life; his imitation of a set of filmic reflections provides him with access to an irresponsible, amusingly defiant mode of existence.

> So supposing the Three Stooges were real and like Cody and me were going to work, only they forget about that, and [. . .] interallied, begin pasting and cuffing each other at the employment office desk as clerks stare; supposing in real gray day and not the gray day of movies and all those afternoons we spent looking at them, in hooky or officially on Sundays among the thousand crackling children [. . .] in the dark show when the Three Stooges [. . .] are providing scenes for wild vibrating hysterias as great as the hysterias of hipsters at Jazz. (304–305)

Becoming one of the Three Stooges emboldens Cody, gives him the confidence that his affective oddness is legitimate, and that he therefore has no reason to regret his unorthodox desires: "all the goofs he felt in him were justified in the outside world and he had nothing to reproach himself for, bonk, boing, crash, skittlely boom, pow, slam, bang, boom, wham, blam, crack, frap, kerplunk, clatter, clap, balp, fap, slapmap, splat, crunch, crowsh, bong, splat, splat, BONG!" (306). To celebrate his pal's achievement, the narrator treats words and grammatical conventions as roughly as Moe treats the bodies of Larry and Curly, brutally pounding away at his medium until meaningful discourse breaks up into material gibberish, reducing sense to sheer sound effects—thus creating a non-jazz sort of bop prosody.[8]

The passage also hints at the pivotal function of images of corporeal aggression in the individual's effort to survive in an inhospitable environment. So practiced are the performers in techniques of repetitive violence that they can endure exceptionally severe assaults. They have trained themselves well to withstand attacks from the outside: "they've been at it for so many years [. . .] and worked out every refinement of bopping one another so much that now, in the end, [. . .] they are finally bopping mechanically and sometimes so hard it's impossible to bear (wince), but by now they've learned not only how to master the style of the blows but the symbol and acceptance of them also, as though inured in their souls and of course long ago in their bodies, to buffeting and crashings" (305). The Stooges' comically polished demonstration of their physical capacity to withstand shocks limns the possibility that ordinary people can learn the somatic skills they need in order to exist in harsh surroundings. As Kerouac grotesquely depicts it, Larry trips and falls "face first on a seven-inch nail that remains imbedded in his eyebone." "Moe yanks it out of his eye," somehow leaving Larry worse off, for now he is impaled "with an eight-foot steel rod." Of course this is all in good fun;

suffering multiple puncture wounds is not cause for anguish in the "sticky dream" universe of early sound comedy (304). The laughter such a description generates does not proceed along the lines of what Tyrus Miller has characterized as the "laughter of late modernism." Taking Wyndham Lewis as his primary example, Miller asserts that the purpose behind the writer's non-mirthful humor was psychic defense; ironic laughter for Lewis was a protective instrument, a device designed to keep him from coming apart.[9] In contrast, Kerouac detects in the Three Stooges a (slapstick) masochism that takes the penetrative infliction of punishment as a prelude to the experience of pleasure. Identifying with the brutally punctured characters, the spectator participates (vicariously) in a process that treats pain as the condition of possibility of the satisfaction of desire.[10]

The reverie on the Stooges in *Visions of Cody* is just the tip of the iceberg with regard to Beat allusions to slapstick materials in the 1950s. Indeed, the surfaces of numerous artifacts associated with the movement confirm this genealogy, indicating the central importance to this generation of postwar writers of comic traditions stretching back to the early decades of the twentieth century. Witness, for example, the "52nd Chorus" in Kerouac's poetry collection *Mexico City Blues,* where the boisterous speaker declares: "I'm crazy everywhere / like Charlie Chaplin / dancing in moral turpitude" (52). Correlatively, in Allen Ginsberg's "Today," the speaker declares, "Tonight I'll call up Jack tell him Buster Keaton is under the Brooklyn Bridge by a vast red-brick wall still dead pan alive" (345).[11] The title of Ginsberg's poem "Laughing Gas" (from *Reality Sandwiches*) may or may not be an allusion to the 1914 Keystone film of the same name (featuring Chaplin), but the slapstick icon is explicitly designated in Lawrence Ferlinghetti's "Constantly Risking Absurdity" as a reflexive figure for the poet himself, "a little charley chaplin man" whose daring linguistic performances are analogous to the "sleight-of-foot tricks" of a circus acrobat balancing on a high wire (30). Bob Kaufman too appealed at times to Chaplin, most notably in "The Enormous Gas Bill at the Dwarf Factory: A Horror Movie to Be Shot with Eyes" (*Golden Sardines*), a poem written to protest the imminent execution of Caryl Chessman. Lastly, of the figure whose *Naked Lunch* (1959) can be said to have bridged the gap between the Beats and black humorists, Kerouac had this to say: "we imitate W. C. Fields, and we imitate Bull [Burroughs. . . .] There's a connection between Bull [and] W. C. Fields" (*Visions of Cody* 181).[12]

John Clellon Holmes, the author of *Go* (1952), once referred to *Naked Lunch* as *1984* as told by W. C. Fields (quoted in Hobbs 117).[13] Indeed, the legendary film comedian finds his literary incarnation in A. J., an "agent" whose cover story is that he is a "harmless practical joker" (Burroughs, *Naked Lunch* 122–23) but who gleefully orchestrates a series of grotesquely obscene events that disrupt high society. Burroughs's most memorable literary creation, the medical maniac Dr. Benway, may also have had his origins in early sound comedy. Groucho Marx easily could have furnished the template for the farcically deranged doctor. When the demented disciplinarian makes his entrance into the novel at the end of a disastrous stint as advisor to the Freeland Republic, it is as if Rufus T. Firefly, the character Groucho portrays in *Duck Soup* (1933; dir. Leo McCarey), has left the nation—Freedonia—he had once led into war and found sanctuary in the geographically indeterminate zones of Burroughs's fiction. In addition, the account of Benway's escape from the debacle he precipitated in Freeland as the misguided director of the Reconditioning Center resembles the "help is on the way" montage near the end of the motion picture. Whereas the latter features fire trucks, a brigade of motorcyclists, long-distance runners, rowers, swimmers, elephants, monkeys, and a school of porpoises rushing to save the beleaguered republic, the former concludes with desperate tourists hurrying away from Freeland "by plane, car, horse, camel, elephant, tractor, bicycle and steam roller, on foot, skis, sled, crutch and pogo-stick" (38). Storming the frontiers of countries elsewhere in the world, the "crazies" insist on being granted asylum on the basis of the "unspeakable conditions obtaining in Freeland," where "Rock and Roll adolescent hoodlums open zoos, insane asylums, and prisons, burst water mains with air hammers, chop the floor out of passenger plane lavatories, shoot out lighthouses, file elevator cables to one thin wire, turn sewers into the water supply, [and] throw sharks and sting rays, electric eels and candiru into swimming pools." Worse, dressed "in nautical costumes" they "ram the *Queen Mary* full speed into New York Harbor," and at other times "play chicken with passenger planes and buses, rush into hospitals in white coats carrying saws and axes and scalpels three feet long, throw paralytics out of iron lungs, mimic their suffocations flopping about on the floor and rolling their eyes up, administer injections with bicycle pumps, disconnect artificial kidneys, [and even] saw a woman in half with a two-man surgical saw" (38).

Yet, as the 1950s came to end, the enthusiasm that had initially enabled the Beats to draw energy and optimism from the obsolete form of popular entertainment began to wane. The most elaborate meditation on the seeming decline in value of the great slapstick comedians is Gregory Corso's elegy "Clown," in which the joy and laughter of the "Old America" of Chaplin and W. C. Fields is sadly said to be gone, the once vital resource depleted, all of their "slapstick gold [. . .] useless" (*Mindfield* 79, 82). Similarly, near the beginning of *The Fall of America*, Ginsberg laments the fact that the great slapstick comedians have gone missing in a time of great need: "Where's [. . .] Chaplin? Harpo Marx? / Where's Laurel and his Hardy/ Laughing phantoms / going to the grave—/ Last time this town I saw them in movies / Ending *The Road to Utopia* / 'O Carib Isle!' / Laurel aged & white-haired Hardy / Hydrogen comic smoke billowing / up from their Kingdom" (10).

Conversely, just as the Beat writers were losing faith in their slapstick predecessors as enduring role models, a new generation of comically inclined novelists (and playwrights) began to demonstrate the benefits of incorporating elements of the film genre into innovative literary enterprises. Two mid-decade paperback anthologies codified this developing tendency under the heading of "black humor." One was edited by Bruce Jay Friedman, who selected a chapter from Céline's *Journey to the End of the Night* to end the collection of otherwise exclusively American writers. (The titular hero of Friedman's first novel, *Stern* [1963], is a Jewish Buster Keaton living a Kafkaesque existence in postwar suburban modernity.) The other, *The World of Black Humor*, published in 1967, was edited by Douglas Davis and contained an excerpt from Elliott Baker's *A Fine Madness* (1964), a literary obscurity today but one that exemplifies the provocative historical trend in question. The novel's hero is Samson Shillitoe, a W. C. Williams–inspired poet whose obstreperous behavior lands him in a mental institution, where an unscrupulous psychiatrist out to make a name for himself subjects the poet to a lobotomy. Notably, an anonymous blurb from the *New York Herald Tribune* accurately describes the narrative as "Fine slapstick that Henry Miller might have whipped up as a script-writer for Mack Sennett" (Baker, n.p.). In this same year Richard Brautigan's countercultural breakthrough *Trout Fishing in America* finally appeared in print (he had finished it in 1961). In the opening paragraph of a chapter titled "The Pudding Master of Stanley Basin," the speaker describes a lake as filled with "silly minnows [. . .] busy putting in hours of Mack Sennett time" (64). One of the fundamental premises of the present book is that such seemingly insignificant details are the historical traces of a momentous change in creative sensibility in this country. *The Freelance Pallbearers,* Ishmael Reed's first novel also appeared in 1967; of this novel, he has stated: "My narrative technique involves a kind of duo that one associates with the vaudeville stage. There's the straight man, the clown, and the joker. Like Laurel and Hardy. And there's a formula for it: one guy is a straight, sophisticated, intelligent, intellectual dude and the other guy keeps breaking into slang, and slapstick or burlesque. [. . .] That's what I attempted to do. I was reading a lot of Bert Williams and Max Sennet [*sic*] scripts at the time, and burlesque, and listening to comedy routines" (quoted in Dick and Singh 36). In the same year, Edward Albee told the cast of *A Delicate Balance*: "Don't forget about the laughs and slapstick so essential to the success of any of my plays" (quoted in Bottoms vi).

This decisive change in the nature of American literature is epitomized by the first three novels of Thomas Pynchon. Again a roughly contemporaneous book blurb conveys what was at stake in this transformation, praising his work as "the most widely discussed and acclaimed books of our time" and that have "been compared to James Joyce and to Vladimir Nabokov, to the Keystone Kops and to the Marx Brothers."[14] And indeed after *V.* (1963) and *Crying of Lot 49* (1966), Pynchon's *Gravity's Rainbow* (1973) arrived in the 1970s as one of the crowning achievements of the phenomenon under investigation. (William Gaddis's *J. R.* [1975] is another.) Reading such a text is obviously beyond the scope of the present book, but it is worth mentioning the exemplary scene in it in which Tyrone Slothrop, riding in a hot air balloon, wards off Major Marvy by hurling golden custard pies at his plane (Pynchon, *Gravity's Rainbow* 332–36).[15] Though less substantial, Philip Roth's 1971 satire of the Nixon administration, *Our Gang*, and Vonnegut's *Slapstick* (1976) should also be listed here, the one invoking the Hal Roach studio product alternately known as the Little Rascals, the other dedicated to Laurel and Hardy on the grounds that the novel approximates the "grotesque, situational poetry" of their films.[16] The New Journalist Hunter S. Thompson's breakthrough novel, *Fear and Loathing in Las Vegas* (1971), also fits into the category of slapstick modernism, with Dr. Gonzo and his partner in crime, Raoul Duke, reminding each other of the sad fate of Fatty Arbuckle when their drug-fueled frenzies get out of hand. Lastly, Robert Coover's *The Public Burning* (1977), in reproducing the events around the Rosenberg treason case as a mass spectacle (thus realizing the rhetorical and aesthetic promise embedded in Dos Passos's *Manhattan Transfer*), brings the pantheon of slapstick performers on stage toward the end of the entertaining show, one skit seizing on "the astonishing resemblance Groucho and Harpo bear to Julius and Ethel" as justification for having the two brothers play the doomed defendants" (454–55).[17]

One can also follow the thread of slapstick through underground film in the United States in the late 1950s and '60s. Bruce Conner, for instance, has said that the idea for his critically reflexive collage, *A Movie* (1958), came from the "Help Is on the Way" montage sequence at the end of the Marx Brothers' film *Duck Soup* (B. Jenkins 188). Ron Rice's 1960 film, *The Flower*

Thief (the cast of which included Bob Kaufman), is an especially significant film document. Characterized by P. Adams Sitney as "the purest expression of the Beat sensibility in cinema" (*Visionary Film* 300), the film negates commercially orthodox narrative conventions in paradigmatically modernist fashion yet is dedicated to those who sacrificed themselves to the cause of laughter, who concocted and clumsily executed daring physical feats. In the program notes to the motion picture, Rice states, "In the Old Hollywood days movie studios would keep a man on the set who, when all other sources of ideas failed (writers, directors), was called upon to 'cook up' something for filming. He was called The Wild Man. *The Flower Thief* has been put together in memory of all dead wild men who died unnoticed in the field of stunt" (quoted in Sitney, *Visionary Film* 300–301). (Rice no doubt happened upon this legendary anecdote in Agee's seminal essay, "Comedy's Greatest Era," where the mythically irrational being in question is linked to the production methods of Mack Sennett at Keystone Studios [8].) Moreover, in *The Flower Thief*, which opens with an homage to *City Lights*, Taylor Mead's acting style (as it will again in Rice's *The Queen of Sheba Meets the Atom Man*) consistently references Chaplin (and Harry Langdon). Also notable is the radicalized filmmaker Saul Levine's *Big Stick / An Old Reel* (1967–1973), an experimentally abstract work of art that also repudiates the state as a force of political oppression. Made with the remnants of 8-mm prints of two short Chaplin films—*Easy Street* (1917) and *In the Park* (1915)—which Levine edited together with images of a televised antiwar demonstration he had himself attended, the film ambiguously commingles pathos-laden scenes of comic brutality with real-life scenes of violent conflict between the police and protesters. The six-reel film Jonas Mekas completed in 1969—*Diaries, Notes & Sketches*, subtitled *Walden*—also registers the impact of silent comedy on the American avant-garde cinema. Near the end of the second reel, as we watch a young child playing on the floor inside a New York City apartment, we can see in the background a poster of a laughing Chaplin on the wall. This seemingly innocuous detail takes on the status of an allusion when the film cuts to wintertime images of ice skaters in Central Park, suggesting that for the moment it is a remake of *The Rink* (1916), in which the Tramp memorably maneuvered his way around a roller-skating rink. Such a correlation is less fanciful than it may seem at first glance when one takes into consideration the rhythmic jerkiness and excessively speedy quality of the images on screen that Mekas's single-frame shooting technique frequently creates.[18] Indeed, the experience of watching *Walden* in its entirety is like watching an especially long-running slapstick motion picture. Finally, there is Ken Jacobs. Besides his reworking of a Buster Keaton short (*Keaton's Cops* [1991]) and dazzling reshaping of Laurel and Hardy's *Berth Marks* (*Ontic Antics Starring Laurel and Hardy: Bye, Molly* [2005]), Jacobs finally finished editing and released in 2004 his eight-hour magnum opus, *Star Spangled to Death* (shot between 1956 and 1960). This impressive collage film (which realizes the compositional and critical promise embedded in W. C. Williams's *Great American Novel*) combines unusually lengthy excerpts of found footage with live-action scenes featuring the deviant foolishness of Jack Smith (who, according to Jonas Mekas, "does as good a job as the early Chaplin" in this film [quoted in Sitney, *Visionary Film* 329]) and his strange associates, generating in the process a fiercely radical indictment of corrupt politicians and the US government's unduly harsh policies on the domestic front and abroad. One of the summary achievements of a slapstick modernism, the film shows that comic delirium, artistic experimentation, and sociopolitical resistance are anything but mutually exclusive. Perhaps it is with the emerging countercultural tendency in mind that Sidney Peterson asserted, in a 1963 piece titled "Note on Comedy in Experimental Film," that "the best introduction to the extravagances of the experimental film are not the works of Ford, Eisenstein, or de Mille. They are those silent comedies, first French and then American, in which people used to experience until their ribs ached, the ferocity and heartlessness of the farcical view of things" (400).

Cody and Comedy: Kerouac's "Imitation of the Tape"

> That the typewriter, which carried the Gutenberg technology into every nook and cranny of our culture and economy should, also, have given out with these opposite oral effects is a characteristic reversal. Such a reversal happens in all extremes of advanced technology.
>
> —Marshall McLuhan, *Understanding Media*

In a letter dated October 12, 1955, Kerouac gave the following advice to his friend and fellow novelist John Clellon Holmes: "write fast, get it all in, or out, up, down, everywhere, throw it, like Céline, like yourself used to tell me to do, great god learn to type a thousand words a minute, buy two tape recorders, upset the silly laws [. . .] instigate revolutions in the bottom of your attic" (*Selected Letters* 221). In the "Imitation of the Tape" section of *Visions of Cody*, adhering to the principles formulated above, Kerouac emphasizes the tactile and the auditory dimensions of writing to produce a slapstick modernist diction that has as its primary task the cracking apart of coherently communicative intercourse. Moreover, if in this portion of *Visions* the writer strives to generate a compositional strategy to match Cody/Cassady's manically improvisational conversational style, he does so in a technologically mediated way. His hero's oral clowning may supply Kerouac with an idealized model for his rhetorical as well as his existential heterodoxy, but ultimately the goal is to reproduce not the real of spontaneous speech but the machinic recording of that real, the revolutionary force of which shatters the words we customarily rely on to ward off non-sense. As typing copies (magnetic) taping, comic writing is updated as a mode of data storage, one that captures the materiality of the embodied voice and the letter as both exceed meaning.

Whereas the lengthy previous section of *Visions*, "The Tape," purports to be a verbatim transcription of the rambling nighttime exchanges between Jack and Cody and a few of their close friends, in "Imitation" Kerouac takes his hero's linguistic eccentricities—his unmotivated changes of topic and penchant for humorously imitating the voices of others—as the inspiration for an inventively aleatory method of writing, one that deliberately disobeys "the silly laws" of rational discourse. Randomly mixed in with a series of frequently unfinished lyric descriptions of the subject's past experiences are reproductions of a few of the narrative fictions he composed on the threshold of adolescence ("I tried to write this at eleven it was called "Mike Explores the Merrimack" [*Visions of Cody* 267]); comic impersonations ("my dear says the British Noble like James Mason at the moon" [250]); assorted literary and journalistic burlesques; obviously fabricated scenarios (such as the story of Christ's leaving of the imprint of his face on a rag [267–68]); decontextualized lines of dialogue; caricatured reproductions of racialized idioms; fragmentary film projections ("REEL TWO. Charlie Chaplin twinkling in an early morning dew, by a garden wall, just as big Two-Time Butch is about to heave a pail of cold water over the wall" [270]); attempts at sociological and self analysis; foolishly anachronistic anthropological speculations ("they [cavemen] must have arranged systems of shuffling and shuttling wives, like through a master male agency [266]); vast amounts of spontaneous free association—much of which exhibits excessive degrees of repetition, alliterative absurdity, and nonsense rhyming before sinking into sheer gobbledygook: "'lot lost a wife, lot lost a wife, lot lost wives or wives lost lots, if not lot lost lots salt'" (263).

Just as disruptive of typical reading processes are the assorted asides or metatextual addresses to the reader, some of which self-consciously disclose the hesitations and uncertainties involved in this spatially and temporally specific act of verbal raving or "completely senseless" babbling: "Oh Mowdelaire! He leaned and gleaned, balcony—say, why did I say balcony?" (252); "the truth is I haven't a single thing to wr—feel foolish" (260); "is that what I meant to say?" (268). Reflexive registrations of the materiality of the printed or typed page also interfere with the text's communicative or expressive dimensions: "aof the ehekdie kdhdke ashout thbut and eyou kdht thekkk, there was no real interruption there or anything but the pour pour pure mechanical faculties and fear, natural, of making noise, amen" (271); and the writer's critical acknowledgment of the physical existence of the vocalizing body, of the real of the throat and lungs, also undermines its more discursive aspirations: "but, ahem, kaff, kaff" (256).[19] Ultimately, this wildly aberrant "monlogo" may be comprehended as Kerouac's willfully imbecilic effort to contribute to the legacy of modernist innovation. Tellingly, Stein, Frost, Hemingway, and Wolfe are alluded to in passing in this section of the text, and Yeats is praised as "a great man because he learned how to write oatutomatically at the behest of little (gragahest?) ghosts" (271).[20] And a productive misunderstanding of Joyce's signature technique is the likely inspiration for what we eventually realize has been a late-night bout of creative improvisation: "but enough, let us sleep now, let us ascertain, in the morning, if there is a way of abstracting the interesting paragraphs of material in all this running consciousness stream that can be used as the progressing lightning chapters of a great essay about the wonders of the world as it continually flashes up in retrospect" (258).

The end result of his drug-fueled experiments in writing automatically (he informs us he is "high on T" [251]) is that literature plunges downward into the realm of what Deleuze would conceptualize roughly a decade later as "infra-" or "under-sense." He diagnoses this as a schizophrenic approach to language, or the mother tongue, a regressive drop into corporeal depths that causes undifferentiated words to pulsate with affective and physical force at the expense of clear-cut meaning (*Logic of Sense* 88). In contrast to Lewis Carroll's status as a surveyor of surfaces as well as a producer of nonsense, Antonin Artaud sinks language down so that it reestablishes contact with the digestive processes of the body. Whereas Carroll's humorously esoteric words tend to circulate between two heterogeneous series of orality, between the alimentary and the semiological (*Logic of Sense* 44), Artaud erases the border line between eating and speaking, obliterating in turn the distinction between denotation, signification, and manifestation on which the language of sense depends. If language, as Deleuze claims, is founded on the separation of sounds from the body, the exceptionally sonorous words of the impassioned schizophrenic absorb or engulf sense (*Logic of Sense* 91), thereby eradicating the frontier that divides propositions and things. Similarly eschewing the opposition between using the mouth to speak rather than to consume food, "Imitation of the Tape" enacts a kind of uncivilized textual vomiting, vulgarly spewing out or regurgitating onto the page bits and pieces of verbal matter that constitutes for the startled reader an unappetizing, all but inedible meal:

> As a printer's son I feel obliged to say that this twaddle—shee—this twaddle—Sheee, plea, sir, plea, chiny towh, town, tow, how, ow, ow, wo, ow, now you done come up and madeitsuch a largerpeforating word that intha doriginal because by gare there my father he was drunk all the time jess like that I can't understoodand eand the feasome and coustiltalk and all those things you was atalking about before I came back from antientam, mm, taint, and found you (why are you hiding vremedeer?)—(they told me, they used to tell me. (Kerouac, *Visions of Cody* 273–74)

The condition of possibility of this act of literary primitivism is a mechanical device, and we have previously heard Kerouac meditating, in the privacy of his room, on "what working people think of me when they hear my typewriter clacking in the middle of the night" (260). In the decade after Kerouac produced *Visions of Cody*, Marshall McLuhan would point out that the typewriter has had a dual function historically. On the one hand, it has aided in the performance of economic tasks; on the other hand, it has contributed to innovations in the creative arts. Whereas the typewriter "brought into business a new dimension of the uniform, the homogenous, and the continuous" that made it "indispensable to every aspect of mechanical industry" (*Understanding Media* 228), it also furnished the impetus for the development of "an entirely new attitude to the written and printed word," encouraging modern poets to conceive of themselves "in the manner of the jazz musician" and "experience performance as composition" (229). The "poet at the typewriter" might even seek audaciously to do what McLuhan credited E. E. Cummings as having done long before Ginsberg: "Chaplin-like shuffles and wiggles" (230). Indeed, in Kerouac's hands, the technical device or instrument allowed him to indulge in a radically undisciplined, grammatically irreverent mode of linguistic unruliness—that is, a slapstick modernist method of playfully mechanized writing: "typing is a goof [. . .] YOU'VE GOT TO MAKE UP YOUR GODDAMN MIND IF YOU WANT TO GOOF OR DON'T WANT TO GOOF OR WANT TO STAY ON ONE LEVEL KICK OR GOOF AND KICK ALONG MISSPELLING AND—" (*Visions of Cody* 255).

Jokes and Their Relation to the Counterculture: *Catch-22*

> No one has been able to pose the problem of language except to the extent that linguists and logicians have first eliminated meaning; and the greatest force of language was only discovered once a work was viewed as a machine, producing certain effects, amenable to a certain use.
>
> —Gilles Deleuze and Félix Guattari, *Anti-Oedipus*

In commenting in 1961 on slapstick film as one of the "decisive" influences on the Theatre of the Absurd, a phenomenon that was aesthetically and historically cognate with black humor fiction in the United States, Martin Esslin pointed out that although "the coming of sound in the cinema killed the tempo and fantasy of the heroic age of comedy," it "opened the way for other aspects of the old vaudeville tradition" to be integrated into the film genre by the Marx Brothers, W. C. Fields, and Laurel and Hardy (335–36). In *Catch-22*, published in the same year, Joseph Heller incorporated the comic dialogues associated with the latter figures into a progressively oriented literary enterprise, one that was designed to generate an ethical modification, to serve as a means of carving out an alternative set of values and beliefs in an era of Cold War aggression and ideological constraint. His jokes were a verbal praxis, an innovative public action aimed at undermining and contradicting "the prevalent belief-system of a community (*éndoxa*), thus revealing the transformability of the contemporary form of life" (Virno 129). If in "Imitation of the Tape" Kerouac converts the typewriter into a "second technology" to gain the upper hand over grammatical and syntactical rules and over the empirical communications these make possible, in *Catch-22* Heller (the onetime copywriter for an advertising firm) treats language itself as a machine, the parts of which can be wittily dismantled and reassembled as a means of producing a still nascent countercultural sensibility.

The intended addressee of the novel was the obedient, decent young man, the kind of person who would allow himself to be drafted (or enlist) because it's the proper, accepted thing to do. Heller envisioned himself writing for the type of individual who respects authority, who accepts the advice of his elders and is ultimately willing to follow orders. This figure takes shape in the novel in the form of Nately and Clevinger, two of the bomber Yossarian's closest friends, who simply refuse to embrace his skepticism, who repeatedly dispute his hostile attitude toward, among others, the discourses of sacrifice and patriotic nationalism. In light of the proliferation of propagandistic discourses, it is crucial to conceptualize Heller's approach to writing as a critical encounter with already circulating clichés, with religious sayings and proverbs, business jargon, official documents, canonical literary materials (Shakespeare, Marlowe, Milton, Whitman, even P. G. Wodehouse), as well as the phrases that constitute common sense in general. This mass of textual verbiage preexists the act of writing as the manufacturing of jokes, and to the degree that such linguistic material both organizes the prospective reader's outlook on the world and conditions his submissive behavior, it must be demolished. This is why the ever elusive Catch-22 is so frustrating: it offers "no object or text to ridicule or refute, to accuse, criticize, attack, amend, hate, revile, spit at, rip to shreds, trample upon or burn up" (*Catch-22* 409). One way to image all this, then, is to say that Heller as an author did not envision himself as approaching a blank page, but as confronting a field swarming with actual utterances, the ideologically coercive power of which he had to find a way to overcome.

Heller's humorous technique can be broken down or simplified into two basic rhetorical procedures. First there is the more or less metaphorical method of substituting an unexpected word for an expected one, which often has the effect of producing additional (or alternative) meanings, of generating a different perspective on existence. Second, he fractures established or conventional signifying chains and then attaches one of the broken parts to a fragmentary piece of an antithetical chain. This more metonymical tactic frequently results in the negation, emptying out, or subtraction of meaning, of the collapsing of common sense into non- or no-sense. Both procedures customarily presuppose and in effect disclose the hidden motivations of a given subject, usually a hypocrite, who claims to be speaking objectively when in truth he is extremely self-interested or brutally egocentric. In such cases we usually observe an officer mouthing platitudes about responsibility as a means of manipulating gullible listeners. The narrator's description of Colonel Cathcart's purported bravery is one of many examples: "Colonel Cathcart had courage and never hesitated to volunteer *his men* for any target available. No target was too dangerous for *his group* to attack" (*Catch-22* 55; emphasis mine). The interpolation of the possessive phrases grammatically acts out a displacement that also occurs in the actual world: the vanished subject (who should have appeared after "volunteer" and "dangerous for" in reflexively pronominal form) evades the risk of bodily harm by putting "his men" and "his group" in place of himself in the sentence and in reality.

The novel's first chapter provides several especially telling examples of the first procedure formulated above. Utilizing free indirect discourse, Heller has Yossarian reflect on the fact that he "had everything he wanted in the hospital. The food wasn't too bad, and his meals were brought to him in bed"

(*Catch-22* 7). The joke derives from the implicit conflation of the hospital with a hotel. The equation transfers the qualities associated with the latter—good service, rest and relaxation, safety—to the former, which in turn generates, by contrast, an unconventional if not unpatriotic attitude toward military service. Remaining on duty becomes a displeasing, stressful situation that one is better off avoiding, and Yossarian does so with no guilt at all, "lying around idly with a clear conscience." Shortly thereafter, in a conversation with the chaplain, Yossarian refers to Nately as "a bit loony" and "as goofy as they come" (12). He then explains his diagnosis: "Nately had a bad start. He came from a good family." Obviously, one would have anticipated, given received wisdom, a repetition of "bad." Merely insert "good" where one expects its opposite and you have expressed, indirectly, a disdain for wealth, social status, and privilege. Badness (in the context of origins) is henceforth linked to attributes we customarily think of as desirable (financial support, prestige, opportunity, etc.). Nately is thus out of his mind because his familial background has paved the way for his internalization of the values and beliefs to which his parents and the class they belong to pay lip service. Next, Yossarian tells the chaplain that Dunbar, another of the bombardier's pals, is "a true prince. One of the finest, least dedicated men in the whole world" (14). Replacing one adjectival superlative with its opposite—"most" with "least"—in effect produces a more countercultural model of anti-heroism whereby what is most admirable is the character's lack of commitment, his cowardly unwillingness to participate in collective undertakings like the war effort. In the next chapter, again via free indirect discourse, the narrator reports that Yossarian is pleased by the fact that he had "not helped build" the new officers club: "Actually there were many officers' clubs that Yossarian had not helped build, but he was proudest of the one on Pianosa. It was a sturdy and complex monument to his powers of determination. [. . .] It was truly a splendid structure, and Yossarian throbbed with a mighty sense of accomplishment each time he gazed at it and reflected that none of the work that had gone into it was his" (18). The insertion of "not" and "none" is a linguistic trace of the subject's rejection of voluntary good deeds; the two parts of speech indicate his ability to escape being suckered into helping out for the good of (a segment) of the community. Working to increase the comfort of the high-ranking members of the squadron is repudiated in favor of private leisure or laziness, and while this might seem to be a limiting stance in many situations, here it resonates with the determination not to conform, to defy the pressure to join in on a project designed by and for those who are already occupying positions of power. Satisfaction comes when one evades exploitation, when one does not contribute with hard work and sacrifice to the well-being of (a part of) the whole. What one glimpses in such one-liners or verbal gags—and they proliferate throughout the text—is the emergence in nascent form of the entire oppositional structure of a countercultural outlook on existence. The simple insertion of signifiers where they don't belong inaugurates the process of fashioning a spirited rebelliousness that ceases to adhere blindly to mainstream or established opinions.

One of the culminating points of the kind of witty procedures under investigation takes place in the chapter titled "Nately's Old Man." Nately, whose name evokes his unworldly credulousness, his naïveté, is troubled by the fact that the dirty Italian man who hangs around the brothel the soldiers' patronize reminds him of his American father. In terms of character, appearance, and epistemological authority, the two stand in stark contrast. One is "sordid," "diabolical," "debauched," and "ugly," "an uncouth bum," "fickle and licentious"; the other is "a courtly white-haired gentleman who dressed impeccably," who was "rich and prominent," "sober, philosophical and responsible." "Nately's father believed in honor and knew the answer to everything; this old man believed in nothing and had only questions." "Nately's father—and everyone else's father Nately had ever met—was dignified, wise and venerable; this old man was utterly repellent" (254). Worse, the opportunistic old man makes "disparaging jokes about America" (252) and taunts the boy, warning him he will not survive the war if he does not become more alert to the dangers threatening him. The old man therefore tries to persuade Nately to interrogate his unwavering faith in admirable parental figures and the codes of conduct they have instilled in him (yet which they ignore). Nately, in turn, remains desperate to repudiate the "vile logic and insinuations" (254) of his interlocutor. Clearly, the former, who cannot accept the advice of the old man, is a figure for the resistant reader, whereas the old man is a figure for the devious yet ultimately well-intentioned author. The cynical old man endeavors one final time to convince the impressionable boy of the risk he is running because of his passionate faith in and willingness to die for his country. "They are going to kill you if you don't watch out, and I can see now that you are not going to watch out" (257). Nately retorts "with triumphant and lofty conviction" that "'it's better to die on one's feet than live on one's knee.'" However, Nately's faith in pithy sayings does not impress "the treacherous old man," who informs his interlocutor that he has it "'backward. It is better to *live* on one's feet than die on one's knees. *That* is the way the saying goes.'" Unsettled but determined to stand his ground, Nately maintains that "'it seems to make more sense my way,'" to which the old man replies: "'No, it makes more sense my way. Ask your friends'" (258; emphasis in the original). Nately doesn't and is killed in action shortly thereafter. The crucial point is that the conversation illuminates the goal toward which the text's wittiness is strategically aimed. The modification or rearrangement of ideological clichés is intended to serve as a means of creating controversial attitudes toward the particular individual's responsibilities in regard to the general well-being of the nation. Here the rhetorical procedure functions as a means of rejecting the traditional, widely accepted judgment that it is better to die with dignity than live in shame.

Lastly, there is the profoundly revealing chapter dealing with the fate of Major Major. The primary intertexts here are homilies, sermons, and biblical proverbs, and it is again a cruel father, a religious hypocrite, who is the main target of the subversive humor. Throughout the chapter, the joining together of incompatible phrases serves to undermine the Calvinist ethos in accordance with which Major Major's father purports to behave: "He was a long-limbed farmer, a God-fearing, freedom-loving, law-abiding rugged individualist who held that federal aid to anyone but farmers was creeping socialism. He advocated thrift and hard work and disapproved of loose women who turned him down" (83). The interpolation of the exception to the rule ("but farmers") in the first sentence reveals his contradictory desire for the kind of help from the government that he argues no one else deserves; in the second sentence, the inclusion of the final clause discloses the degree to which his evaluation of others is determined by his own subjective lust rather than objective criteria. Similarly, when Major Major's father preaches that "the Lord gave us good farmers two strong hands so that we could take as much as we could grab with both of them" (84), we immediately register public puritanism as a pretense, as a mask for private greed. The mechanical aspects of Heller's rhetorical tactic are apparent in the following sentences, which mock the marketplace dynamics that makes it at times economically advantageous to diminish the supply of certain agricultural products: "His specialty was alfalfa, and he made a good thing of not growing any. The government paid him well for every bushel of alfalfa he did not grow. The more alfalfa he did not grow, the more money the government gave him, and he spent every penny he didn't earn on new land to increase the amount of alfalfa he did not produce" (83). Once the first "not" is punched in, the rest of the satiric routine follows (il)logically.

Importantly, the malignant father himself possesses a (mean-spirited) sense of humor. He loves practical jokes, his finest hour coming in his secretive naming of his son. The surreptitious designation supplies the father with considerable pleasure at the expense of his son, whose life is wrecked when he learns of the verbal act that in effect creates a new alienating identity for him. Upon enrolling in kindergarten, he realizes that he is not, "as he had always been led to believe, Caleb Major, but instead was some total stranger [. . .] about whom he knew absolutely nothing" (85). Eventually the docile and compliant boy enlists and applies for aviation cadet training as he has been instructed to, whereupon "an I.B.M. machine with a sense of humor almost as keen as his father's" (86) promotes him to the rank of major. How are we to defend ourselves against the arbitrary acts of power carried out by language machines, whether these machines take shape as intimidating parents, officers in the military, or computer assemblages? Caleb eventually learns the virtues of duplicity, which provides him with a measure of relief from the burdens of paperwork. He tentatively signs "Washington Irving" to a series of official documents rather than his own name, thus engaging in an "an act of impulsive frivolity and rebellion for which he knew afterward he would be punished severely" (92). However, the punishment never comes; instead, his act of forgery halts the bureaucratic machine, removing him from the communicative loop and resulting in paper flowing elsewhere. Deceitfulness surprisingly leaves him free to indulge in more of the same: "He had sinned, and it was good, for none of the documents to which he had signed Washington Irving's name ever came back! Here at last was progress, and Major Major threw himself into his new career with uninhibited gusto" (93). We are witnessing here, of course, the birth of the countercultural author as insubordinate black humorist, or rather the genesis of the slapstick modernist as sociopolitically motivated liar.

The commentary above does not account for the novel as a whole. Indeed, from the point of view of Yossarian's horrific encounter (in the form of a flashback) late in the book with Snowden's torn body, it is reasonable to diagnose the witty wordplay that saturates the first two-thirds of the text as a symptomatic mode of defense against a traumatic event that has not yet been adequately comprehended. Still, to bring this study to a close, it is sufficient to remark that Heller's jokes are designed to function as a machinic method of counteracting the repetitious orders that cause the pilots and their crews to suffer psychically and corporeally. If language (as a first technology) acts as an ideological force of aggression in the world, it does so (in *Catch-22*) most commonly in the form of the command, the perlocutionary force of which must be countermanded. Jokes (as a second technology) seek to discredit such imperative speech acts (which often masquerade as impartial statements of fact) by attacking them at their most vulnerable point: the subject as self-absorbed commander. The overarching aim of the witty novelist is thus to help facilitate his prospective readers' adjustment to their discourse-saturated environment, a pedagogical task that is accomplished when they are taught not to trust respected authority figures and the institutions they control. Writing, as an inventive mode of verbal play, has as its dialectical goal the rhetorical mastery of a medium that military (and business) leaders, when left in charge, utilize to satisfy their drives to the dismay of those serving under them (from the recruits that Lieutenant [soon-to-be General] Scheisskopf brutalizes physically during basic training, due to his obsession with parade-ground victories, to the men killed in combat as a result of Colonel Cathcart's lust for public acclaim).

The "miraculous achievement" of an ostensibly minor character images in the text the (counter)cultural enterprise the novel as a whole pursues. From his tent mate Yossarian's perspective, Orr exists in a state of vulnerability and is therefore to be pitied: "Yossarian felt sorry for Orr. Orr was so small and ugly. Who would protect him if he lived? Who would protect a warmhearted, simpleminded gnome like Orr . . . ?" Yossarian does realize that this "eccentric midget, a freakish, likable dwarf" possesses "a thousand valuable skills," that he can "use a soldering iron and hammer two boards together"; "drill holes"; construct "andirons for the fireplace out of excess bomb parts"; and repair broken gasoline lines" (323). And he can "engross" himself in such seemingly inconsequential tasks "for hours without growing restless or bored, as oblivious to fatigue as the stump of a tree" (323). Yet the bricoleur's predilection for becoming patiently absorbed in the most mundane of mechanical activities strikes his tent mate as further evidence of Orr's poor prospects, guaranteeing only that he will remain "in a low income group all his life" (323). As Yossarian sees it, the resources of a handyman are useless when it comes to defending oneself against the aggressive nature of an unjust and cruel social system. The "happy imbecile's" compulsively repetitive tinkering, his fanatical attention to tiny details when laboring on mechanical devices, tend to drive Yossarian crazy and certainly do not seem to him to constitute a solution to their shared predicament. Forced to watch Orr once again take up his endless project of fixing his stove, Yossarian begs him to stop: "'You're about to take it apart. I know what you're doing, you bastard. I've seen you do it three hundred times'" (320). To his tent mate's dismay, Orr gleefully explains that he has just about finished the job: "'I want to get the leak in this gasoline line out' [. . .] I've got it down now to where it's only an ooze.'" Protesting in anguish—"'If you want to work with something big, that's okay. But that valve is filled with tiny parts, and I just haven't got the patience right now to watch you working so hard over things that are so goddamn small and unimportant'"—Yossarian remains deaf to the life lesson embedded in Orr's rejoinder: "'Just because they're small doesn't mean they're unimportant'" (320–21).

It turns out that the odd pilot is a literary descendant of the silent screen comedians of the interwar years, is the only person in the novel who is able to successfully flee the dictates of his military rulers, who keep escalating the number of bombing missions the members of the squadron must fly before they can be sent home. Yossarian finally realizes that Orr's apparent ineptness in the air, the fact that he keeps getting shot down, is part of the latter's plan; he has been practicing crash landings, has been rehearsing them so that when the time is right he will be ready to put his survival skills to use. He eventually succeeds, rowing across the ocean in a raft to safety. His exemplary accomplishment, then, is predicated on his success at converting a weapon of destruction into a vehicle of escape.[21]

Taking the ultimately wise character as a surrogate for the writer—Orr as a figure for the author—makes available an understanding of Heller's literary method as an amusingly subversive endeavor. Just as the pilot meticulously dismantles and ingeniously reassembles mechanical contraptions, utilizing pieces of one device in the process of fabricating another, the novelist relentlessly takes apart and recombines linguistic utterances, appropriating in deviously twisted fashion fragmentary elements of the spoken phrases and written enunciations of others in the process of constructing his dysfunctional verbal gag apparatus. A kind of critical joke machine that runs by repeatedly ruining referentially authoritative discourses, *Catch-22* takes full advantage of the fact that "words come at many of the things which they alone can do by such a Rube Goldberg articulation of frauds, compromises, artful dodges and tenth removes [as] would fatten any other art into apoplexy if the art were not first shamed out of existence" (Agee, *Let Us Now Praise* 236).

Coda: Mimesis Takes Command

> What "influence" means is still unclear even today. Is it perhaps something like [. . .] the rotation of a dynamo rotor in an electric field that, as a result, creates a new kind of electricity?
>
> —Viktor Shklovsky, *Bowstring: On the Dissimilarity of the Similar*

At the start of "Thought and Cinema," the seventh chapter of *Cinema 2: The Time Image,* Deleuze briefly reflects on the historical goal that "cinema as industrial art" did *not* attain as it developed during the first half of the twentieth century: "Everyone knows that, if an art necessarily imposed the shock or vibration, the world would have changed long ago, and men would have been thinking for a long time. So this pretension of the cinema, at least among its greatest pioneers, raises a smile today. They believed that cinema was capable of imposing the shock, and imposing it on the masses" (157). The conviction that automatically moving images, in "*communicating vibrations to the cortex, touching the nervous and cerebral system directly,*" would give rise to what he calls "a *spiritual automaton* in us," a sort of collective mind possessed of the power to think actively, turned out to be unfounded. Worse, this utopian dream persistently ran the risk of turning into its dystopian inverse: the fear that the masses would become "the dummy of every kind of propaganda," would be robotically programmed to passively accept whatever their leaders instructed them to believe. Rather than gain access to "the status of the true subject," cinema as mass art "degenerated into state propaganda and manipulation, into a kind of fascism which brought together Hitler and Hollywood" (164; emphasis in the original). One wonders, however, whether a less dismal evaluation of the past can be secured if one looks to developments in a different cultural medium, for by the late 1960s, rock music had replaced the movies as the dominant means through which the libidinal energy of the masses might be amplified.

The achievement of the proto-punk band the Stooges is significant in this regard. Releasing their eponymously titled first album in 1969 (the year Kerouac died), the band's performances, whether recorded or live, in effect furnish the basis for a response to the Beat writer's conjecture in *Visions of Cody*: "supposing the [Three] Stooges were real." Initially reviled by critics and consumers alike, the group has retroactively been appreciated for having been one of the bands (like the Velvet Underground) to introduce into rock music a modernist willingness to defy audience demands for familiar generic pleasures in favor of pain-inducing onslaughts of high-volume stimuli. The aural cacophony that is "L.A. Blues," the last cut on their second LP, *Fun House* (1970), is one of several cases in point—screeching vocals and a caterwauling saxophone compete to be heard throughout the five-minute song amid the feedback-drenched sludge of heavily distorted guitars.[22] Yet at the same time, the band remained, as their name attests, attuned to the enduring tradition in this country of comic foolishness, of slapstick idiocy.[23]Indeed, as Ray Manzarek (keyboardist for the Doors) put it: "The Stooges were just like raw-energy maniacs. That was the perfect name for them—the Stooges—like if the Three Stooges played rock & roll, what would it sound like? It would sound like the Stooges (McNeil and McCain 249). The question the short-lived group allows us to pose (again without answering definitively) is whether or not the social function of certain cultural practices has been to hasten collective appropriations of the power of technology for progressive, if not revolutionary, purposes.

In interviews the band's lead singer, Iggy Pop (James Osterberg)—who David Bowie felt personified "the next generation after Kerouac and Ferlinghetti and Ginsberg" (quoted in Palmer 280)—has spoken of his youthful fascination with the "industrial hum" produced around him by, among other things, electric shavers and the space heater in the metal mobile home in which he was raised. He has also pointed to a tour he took (when nine years old) of the Ford Motor Company's main assembly plant at River Rouge as a formative experience, as something of a primal scene for his subsequent career. It was there that he saw his "first drill press" stamping out car fenders and just fell in love with "that sound." Elsewhere he reiterates this point, claiming that in searching for that "added element," "something monolithically simple, metallic, like a big machine," the group as a whole relied on his memory of the giant press as having generated a sound so regular "that even we could master it."[24] In "Of Pop and Pies and Fun: A Program for Mass Liberation in the Form of a Stooges Review; or, Who's the Fool?" occasioned by the release of *Fun House*, the legendary rock critic Lester Bangs asserted that the group finally delivered what was wanted at the time, something approximating "the mechanical mindless heart of noise and the relentless piston rhythms which seemed to represent the essence of both American life and American rock 'n' roll" (44).

Did Iggy's spastic gyrations on stage, then, constitute a comic act of corporeal mimesis motivated by a desire to master the degrading impact of mechanized labor processes? Were the band's sonic performances oriented toward the conversion, via a technologically mediated mode of play, of the forces of production into an innervating instrument of mass emancipation?[25] Or did their avant-garde minimalism, alongside Pop's unusual, aggressively pulsating style of dancing, amount to nothing more than a behaviorist adaptation, one that signals and contributes to the paralysis of "the organism, robbing it of its capacity of imagination and therefore of active response?" (Buck-Morss, "Aesthetics and Anaesthetics" 17).[26] In reproducing the brutally thunderous sounds associated with the economic base, were the Stooges doing nothing more than perpetuating the subjugation of already exploited persons to the present industrial regime? Was the band's music a mere "echo of the machines made by lumps of flesh convulsed with vibrations?"[27] Did the Stooges' songs serve the function of "a work song,'" which "replaces the need for an order from a supervisor by its rhythmic chant," or did their sloppily erratic tunes impede this automatizing process? (Shklovsky, "Art as Device"

13).[28] Was Iggy's "egregious merit," as T. S. Eliot once put it in reference to Chaplin, to have "invented a rhythm"? (306). Did Iggy, as Edwin Rolfe put it in the 1950s, also in reference to Chaplin, simply mirror the "motions of our regimented lives, / our nerve-ends, our goose-stepping muscles," or did his "body, fluid, and flowing [. . .] all music" furnish a glimpse of a glorious future? (174). In sum, can the band's bludgeoning, droning, sometimes excruciating noisiness—whether experienced live or as recorded on vinyl—be considered a genuine overcoming (or sublation) of the repetitive rhythms of mechanized labor processes?

In the 1920s William Carlos Williams, after attending a performance of George Antheil's *Ballet Mécanique*, praised the composer for having successfully accomplished this type of dialectical task: "I felt that noise, the unrelated noise of life such as this in the subway had not been battened out as would have been the case with Beethoven still warm in the mind but it had actually been mastered, subjugated. Antheil had taken this hated thing life and rigged himself into its power over it by his music. [. . .] By hearing Antheil's music, seemingly so much noise, when I actually came upon noise in reality, I found that I had gone up over it" ("George Antheil" 58). A half century later, Robert Christgau interpreted the significance of the New York Dolls' first two albums (1973 and '74) in cognate terms. Noting that the "joy in the Dolls' rock and roll was literally painful," he describes them as

> ambitious kids who'd drifted in from the outer boroughs of Communications Central and devised new ways to cope with information overload. [. . .] They lived in the interstices of the Big Apple war zone on their wit and will, their music at once a survival tactic and a kind of victory. [. . .] They rarely complained about their powerlessness because they were too busy taking advantage of what ordinary power the city provided its citizen denizens—mobility and electricity especially. That's why it seems completely appropriate to me that their music evokes nothing so much as the screech of a subway train. (133–35)

Christgau adds that on stage "Syl [Sylvain, one of the band's guitarists] would turn into Liza Minnelli doing a Charlie Chaplin impression" and that lead singer David Johansen's "pursuit of the funny move" suggested "that human possibility was hilarious" (133–35).[29]

For Bangs, the Stooges' undisciplined music was defiantly rebellious. Echoing Kerouac on the Three Stooges and Cody, Bangs writes that Iggy "has finally stepped out of the night of inertia into his own strange madmanhood, schooled in blows and ready to take on the world" (50). And the critic would add a few years later: "Yeah, Iggy's got a fantastic body; it's so fantastic he's crying in every nerve to explode out of it into some unimaginable freedom. It's as if someone writhing in torment has made that writhing into a kind of poetry" ("Iggy Pop" 207). Borrowing the title of the Stooges' third album (released in 1973), it is reasonable to float the notion that Iggy's jerkiness and his saccadic gestures amounted to a corporeal poetry of raw power. Correlatively, his weird manner of moving may be called mimetic, assuming the term is utilized—as it was for the Greeks (for whom it "meant anything but imitation")—to refer to physical acts such as dancing (Kittler, "From Poetry to Prose" 262).

In sum, Iggy and the Stooges may be considered an embodiment of the idea of slapstick modernism as a countercultural site at which otherwise malleable persons enacted their resistance to the microphysics of biopower, refusing to be brought under control and made into harmoniously automatized workers. In light of his notoriously disparaging assessments of prewar jazz, we may safely assume that Theodor Adorno would turn over in his grave at the mere thought of affirming the positive hypotheses delineated above. In "On Jazz" (1936) he characterizes certain silent screen comedians as clownish versions of the jazz ego, as victimized subjects who willfully subordinate themselves to externally prescribed, normalizing standards of behavior, albeit in a faulty and inept manner. "As a clown, the 'hot' ego begins to follow too weakly the standard of the collective that has been unproblematically set, reeling with uncertainty like many of the figures of the American grotesque genre, such as Harold Lloyd and occasionally Chaplin himself." The pernicious consequences of jazz, then, are that the "subject of weakness takes pleasure precisely in its own weakness" (66–67).[30] Or as Adorno put it more summarily elsewhere, "The adaptation to machine music implies a renunciation of one's own human feelings."[31] Nevertheless, Adorno (with Max Horkheimer) was willing on at least one occasion to entertain the opposite notion that "amusement, if released from every restraint, would not only be the antithesis of art but its extreme role: The Mark Twain absurdity with which the American culture industry flirts at times might be a corrective of art." Unfortunately, such "pure amusement," with its "relaxed self-surrender to all kinds of associations and happy nonsense, is cut short by the amusement on the market." For this reason the inevitable effect of amusement "under late capitalism" is "the prolongation of work. It is sought after primarily as an escape from the mechanized work process, and to recruit strength to be able to cope with the demanding regimes of capitalist labor. Worse, mechanization exerts so much control over a man's leisure and happiness, and so profoundly determines the manufacture of amusement goods, that his experiences are inevitably after-images of the work process itself. The ostensible content is merely a faded foreground; what sinks in is the automatic succession of standardized operations" (Adorno and Horkheimer 137). The growth and development of the entertainment business has thus sadly eliminated the "tendency mischievously to fall back on pure nonsense, which was a legitimate part of popular art, farce and clowning, right up to Chaplin and the Marx Brothers" (137).

A key contention of this book has been that such Depression-era reports of the death of comically affective zaniness turned out to be premature given what happened in the United States and elsewhere in the world in the 1950s and '60s. A final return to Lester Bangs on the Stooges helps underscore the socially beneficial promise of such appeals to slapstick lunacy. For Bangs, the group's music functioned as a dialectical remedy for contemporary ills, or at least was intended to serve as a homeopathic treatment for the "sickness in our new, amorphous institutions" ("Of Pop and Pies" 32). Admittedly, aspects of the band's music exhibit "a crazed quaking uncertainty, an errant foolishness that effectively mirrors the absurdity and desperation of the times," but it nevertheless carries "a strong element of cure, a post-derangement sanity." The Stooges return to the exhausted masses their exploited energies, in effect recharging them: "Power doesn't go to the people, it comes *from* them, and when the people have gotten this passive, nothing short of electroshock and personal exorcism will jolt them and rock them into some kind of healthy interaction" (38). The Stooges work deftly within the "seemingly circumscribed confines of this fuzz-feedback territory" (39) to reenergize their audience. The "'mindless' rhythmic pulsation repeating itself to infinity" that they produce is a key element of "one of the most powerful esthetic experiences of our time" (51). Putting on stage "the secret core of sickness" we all share, the band poses a threat, albeit one that "is cathartic." The final goal is freedom: "the end is liberation" (52). For Bangs, then, the group's raucous music had a restorative thrust, was designed to function as a remedy for modern maladies. On the basis of their curative aspirations, the Stooges' "super-modern" intervention merits high praise, though "you better never call it art or you may wind up with a deluxe pie in the face" (32).

Notes

Introduction

1. The authorial pseudonym derives from Kerouac's birth name (Jeak-Louis Kérouac.)

2. Heller remarked in a 1962 interview that "Céline's book, *Journey to the End of the Night*, was one of those which gave me a direct inspiration for the form and tone of *Catch-22*" ("Impolite Interview" 277).

3. All bracketed ellipses are mine; those without brackets are in the original.

4. "Jack was just the right age to catch the end of vaudeville. His father printed the programmes for the Keith Theatre[. . . .] He was able to see WC Fields and the Marx Brothers live. Jack was seven when talking pictures took over from the old silent movies and made the Marx Brothers and WC Fields international stars." Given "free entry" because of his father's "connection with the theatre," Jack "spent much" of his "spare time absorbing the early offerings of Hollywood" (Miles 15).

5. In a 1949 letter to Ginsberg, Kerouac, in the context of a discussion of the improvements he had been making in his prose style, mentions a vision one of his characters had of watching "the Marx Brothers on the screen with everything going mad and almost exploding" (*Jack Kerouac* 94).

6. Andre Breton's 1939 definition of *humor noire* held greater semantic promise insofar as for him the category encompassed "the early comedies of Mack Sennett, certain films of Chaplin's, and the unforgettable 'Fatty' Arbuckle" (xvii).

7. Similarly, four years earlier, in his introduction to *The Moderns: An Anthology of New American Writing in America*, Leroi Jones had justified his editorial selections for this volume as an effort to do justice to a "continuing tradition of populist modernism that has characterized the best of twentieth-century American writing." Elsewhere in the introduction, Jones comments on the disparate ways in which the

current work of Kerouac and William Burroughs had "paid homage" to the "model" James Joyce's *Ulysses* supplied them (xiv–xv). For an excellent study of the degree to which "avant-garde and modernist aesthetics often arose from a selective appropriation of popular expressive forms," see Suarez (3).

8. For a more recent, broader articulation of a historical stance that is roughly comparable to the one I am taking, see David James, "Mapping Modernist Continuities." My concept of a slapstick modernism might be profitably aligned with Pop Art, which Hal Foster locates in the interval "between the decline of modern art and architecture on the one hand and the rise of postmodern art and architecture on the other" ("Survey" 19).

9. A singular exception to this general rule, one I will deal with at the end of this introduction, is Stan VanDerBeek's "Culture: Intercom and Expanded Cinema."

10. What are we to make of the fact that the titular hero of *Pnin* is bored one night by three movie shorts featuring Chaplin? Could the author's point be that the "humorless" indifference of the novel's protagonist marks his failure to recognize his own (inter-medial) mirror image? His surname encourages one to assume so (Nabokov 80).

11. Correlatively, Dean as listener figures the ideally energized reader: he stands in front of the performer "oblivious to everything else in the world, with his head bowed, his hands socking in together, his whole body jumping on his heels" (Kerouac, "Jazz of the Beat Generation" 12).

12. See also Dos Passos's praise of John Howard Lawson's "jazz play" for its rejection of "real life honestly set down" in favor of "crude and comic and grotesque" scenes that "attempt to invade the audience's feelings[. . . .] The fact that it does move and excite us, and succeeds thereby in reinstating the stage, makes it extraordinarily important" ("Is the 'Realistic' Theatre Obsolete?" 77).

13. For a suggestive reading of the poem from the perspective of this statement authorizes, see Kane (111–16).

14. See also Coffman (3–25); Zach (230); and Bornstein (22–32).

15. One exhibitor who was quoted in a November 1913 *Variety* article asserted that he and his colleagues felt that "to-day none of the companies save Keystone [. . . is] living up to the old laugh standards" (Riblet 171).

16. See Hounshell (217–61); Giedion (115–17); and Flink (177–89).

17. See also Sitney, "Sentiment of Doing Nothing" (149); and McCabe (3).

18. For a related evaluation of the disruptive force of "the culture of shocks" that "constituted the critical underside of modernity as a systematic process of rational and scientific planning," see Gunning, "Modernity and Cinema" (309).

19. For more on Kracauer and slapstick, see M. B. Hansen, "White Skin, Black Hair."

20. For a critique of the purportedly suppressed desire of modernist artists to achieve financial success or fame, see Dettmar and Watt.

21. See also Cohen.

22. For a valuable explication of the pertinence of Benjamin's ideas to an understanding of the affective dynamics of modernism, see Nieland (2–5).

23. Benjamin's endorsement, in "On Some Motifs in Baudelaire" (1939), of the thesis that the French poet's mission was to help train his readers to handle the excessive sensory stimuli of their urban milieu in a non-traumatic fashion suggests that, for the critic, the homeopathic effects of a shock aesthetic were something modernist writing had pursued at its inception, before the invention of cinema.

24. On Chaplin's comic "resistance to 'productive' labor," see Musser, "Work, Ideology" (36–66); and M. B. Hansen: "If his [Chaplin's] early films had a radical function for immigrant working-class spectators and might have encouraged fantasies of resistance and autonomy, it was in his anarchic protest [. . .] against the regimentation of the industrial-capitalist workplace, the discipline of the clock, and the conveyor belt, through a subversive mimicry of processes of reification and alienation" (*Babel and Babylon* 76).

25. In discussing Chaplin's rapid movements in the short film *Dough and Dynamite*, Raymond Durgnat asserts that we "are not so far from the preoccupations of Muybridge and Marey" (70).

26. On Gilbreth's use of "a motion picture camera to take 'chronocyclegraphs,'" see Kern (116); and Giedion (102–104).

27. See McDonald (236). For Steinman, Pound's definition of Imagism was in "accord with the language in which a machine style was being described" (46); see also Raitt: "Efficiency, economy, organization [. . .] are [. . .] central to the evolution of modernist theories of literature" (840); see also Tichi (91–96); Banta (3–36); and Knapp (1–18).

28. See Knapp (30–32).

29. Crane may have been preceded by Mina Loy here. Composed in 1915 though not published until 1923, the central figure in her poem "Ignoramus" is, in the words of Roger Conover, "very much in the spirit of Charlie Chaplin's tramp" (Loy 186). This "Clown of Fortune" carries "a walking-stick" (44–45).

30. A year later, Crane added that to him Chaplin is "the prime interpreter of the soul imposed upon by modern civilization" (Weber 85).

31. Laurence Goldstein notes that "the poem's phrasing is certainly a comedy of language" and that the "continuous stream of invention in the films cannot help but impress the poet as similar to the linguistic play he practices in excess of what is minimally required by the declarative character of his address" (42–43).

32. See Blackmur.

33. R.W.B. Lewis admits "that what Crane really meant was 'obsequiousness,' and that 'obsequies' is simply an example of a muddled and ignorant use of language. But it is always a sounder policy with Crane to assume that he knew what he was doing in his selection of words." Thus out of the historical confusion of two Latin sources (*obsequium* as compliance and *exsequiae* as funeral rites), "Crane drew a word with a packed and paradoxical significance" (49–50). On Crane's "flickering slapstick diction," see G. Stewart (312).

34. "Chaplin may be a sentimentalist, after all," Crane writes, "but he carries the theme with such power and universal portent that sentimentality is made to transcend itself into a new kind of tragedy, eccentric, homely, yet brilliant" (Weber 69).

35. Susan Stewart argues that the "realization of expression depends on the *bind*, the implicit tie of intelligibility between speaker and listener that links their efforts toward closure[. . . .] Lyric, no matter how joyous or comic, expresses that seriousness, the good faith in intelligibility, under which language proceeds and by means of which we recognize each other as speaking persons" (104–5). That Crane was aware that his sonorously erratic aesthetic performances tended not to conform to the dictates of straightforward communication is again apparent in his correspondence. "I realize," he wrote to Gorham Munson on November 3, 1921, "that the technique of the thing ["Chaplinesque"] is virtuosic and open to all kinds of misinterpretation" (Weber 69).

36. René Clair's *Entr'acte* (1924) is another important interwar prefiguration of a properly slapstick modernism; see Sitney (*Visionary Film* 53).

37. One senses Thomas Wolfe's impatience in the Depression era with such an attitude, for in *You Can't Go Home Again* (1940) he has his autobiographical protagonist, George Webber, defend his friend Fox (based on Maxwell Perkins) on the grounds that he "did not write nine-page reviews on 'How Chaplin Uses His Hands in Latest Picture'—how it really was not slap-stick, but the tragedy of Lear in modern clothes." George then repudiates those who claim that "Crane's poetry can only be defined, reviewed, and generally exposited in terms of mathematical formulae" (442).

38. See G. Stewart's "Modern Hard Times" and "Keaton through the Looking Glass."

39. Benjamin goes on to quote Philippe Soupault, who claims that making "people laugh," as does Chaplin, is "the hardest thing to do" and "socially also the most important" ("Chaplin in Retrospect" 224).

40. Equally telling is the fact that VanDerBeek explicitly invokes his allegiance to the tradition of silent screen comedy by dedicating the similarly motivated *Breathdeath* (1963), which he called a "black comedy," to Chaplin and Keaton (*Visibles* 5). Also, one of the print collages he attached to his manifesto contains an image of Chaplin holding a giant fingerprint.

Chapter 1. The Work of Art in the Age of Mechanical Transportation

1. "All that the Ford industries have done—all that I have done—is to endeavor to evidence by works that service comes before profit and that the sort of business which makes the world better for its presence is a noble profession" (Henry Ford 271).

2. Earlier Bataille had figured the binding of human aggregates using technological terminology: "Being, in man's definition and as instantiated by him is [. . .] present in the fashion [. . .] of [an] electric current. If there does exist some unity within pres-

ence, it is that [...] of circuits which tend toward stability and closure." Correlatively, "an inner change of state is easily grasped when I communicate with another—when I talk or laugh, or lose myself within some turbulent group. [...] This change is caused by the passage of a live current from one to the other." In those instances when the elements of isolated individuals "fuse with each other," it is as if they become points "within a network of electric forces" ("Sacrifice" 62). On laughter, communication, and community in Bataille, see Parvulescu (79–99).

3. Trahair does not mention this cinematic allusion in her account of Bataille's theory of comedy.

4. In fact, Bataille has misremembered *The Gold Rush*, conflating two different scenes, one appearing at the beginning and the other at the end of the film. In the first, Chaplin and Big Jim (Mack Swain) battle against Black Larsen (Tom Murray) during a storm while the shack remains on solid ground; in the second, the Tramp and Big Jim are trapped together in the shack as it hovers above an abyss, but they are not combatants. The distinction is not germane to Bataille's argument.

5. On the motor company's achievement at its Highland Park plant, see Smith (15–55).

6. See also King, "Uproarious Inventions" (180–209).

7. On the perilous nature of everyday life in urban environments around the turn of the century, see Singer. Eileen Bowser speculates that the surge in the number of pedestrian deaths in New York City in the 1920s was due to "the advent of the Model T" (109).

8. I will revisit this claim of Benjamin's in the "Theoretical Interlude."

9. See Karen Beckman's excellent analysis of a few turn-of-the-century British films (Cecil Hepworth's *How It Feels to Be Run Over* and *Explosion of a Motor Car* and Walter R. Booth's *The "?" Motorist*) as well as her comparative assessment of Lloyd's *Hot Water* and the Laurel and Hardy film *Two Tars* (25–101). She mentions *Lizzies of the Field* in passing as an example of the way Keystone comedies were "prone to escalate into the total destruction of a demolition derby" (62). For a brief but trenchant reading of excess from a Freudian perspective in *Super-Hooper-Dyne Lizzies*, see Bilton (73–77).

10. On the evolution of the studio's formal system, see Riblet (168–89).

11. See also Mast (56).

12. Axelrod cites Ashleigh Brilliant's *The Great Car Craze: How Southern California Collided with the Automobile in the 1920s* (1989) on this topic: "The automobile became firmly established during the 1920s as one of the standard comic props of the Hollywood film comedy. Audiences never seemed to tire of seeing cars colliding, overturning, falling apart, tumbling over precipices, being squashed by trains, flattened by steam rollers," etc. (Axelrod 79).

13. No such contradiction arises in the case of Williams's avant-garde writing due to the access he had to an alternative mode of literary production; *GAN* and several other of his early experimental writings were published by privately owned,

nonindustrialized small presses. See Hugh Ford (34–116); White (285–306); and, more generally, Rainey (1–9). Williams himself was well aware that the extreme acts of critical negation in which he wished to engage depended on the existence of such small presses. As he put it late in life, after enduring a set of discouraging set of defeats in the domestic literary marketplace, "McAlmon in Paris along with Bill Bird and his Three Mountains Press came to my rescue with books printed abroad" (*Autobiography* 237).

14. For a related approach to what he aptly calls Williams's "poetry of unclogging" and correlates with the economic solutions floated in C. H. Douglas's treatise *Social Credit*, see Tratner, *Deficits and Desires* (121–72).

15. See in particular Williams's critical assertion in the prologue to *Kora in Hell* that "the coining of similes is a pastime of a very low order" (18); this is commented upon by J. Hillis Miller (358). See also Marjorie Perloff's discussion of the practical repudiation in *Spring and All* of "strained associations" (114–15).

16. Though it is not as insistently self-referential, *Kora in Hell* precedes *The Great American Novel* in its utilization of an *allegorical* strategy in the sense that in the earlier text the subsequently adjoined commentaries (in italics) supply the keys that enables one to grasp what the spontaneous compositions are more or less covertly about.

17. Elsewhere, discussing the tenets of primary education in this epoch, Kittler quotes the assertion that the mother "'must be an educator'" because "'the child sucks in its first ideas with the mother's milk'" (*Discourse Networks* 55). Williams praises his own mother as "a creature of great imagination" in the prologue to *Kora in Hell* (6–8).

18. For a different interpretation of this passage, see Boone (13).

19. Williams's interest in analyzing the codes of narration is lackluster in comparison to his sustained attentiveness to the materiality of his medium. He expresses his disdain for the basis of a conventional crime novel—"Oh catch up a dozen good smelly names and find some reason for murder, it will do" (*GAN* 159)—in what amounts to little more than a throwaway acknowledgment of generically prescribed expectations.

20. April Boone notes that this "sounds conspicuously" like Ezra Pound (10).

21. The quoted phrase comes from Hart Crane's posthumously published "Modern Poetry" (1930) and supplies the title for Tichi's study. Her extended discussion of Williams's "rapid-transit poetics" pays close attention to the conceptual link between driving and writing in his work. Her argument is antithetical to the one I am unfolding here; for her, Williams's investment in automotive speed and mobility was indicative of his literary assimilation of the (engineering) values informing economic rationalism: efficiency, productivity, the elimination of waste, etc. (230–88). Susan McCabe reads the moving car in *Spring and All* as a figure for the poet's eye as mobile camera (126–27). James Clifford seizes on the driverless car in "The Pure Products Go Crazy" as a figure for a Western world careening into modern inauthenticity (1–17).

22. See also Baldwin (125). Lisa Gitelman lists Williams, alongside Henry James, Stein, and Pound, as an author for whom the typewriter "reportedly became a sort of object-muse, a fetish, in the creative" process (218).

23. In *Descent of Winter* (1928), Williams will assert that "poems are small and [. . .] they eat gasoline" (239).

24. Though he devotes the bulk of his essay to a comparison of one particular case of "borrowing," Hugh Witemeyer offers a valuable account of this aspect of Williams's rhetorical technique (1–13).

25. Burroughs mentions the "Camera Eye" device in this context, but he almost certainly meant to refer to the "Newsreels" (*Writers at Work* 153).

26. Sennett "took his comics out of music halls, burlesque, vaudeville, circuses and limbo, and through them he tapped in on that great pipeline of horsing and miming which runs back unbroken through the fairs of the Middle Ages at least to Ancient Greece" (Agee, "Comedy's Greatest Era" 7).

Chapter 2. The Politics and Poetics of Attraction I: Dos Passos

1. On this matrix, see Gaudreault (62–69).

2. See also Bordwell (119). On the degree to which Eisenstein's investment in reflexology (and scientific management) compromised his postrevolutionary undertaking, see Beller (88–149). For Beller, the Soviet director's "synthesis of neuronal and industrial research, of Pavlovian logic" and "Taylorization," amounted to "an extension of capital logic into the cinema" (120).

3. For more on the disappearance in the mid-1920s of the term "attraction" from Eisenstein's conceptual vocabulary, see Aumont (44, 48). On ecstasy in Eisenstein, see Nieland (67–101).

4. See also Wollen, "Modern Times" (47–54). Miriam Hansen has touched on Eisenstein's probable influence (via Asa Lacis) on Benjamin ("Benjamin and Cinema" 317–18).

5. Also, in a convoluted discussion of the "model actor's" capacity to preserve "inertia," Eisenstein posits the Keystone Kops ("'Fatty' Arbuckle's film group") as an exemplification of the incorrect way of handling this principle; they demonstrate what happens when one breaks this rule ("Montage of Film Attractions" 50). In the following decade, Eisenstein would endorse Alexander Medvedkin's truly demented film *Happiness* (1934) as a move beyond Chaplin, since the gags have become socialist rather than individualist ("*Happiness*" 52–55).

6. For an anthropological approach to the topic of "affective mimicry," see Stromberg (esp. 77–91). In addition to furnishing a valuable bibliography on "simulation theory," Stromberg explicates lucidly a good deal of recent neuroscientifical research on the way humans learn through imitation. See also Plantinga (esp. 1–16, 48–77).

7. George M. Cohan and George J. Nathan's "The Mechanics of Emotion" (1913) is an oft-cited early twentieth-century variant of a rationalized approach to controlling audience reactions. See also Alfred Hitchcock on his method: "Do you realize

what we're doing in this picture? The audience is like a giant organ that you and I are playing. At one moment we play *this* note on them and get this reaction, and then we play *that* chord and they react *that* way. And someday we won't even have to make a movie—there'll be electrodes implanted in their brains, and we'll just press different buttons and they'll go 'oooh' and 'aaah' and we'll frighten them, and make them laugh." Quoted (from Donald Spoto's *The Art of Alfred Hitchcock*) in Žižek (240; emphasis in the original).

8. I am preceded here by E. D. Lowry's excellent essay "The Lively Art of *Manhattan Transfer*" (1969); his more frequently cited "*Manhattan Transfer*: Dos Passos' Wasteland" (1963) is less valuable.

9. Previous accounts of *Manhattan Transfer* that take into consideration Soviet cinema include Spindler (402–405); G. Foster (1986); and Shloss (143–49). Dos Passos himself helped set the stage for subsequent readings by offering, later in life, uninspired reflections on the novel's inception. See, for instance, his "The Desperate Experiment" (1963): "Direct snapshots of life. Reportage was a great slogan. The artist must record the fleeting world as sharply as the motion picture film recorded it. By contrast and juxtaposition he could build his own vision into reality: montage." Quoted by Martin (326). On Dos Passos's montage strategies, see also Dow (405–408).

10. Jameson also recognizes the discontinuous structure of the variety show as the basis for the affinity between "the operations of the comic," as epitomized by the farces of Chaplin, Keaton, and Jacques Tati, and the "episodizing logic of the various modernisms" ("Existence of Italy" 211).

11. For more on this topic, see the essays collected in Strauven.

12. In "An Aesthetic of Astonishment" (1989), Gunning solidifies this comparison, positing that early cinema sought to supply its audience with a "dose of scopic pleasure" (869) and to fulfill "the curiosity it excites." Yet "it is in the nature of curiosity, as the lust of the eye, never to be satisfied completely. Thus the obsessional nature of early film production and the early film show the potential endless succession of separate attractions [. . .] the unlimited metonymy of curiosity" (873). In the headnote to a chapter of *Manhattan Transfer* titled "Nickelodeon," Dos Passos registers the sexually stimulating aspects of early cinematic materials: "*On Sixth Avenue on Fourteenth there are still flyspecked stereopticons where for a nickel you can peep at yellowed yesterdays. Beside the peppering shooting gallery you stoop into the flicker* A HOT TIME, THE BACHELOR'S SURPRISE, THE STOLEN GARTER . . . *wastebasket of tornup daydreams . . . A nickel before midnight buys our yesterdays*" (248; emphasis in the original).

13. Eisenstein wrote his second essay titled "The Montage of Film Attractions" after having finished shooting his first feature-length film (*Strike*). This second article appeared in print posthumously.

14. Wollen mentions "that the word 'attraction' may well have been suggested to Eisenstein by the roller-coaster in the Petrograd Luna Park, which carried that name" (*Signs and Meaning* 32).

15. On this topic, see Kittler, *Gramophone, Film, Typewriter* (3, 12–14).

16. In truth, Dos Passos's employment of the "mythical method" does supply an implicit model for understanding the impending fate of the nation. As a couple of early headnotes indicate, the novel presupposes a theory or law of history (a modification of the premise informing D. W. Griffith's *Intolerance* [1916], subsequently parodied by Keaton in *Three Ages* [1923]), in which the centers of great civilizations rise and then fall. Ultimately, the text thematically discredits such a prophetic stance, but deconstructing *Manhattan Transfer* in this fashion would add little to the present discussion.

17. For a different take on oceanic imagery in the novel, see Moore.

18. The internal quote is cited by James from Vorkapich's 1934 article "The Psychological Basis of Effective Cinematography."

19. Crary notes that Eisenstein and the French painter may "be associated as artists who struggled to reconcile rational formal clarity with techniques for stimulating emotional response" (*Suspensions of Perception* 173n48; see also 198n106 and 222).

20. The quote comes from a 1926 article in *Advertising and Selling*; it is quoted by Marchand (vii), who comments: "Advertisers recognized that consumers would rather identify with scenes of higher status than ponder reflections of their actual lives."

21. As Dos Passos was no doubt aware, the business acumen of King Camp Gillette—the inventor of the modern safety razor—was legendary, especially in the realm of advertising. Gillette was also the author of *The Human Drift* (1894), a utopian socialist fiction in which everyone is sent to live together in a huge city named Metropolis.

22. See Wicke (172). Jackson Lears mentions the convergence of advertising with "suggestion psychology," tracing this meeting back to Walter Dill Scott's 1908 study *The Psychology of Advertising* (Lears 208).

23. Dos Passos was an undergraduate at Harvard between 1912 and 1916, though to my knowledge he never crossed paths with Munsterberg, who was on the faculty there until his sudden death in 1916. Carr lists Munsterberg as one of the prestigious members of the philosophy department with whom students like Dos Passos customarily selected courses to take (52).

24. For Moretti, advertising functioned as a panacea for the woes of the urban masses: "The billions of human beings who have ended up in big cities—have they really lived better? Hard to say. But they have *dreamed* better, of that I am sure. And the credit, if credit it is, goes to these: advertising, the stream of consciousness, the preconscious" (167; emphasis in the original).

25. In *U.S.A.* Dos Passos revisits the issue of advertising in great depth; see especially the narrative sections devoted to the ultimately despicable expert in public relations J. Ward Morehouse and his ethically bankrupt protégé, Richard Ellsworth Savage. For an account of the trilogy from this point of view, see Stratton (101–143). Particularly relevant is his treatment of the Committee on Public Information, the

creation of which was authorized by Woodrow Wilson in 1917 to sell the war effort to the general public (116–21).

26. Marcus, quoting and commenting on Harry Levin's account of *Ulysses*, writes: "Leopold Bloom's mind is a motion picture, cut and edited 'to emphasize the close-ups and fade-outs of flickering emotion, the angles of observation and the flashbacks of reminiscence.' The organization of the raw material of Joyce's fiction [. . .] entails the operation of *montage*" (91; emphasis in the original).

27. McLuhan found fault with Dos Passos's treatment of suffering in *Manhattan Transfer* as insufficiently attuned (in contrast to Joyce in *Ulysses*) "to the interior landscape which is the wasteland of the human heart" ("John Dos Passos" 152). Eisenstein reported that when he met Joyce in Paris, the latter "was intensely interested in my plans for the inner film-monologue, with a far broader scope than is afforded by literature. Despite his almost total blindness, Joyce wished to see those parts of *Potemkin* and *October* that, with the expressive means of film culture, move along kindred lines" ("Course in Treatment" 104).

28. Dos Passos's influence is especially strong in the "Manhattan Sketches" portion of *Visions of Cody*. This is not to say that Kerouac was fully aware of the debt he owed Dos Passos. In a 1949 journal entry, he wrote: "Who wants Dos Passos' old camera eye? [. . .] Everybody wants to GO!" (*Windblown World* 252). Kaplan and Roussin identify the American novelist's version of Broadway in *Manhattan Transfer* as the key intertext for scenes in Céline's *Voyage* and mention that the French novelist tried to arrange a meeting with Dos Passos in 1934 while on a publicity tour of the United States ("Céline's Modernity" 440n3).

29. In 1932 Dos Passos recalled that at the end of the First World War "whenever you went to the movies you saw Charlie Chaplin" ("Introduction" 146).

30. Stevens had submitted "From the Journal of Crispin" two years earlier in a competition to win the Blindman Prize.

31. Though R.W.B. Lewis, without the help of the excised passage, managed to intuit the presence of silent comedy in the background of "Comedian," designating Crispin "the Buster Keaton of poets" (73), Stevens's selection of Harold Lloyd was perhaps determined by the coincidental resemblance between the name Harlequin and a portion of the screen star's proper name, but if a pun was the only determining factor then Harry Langdon would have fit the bill just as well.

Chapter 3. The Politics and Poetics of Attraction II: Harold Lloyd's "Thrill" Films

1. See also Lacan's account of the role that visual idealization plays in the process of motor development. "His [the child's] joy [in front of the mirror] is due to his imaginary triumph in anticipating a degree of muscular co-ordination which he has not yet actually achieved" (76); and Schwartz: "Having hypothesized that "the indirect impact" of the physical movements of silent-movie stars such as [. . .] Chaplin and Stan Laurel "must have been enormous" "upon audiences sitting year after year

in front of the silver screen [. . .] the glamour of the stars came to be equated with a dynamism that drew on a new kinaesthetic" (101).

2. Elsewhere in the essay Tretyakov proposes that at those times when a "vigorous gymnastic pace replaces the rocking of the cradle [. . .] the 'kino-illusorium' is transformed into a 'kino-affectorium,' a place where people are loaded with social gunpowder" (30). Previously, he had formulated this shift as an embrace of "*organizational* and *constructive*" tasks in lieu of traditional art's pursuit of "*representation* and *reflection*" ("Art in the Revolution" 14; emphasis in the original).

3. Naremore quotes Andrew Bergman's observation that "what [Hitchcock] did in his thrillers is very close to what one attempts in comedy—placing characters in extraordinary situations" (126).

4. Kerr asserts that Lloyd "wanted the 'glasses' on the screen every week of the year and was determined to saturate the country with the image" (104). That by the end of the decade Lloyd had succeeded in his quest for popularity is evident in Robert S. and Helen Merrell Lynd's report in *Middletown: A Study in Contemporary American Culture* (1929) that "Harold Lloyd comedies draw the largest crowds" (cited in Dale 69). Lloyd's movies outdrew Keaton's, but Lloyd grossed more than Chaplin in the 1920s only because the latter produced merely four features whereas the former released eleven. See Dardis (200–201).

5. By this time, Lloyd had a considerable amount of control over the filmmaking process. Having signed a new contract with Hal Roach in November 1921, the creative staff he employed was increasingly autonomous. In July 1923, shortly after completing *Safety Last!* Lloyd left Roach's studio to form an independent company, taking with him twelve employees, including Sam Taylor, Fred Newmeyer, and Ted Wilde, all of whom would continue to be credited as directors of the pictures in which Lloyd starred; see Ward (44–45).

6. *Why Worry?* (1923), Lloyd's fifth feature, applies this same diagnosis to its male protagonist. Lloyd plays a rich pill-popping hypochondriac who takes a voyage to Paradiso—a resort off the coast of South America that is unknown to tourists—in the hopes of improving his health. After getting caught up in an attempt by revolutionary forces to overthrow the government, however, he discovers that vigorous action in a dangerous situation is all he requires to feel better.

7. Cummings hyperbolically predicts in the article that were "Congress to pass a bill compelling every adult inhabitant of the United States of America to visit the circus at least twice a year [. . .] hundreds of cripples—lame, halt, and blind—would toss their infirmities to the winds [. . .] and millions of psychoanalysts would be thrown out of employment" ("Adult, Artist, Circus" 253.)

8. Amusement park attractions are, on the other hand, even more exemplary in this respect. For at that "incredible temple of pity and terror, mirth and amazement, which is popularly known as Coney Island [. . .] we [. . .] dare all the delirious dangers conceivable; and when, rushing at horrid velocity over irrevocable precipices [. . .] no acrobat [. . .] can compete with us" (Cummings, "Coney Island" 258).

9. *Too Much Johnson*, a recently unearthed forty-minute film directed by Orson Welles in 1938, includes footage alluding to Lloyd's slapstick classic (Joseph Cotten fumbling around on the ledge of a skyscraper), as well as a Keystone-like chase across Lower Manhattan. It would seem that before setting to work on *Citizen Kane* (1941), his masterpiece of cinematic modernism, Welles served a brief apprenticeship in silent comedy.

10. Such demonstrations may have undesirably antithetical consequences due to copycat behavior. Merrill Schleier mentions that conquering skyscrapers was made illegal when a man fell to his death while publicizing *Safety Last!* (31). In her lengthy account of the film, she argues that the film vividly renders how (white) manhood and upward mobility could be conceptualized at the time through displays of physical prowess. Scaling the tall edifice figures the attainment of a masculine identity as well as a socioeconomic elevation (Schleier, esp. 25); see also Jacobs (152–68).

11. On the twentieth-century emergence of an "adrenaline aesthetic," see Duffy.

12. On the function of "vertigo and simulation" in noncapitalist societies, see Caillois (81–97).

13. For a reading of these two films, see Gunning, "Mechanisms of Laughter" (137–51); and Beckman, *Crash* (68–81).

14. On the fifty-year time span it took to perfect "the tracking frontal shot from a moving vehicle," see Rees (86, 91–92). Significant exceptions to the general tendency to delimit the use of this type of shot include the opening scene of Jean-Luc Godard's *Breathless* (1960) and portions of the chase scene in Hitchcocks's *Foreign Correspondent* (1940). On the equation of windshield and screen, and by extension driving and watching films, see Virilio, "Dromoscopy."

15. On turn-of-the-century reactions to the hazards of big-city traffic, see Singer (72–84).

16. See also Isenstadt.

17. All internal citations are from Balint's *Thrills and Regressions* (1959).

18. See also Fielding; and on the precursors to Hale's Tours, see Nead.

19. The gap between Hale's Tours and Lloyd's feature films was filled by Mack Sennett, whose films had a "common tendency, fully developed in the studio's (Keystone's) post-1914 output [. . .] to stage elaborate race-to-the-rescue climaxes in which multiplying modes of transportation intersect along chaotic, intersecting paths of pursuit" (King, *Fun Factory* 188).

20. Jonathan Crary glosses this distinction as follows: "haptic refers to the eye-fulfilling 'non-optical functions,' including tactility but other senses as well [. . .] where optic refers to a distance through static points of reference" (*Suspensions of Perception* 340). See also Rheingold (27). For an application of this model (by way of Merleau-Ponty) to film in general, see Barker.

21. Similarly, in "Just Gaming," Stallabrass proposes by way of a reading of Benjamin's *Trauerspiel* that the critic's "shade seems to haunt the virtual world" (92).

22. Ed Link patented his original design for a flight simulator in 1929 (Rheingold 202), one year after *Speedy* was released.

23. I assume that the final word in the passage should read "situations" rather than "simulations." A January 22, 2010, article by James Dao in the *New York Times* titled "Simulator's Prepare Soldiers for Explosions of War" describes the implementation of new technologies as a means of preparing soldiers for the hazards of combat, including driving. See also Pollack; and Lenoir. Friedrich Kittler asserts along these lines that strobe lights in discos function "to train the speed of our perception—in defiance of all physiology—for the extreme requirements of a technical war" (*Optical Media* 152).

24. Research in the newly constructed (and unproven) field of neurofeedback pursues a comparable end. In one study, children were monitored while playing a race-car video game in which "the ability to speed up the car and steer it was contingent on maintaining brain waves in a more favorable ratio." "Train the Brain: Using Neurofeedback to Treat ADHD," National Public Radio, "Morning Edition," November 1, 2010, http://www.npr.org/templates/story/story.php?storyId=130896102. The agenda Hart Crane set in "Modern Poetry" is cognate though not identical to such an undertaking. The responsibility of the machine-age poet is to "absorb the machine, i.e., *acclimatize* it," for machinery cannot "act creatively in our lives until, like the unconscious nervous responses in our bodies, its connotations emanate from within" (261–62; emphasis in the original).

25. Lloyd's erotic work in this field can be seen, with the help of an enclosed pair of special glasses, in *Harold Lloyd's Hollywood Nudes in 3-D* (2011). Most of the information in the above paragraph is derived from "3D," HaroldLloyd.com, http://www.haroldlloyd.com/cms/index.php?option=com_content&view=article&id=136:3d&catid=55:updates&Itemid=174.

Chapter 4. Becoming-Child: Harry Langdon

1. Less hostile than Lewis, Eisenstein nevertheless has his reservations about Chaplin's decision to retain in the adult "infantile features in all their undisciplined glory" on the grounds that this procedure also explains the "monstrous" reality of Hitler ("Charlie: The Kid" 264–65).

2. Also, in speaking of James Broughton's "classically comic sensibility" as manifested in a film like *Mother's Day* (1948), P. Adams Sitney asserts that the "childlike man is Broughton's favorite metaphor" and then quotes the filmmaker's notes on the film: "I deliberately used adults acting as children, to evoke the sense of projecting oneself as an adult back into to memory, to suggest the impossible borderline between when one is child and when one is grown-up" (*Visionary Film* 54–55). See as well the section titled "'Like a Playful Child': The Anarchistic Comedy" in Henry Jenkins's *What Made Pistachio Nuts?* (144–47), and the chapters on Keaton and Lloyd, titled the "Most Memorable as the Eternal Juvenile" [Dale, *Slapstick* 60]) and "Junior" respectively, in Alan Dale's *Slapstick Is a Man in Trouble.*

3. See also Deleuze and Guattari, *A Thousand Plateaus* (233–309).

4. Langdon's reputation has not yet benefited from the revived interest in silent screen comedy, although it is generally acknowledged that he remains the primary

precursor of actor Paul Reuben's Pee Wee Herman persona. Deleuze mentions Langdon in passing in *Cinema 1* as "the affection-image in a purer state than it is actualized in any other matter or milieu" (199). His point seems to be that Langdon's appearance on screen corresponds to a state of sheer submissive consciousness without the capacity for action in the world.

5. See also Durgnat: "His [Langdon's] gestures, vague yet clipped, brightly hopeful yet squidgily inept, sketch, vividly, a baby attitude untranslatable into any adult code, a strange condition of being pampered and lost, expectant and malicious" (91); and Mast (165–78).

6. Kerr relies on linguistic analogies to account for Langdon's novelty within the tradition of silent comedy. To the extent that by the 1930s audiences had become familiar with the "grammar" of the film genre, Langdon functioned "as a comma," as a reflexive pause in a form conventionally devoted to acceleration. Consequently, only those with sufficient spectatorial competence can appreciate his singularity. "Langdon's special position as a piece of not quite necessary punctuation inserted into a long-since memorized sentence means that he remains, today, dependent on our memory of the sentence" (264–65).

7. For a cognate exploration of the process of becoming woman, see Langdon's 1929 film, *The Chaser*. There, Langdon is an irresponsible husband whom the courts sentence, in a "freak decision," to be "deprived of all privileges of manhood" and who must therefore "take his wife's place in the kitchen." Although the character wears a skirt, it is less transvestitism that is at stake than it is an entry into a zone of indiscernibility between man and woman. Langdon does not resemble a woman (in contrast to Tony Curtis in *Some Like it Hot)*, yet he nevertheless receives (to his dismay) the amorous attentions of a bill collector and the iceman. When he finally submits to the milkman's kiss, he is indicating his acceptance of this unusual metamorphosis.

8. Noel Burch traces "the blossoming of the Institutional Mode of Representation" to around 1910. He defines this mode as ideologically grounded in the aspiration to recreate reality, to realize "a perfect illusion of the perceptual world" (6–7).

9. Langdon's second short for Sennett, *Smile Please* (1924), also disobeys the laws of gravity. While chasing a runaway horse, an automobile follows the animal's lead, jumping over any obstacles in its path.

10. The title of Philip Roth's 1971 satire of the Nixon administration, *Our Gang*, suggests the endurance of the Little Rascals in the memory of at least one American black humorist.

11. Just as "the adult is captured in a childhood block without ceasing to be an adult [. . .] the child can be caught up in an adult block without ceasing to be a child" (Deleuze and Guattari, *Kafka* 79).

12. Susan Sontag describes Mead's acting style as a result of his having given himself, as Harpo Marx, Langdon, and Keaton did before him, "to some bizarre autistic fantasy," an appealing type of behavior, albeit one that is "extremely rare after the age of four" (157–58). See also Sargeant (71–72).

13. For more on Benjamin and children, see Buck-Morss, *Dialectics of Seeing* (262–79).

14. In the audio commentary for the DVD version of *Three's a Crowd*, film historian David Kalat mentions that Beckett greatly admired Langdon's work and conceived *Film* with the latter in mind. Since Langdon was dead by the time Beckett was ready to shoot it, he hired Keaton instead.

15. Oscar Metenier, the founder of the Grand Guignol, reportedly named his theater of humorously exaggerated, sensationalist violence and over-the-top madness after "the Punch and Judy puppet character from Lyons, which had become a generic name for all puppet entertainments" (M. Gordon, *Grand Guignol* 14).

16. Many film historians have explored Dahlberg's sense that Bergson's ideas are applicable to the practice of slapstick cinema; see Durgnat (70–71); Mast (50–52); and especially Winokur 99–106). Langdon himself defined his technique in Bergsonian terms. In "The Serious Side of Comedy Making" (1927), he asserted that "systematic absentmindedness is the most comical thing imaginable [...] the four greatest stimuli to laughter are rigidity, automatism, absentmindedness, and unsociability." Quoted in Urish, "The Case for Harry Langdon" (157).

17. Hal Foster is commenting on surrealism's uncanny image repertoire (which includes the mannequin, the automaton, the wax figure, and the doll). Benjamin Buchloh interprets such figurations in European painting in the 1920s as "self-pitying expressions of artistic impotence" (118).

18. Burroughs declared in "Les Politiques de l'écriture" (1975), "I situate myself clearly in the picaresque tradition, a tradition which includes Louis-Ferdinand Céline's *Journey to the End of the Night*." Translated and quoted in Kaplan and Roussin, "Céline's Modernity" (437). Kaplan and Roussin add in the introduction to the essay collection *Céline, USA*: "Through figures like Jack Kerouac, Kenneth Rexroth, William S. Burroughs, and Allen Ginsberg, Céline is tied to a vibrant postwar American avant-garde" (200); see also Ostrovsky (20–24).

19. On the relationship between the American and the French writer, see Dickstein, "Sea Change" (210–12); and Ibarguen, "Céline, Miller, and the American Canon" (489–505).

20. On the situation of West's *Miss Lonelyhearts* vis-à-vis "the vernacular tradition of slapstick comedy," see Nieland (195–218).

21. On the basis of Flaig's excellent essay "Brecht, Chaplin and the Comic Inheritance of Marxism," one may consider the German dramatist to have been another important European predecessor to the post–WW II generation of slapstick modernists in the United States (39–58).

Chapter 5. The Emergence of Slapstick Modernism

1. See also Paraskeva (224).

2. See also Frohock (245). Céline mentions Chaplin innocuously in *Castle to Castle* (1957); however, the references to Chaplin in *Bagatelle Pour Une Massacre* (usually

in the context of a hysterical diatribe against the Jewish conspiracy in Hollywood and once in conjunction with the Marx Brothers) are by no means favorable.

3. In "Caesura of the Speculative," Philippe Lacoue-Labarthe wonders whether Aristotle's doctrine of catharsis "furnished the scheme which is the matrix of dialectical thought," whether the dialectic of Absolute Idealism "were the echo, or the reason, of a ritual" (214, 209). In "On Catharsis, or Resolution," Kenneth Burke mentions but chooses not to pursue "the overlapping relationship between *dramatic catharsis* and *dialectical transcendence*" (362; emphasis in the original).

4. According to Jonathan Lear, the only evidence for interpreting catharsis as an expelling or getting "rid of unhealthily pent-up emotions or noxious emotional elements" is in Aristotle's comments in the *Politics* on the cathartic effects of music rather than in the *Poetics,* where the object is drama (316). Julia Kristeva also correlates Aristotle's aesthetic concept of "poetic catharsis," which she considers closer to "sacred incantation, with "rhythm and song" (26–31).

5. Benjamin traces the "spirit in which Céline wrote his scandalously anti-semitic pamphlet to a diary entry by Baudelaire." For the critic, the latter's "macabre humor" and provocative penchant for "*the culte of the blague*" eventually became "an integral part of Fascist propaganda" ("Paris of the Second Empire" 5; emphasis in the original). Also, in a 1937 letter to Gerhard Scholem, Benjamin stated his intention to "analyze the peculiar figure of medical nihilism in literature: Benn, Céline, Jung" (*Correspondence* 540, 558).

6. On this topic, see Solomon (170–88).

7. Courtial was modeled on Hendry de Graffigny; see Kaplan (117–18).

8. In this section of the book the novelist indicates his awareness of the slapstick tradition—at least in one of its native variants—when he has Courtial advise his young protégé to hit the Boulevards as if he were "Max Linder" (Céline, *Death* 369). Linder was an important influence on Chaplin early in his career. For an in-depth interpretation of the two-reel Keaton comedy mentioned above, see Trahair (35–57).

9. In France in the 1960s, Jean-Luc Godard's films would take aspects of this motion picture tradition back from the modernist writer; see especially *Pierrot le Fou* (1965), in which a character named Ferdinand reads aloud a lengthy passage from *Guignol's Band.* Godard dedicated his first film, *Une histoire de l'eau* (1961; made in collaboration with François Truffaut), to Mack Sennett. The most splendid incarnations of slapstick modernism in postwar French cinema are the films of Jacques Tati and his protégé Pierre Etaix.

10. In the 1930s Miller also turned to modern technology to trope literary power. In *Tropic of Cancer* he figures his task as putting "the live wire of sex right between the legs," as hitching "one's dynamo to the tenderest parts" (249–50). Antonin Artaud's therapeutically oriented enthusiasm in the Depression era, both for the Marx Brothers and for a poetry that, in catering to violent satisfactions and appealing to the nerves and heart, would exploit language's "possibilities of producing physical shock," is equally well known (esp. 41–46, and 81–85). A variant of this aesthetic can

be found in Ginsberg: "The interesting thing would be to know if certain combinations of words and rhythms actually had an electrochemical reaction on the body. [. . .] There's a statement by Artaud on that subject, that certain music when introduced into the nervous system changes the molecular composition of the nerve cells" (*Writers at Work* 226).

11. Céline's reflexive analogy converts a mechanized force that in the previous century was held responsible for causing nervous disorders into an emblem of literary power. A literal agent of accidental trauma, the railway is reconfigured as a source of aesthetic energy. See Schivelbusch (124–70).

12. As Deleuze put it elsewhere, in *Guignol's Band* the writer "achieves the ultimate aim: exclamatory sentences and suspensions that do away with all syntax" because the shattering of sentence structure allows its meanings to fall into the void ("He Stuttered" 112).

13. Kaplan also considers Céline a "practitioner of 'social medicine,'" but places him in the tradition of the "neighborhood doctor" who listens sympathetically to his patients as they diagnose and complain "about illness" (110).

14. The compatibility between Gombrowicz's literary preoccupations and Deleuze and Guattari's philosophical concerns has not gone unnoticed. See Goddard (esp. 32–64).

Theoretical Interlude

1. On the distinction between this version and the canonical version in *Illuminations*, see Miriam Hansen, "Benjamin and Cinema"; "Of Mice and Ducks"; and "Room-for-Play." My explication remains indebted to these articles, as well as to Hansen's synthesis of them in the posthumously published *Cinema and Experience* (75–204). Also valuable is Leslie (80–122).

2. It may seem that a leap in logic occurs here insofar as Benjamin moves from the declaration that second technology aims "at an interplay between nature and humanity" to a discussion of how it helps resolve the central predicament of capitalist modernity (collective subordination to the apparatus). This shift seems less abrupt if "nature" in the citation is understood as what Georg Lukacs termed "second nature," the problems of which, according to Benjamin in "A Different Utopian Will," have to do with "social and technological" matters (134).

3. Conversely, Adorno condemns play as designating "the regressive, archaic element of art; secretly in complicity with fate and the mythical" and therefore tied to repetition and discipline in ways that make it "the afterimage of unfree labor" (*Aesthetic Theory* 318).

4. I. A. Richards had speculated a decade earlier on "the immense practical utility of most forms of play," which he considered "the preparatory organization and development of impulses." However, in contrast to Benjamin, Richards emphatically denies such anticipatory functions to "The Cinema" (231–34).

5. Benjamin had been thinking about this matter for quite some time. As early as 1922–1923, in a fragmentary essay titled "Outline of the Psychophysical Problem," he had argued, from a more theological standpoint, "In addition to the totality of its living members, humanity is able partly to draw nature, the nonliving, plant, and animal into this life of the body of mankind, and thereby into this annihilation and fulfillment. It can do this by virtue of the technology in which the unity of its life is formed. Everything that subserves humanity's happiness may be counted part of its life, its limbs" (395).

6. As Miriam Hansen ("Benjamin and Cinema" 315–16) notes, J. Laplanche and J. B. Pontalis define innervation as a physiological process in which "energy is transported to a particular part of the body where it brings about motor or sensory phenomena."

7. Also pertinent is Benjamin's "To the Planetarium," in *One-Way Street*, where he asserts, "In technology, a *physis* is being organized through which mankind's contact with the cosmos takes a new and different form from that which it had in nations and families" (487).

8. In a discussion of Jules Romain's 1911 essay, "The Crowd at the Cinematograph," Pasi Valiaho argues that early cinema sought to create "its own sphere of rhythmic being," one requiring "a mode of assimilation in experience in which our corporeal rhythms become those of the silver screen" (58). For him, individuals are invisibly shaped in accordance with the technical media insofar as the kinetic forces and affects figured on screen are converted through vision "into various kinds of muscular tensions and pressures" (74).

9. On the politicized preoccupation within Anglo-American modernism with the (unconscious) collective mind as opposed to the body of the masses, see Tratner (*Modernism and Mass Politics* 1–76); and Shail (146–94).

10. Parker Tyler notes that Karl, the protagonist of "Kafka's "The Stoker" (1913), finds the United States to be a land of "phantasmal mechanisms." Given that "derivation" is out of the question, Tyler takes this is as evidence of the "mutually illuminating sensibilities" of Chaplin and the modernist writer (300–304). On Chaplin and Kafka, see also Weitzman (111–15).

11. Noting that in "German, the word *Motiv* connotes both the English 'motive' [as causal motivating ground] and 'motif,'" Ranier Nägele points to an etymological justification for the welding together in Benjamin's thought of a concern with formal traits and functional aims (122–24).

12. Elsewhere, Benjamin associates the notion of shock as a poetic principle with "the strident laughter characteristic" of Baudelaire's "The Essence of Laughter" (*Arcades Project* 325).

13. Michael North takes this question as the point of departure for his inquiry in *Machine-Age Comedy*. Garrett Stewart mistakenly identifies these sentences as an indirect commentary on *Modern Times* when in fact the fragment containing them predates the release of the film (*Between Film and Screen* 312). For a valuable approach (one quite different from mine) to the Benjamin/Chaplin intersection, see Tom Mc-

Call (74–94), who aptly notes there is "a critical levity running above gravity-laden tragedic critique" in Benjamin's oeuvre.

14. See also Benjamin's preparatory studies for his book on the poet. "Modernity finally became a role which perhaps only Baudelaire himself could fill. A tragic role, in which the dilettante [. . .] often cut a comical figure [. . .] he had about him something of the mime who apes the 'poet' before an audience and society which no longer need a real poet, and which grant him only the latitude of mimicry" ("Central Park" 166).

15. Drawing on Roger Callois and Andre Bazin (and Wyndham Lewis), David Trotter utilizes the notion of "hypermimesis" to produce a very different account of Chaplin's historical significance (as a kind of prefiguration of Andy Warhol). For Trotter, the mechanized movements of the Tramp's body amount to an "enactment and critique" of the compulsion to imitate, of the drive "of a person who wants to behave like a machine" (192, 198). For a valuably wide-ranging analysis of mimesis in relation to Chaplin as a historical icon, especially as this pertains to theories of identity, see Bean.

16. The Chaplin reference appears in neither the second nor the third version of the essay.

Chapter 6. The Rise of Slapstick Modernism; or, the Birth of the Uncool

1. In the 1930s Zukofsky had written an appreciative review of *Modern Times*, arguing against the "half-baked idea" that the film simply shows that "humanity has become mechanized by civilization." Instead, the critic asserts, we observe in Chaplin's oeuvre "an intelligence working itself out in the concrete," an "inventive existence interacting with other existences in all its ramifications: sight, hearing, muscular movement, coordination of all the senses acting on the surrounding world and rendering it laughably intelligent" (53–54).

2. Stan Brakhage describes Broughton's cinematic art as an attempt "to make a bridge between the black humor of surrealism and Freudian humor, all the way to the early comedies of Chaplin, Keaton, and Sennett" (75–76).

3. Agee's *The Tramp's New World* is reproduced in Wranovics (159–238). In 1962 Allen Ginsberg and Peter Orlovsky came up with the same plan, providing their ostensible correspondent ("Our Dear Friend Charles") in the aforementioned collaborative letter with a short synopsis of the "great picture" they felt he could make "about the Atom Bomb" (441–42); see also Kane (112).

4. The opening scene of his *A Death in the Family* recapitulates the experience of viewing an early Chaplin short with his father. In the mid-1990s, Henry Jenkins and Kristine Karnick seized on this fond recollection as an example of the nostalgic attitude that historical scholarship must forego in order to reconstruct and interpret the past correctly (1–2).

5. In a 1963 letter, Flannery O'Connor wrote: "The other day I postponed my work an hour to look at W. C. Fields in *Never Give a Sucker an Even Break*. This indicates the measure of my respect for Mr. Fields. [. . .] I think I might have written a picture that would be good for him" (213). O'Connor told James Tate she thought Fields was "the funniest man ever created," though she "did not like Chaplin," finding him "quite unfunny and bereft of talent" (Tate 67). "Reading Flannery O'Connor," her friend Robert Fitzgerald once wrote, "is sometimes like watching a perplexing slapstick" (36).

6. Five years later, in the notes to his musical comedy, *Simply Heavenly*, Langston Hughes described his resilient leading man (Jesse B. Simple) as "a Chaplinesque character" (4). The fictive figure first appeared in 1942 in a column Hughes was writing for the *Chicago Defender*.

7. For an antithetical take on the Beats, see Liu (130–38).

8. On the Three Stooges' refusal of the signified in favor of the signifier, see Brunette; and Chamberlain.

9. See T. Miller (46–62).

10. For a Bakhtinian reading of the passage, see Sterritt (83–98). Kerouac supplies "further Three Stooges adventures" via the character Morely (based on Gary Snyder) in *Dharma Bums* (41).

11. Ginsberg composed this poem after watching the first day's shooting of Beckett's *Film* on location in Brooklyn; see Meade (295).

12. Also in 1959 the New York School poet Kenneth Koch published *Ko; or, A Season on Earth*, a long poem the fast-paced action of which he subsequently explained in an interview as having derived from "certain Mack Sennett comedies. I loved that quality." David Shapiro, "A Conversation with Kenneth Koch," *Jacket*, http://jacketmagazine.com/15/koch-shapiro.html.

13. Speaking of Burroughs's humor, Mary McCarthy, after comparing him to a vaudeville comedian, states that at their best his skits "rise to a frenzy," as if one were watching a "Marx Brothers" movie. She adds that the book delivers "not just messages" but also "prescriptions," possible remedies for widespread conditions of ill health (457–61). Tony Tanner avers that *Naked Lunch* contains "slapstick scenes from some dark carnival" (114).

14. See the inside cover of Slade's *Thomas Pynchon*.

15. Elsewhere in the novel a German cocaine dealer figures the drug trade in Berlin as "a gigantic Laurel and Hardy film, silent, silent," a shortage of permanganate forcing even friends to burn one another, to "*push a pie*" in each other's faces (Pynchon, *Gravity's Rainbow* 375; emphasis in the original). Conversely, Gaddis provides no such internal indications that the comic genius he displays in *The Recognitions* and *J.R.* was indebted to the tradition of slapstick film. The same goes for John Barth, though reflexive analogies in *The Floating Opera* (1956) and *Lost in the Funhouse* (1968) root his fictive performances in forms of American popular entertainment: blackface minstrelsy and amusement park attractions respectively.

16. Roth has "also mentioned as models for his 'broadly comic' book the antics of Charlie Chaplin, Laurel and Hardy [. . .] Abbott and Costello, and the Three Stooges" (Blair and Hill 475).

17. In *A Night at the Movies, or, You Must Remember This* (1987) Coover revisits slapstick, verbally recreating an imaginary Chaplin film and taking Keaton's *Sherlock Jr.* as the touchstone for "The Phantom of the Movie Palace." The Cuban modernist G. Cabrera Infante's *Three Triste Tigres* (1966) suggests the global or transnational scope of the cultural phenomenon under investigation. "Nothing," Infante once declared, "was closer to my purpose in *TTT* than the philosophy of life expressed by the Marx Brothers" (Guilbert 411). See also the work of the Czechoslovakian writer Bohumil Hrabal, which inspired, among other Czech New Wave directors, Vera Chytilova, whose 1966 film, *Daisies,* stands as a feminist appropriation of elements of the predominantly (but not exclusively) male tradition of American slapstick; on preceding exceptions to this rule, see "Girl Heroes" in Dale (92–131); and Bilton (137–54). In his introduction to Hrabal's *The Little Town Where Time Stood Still* (1973), Joshua Cohen informs the reader, "You're supposed to laugh, you're supposed to read fast—like this is all just [. . .] a fast-forwarded slapstick sequence" (xii).

18. Marie Menken was a pivotal influence on Mekas in this regard; see in particular her short film *Go! Go! Go!* (1962–1964).

19. Kerouac is imitating the phlegmatic speaking style of Major Hoople, a character in the newspaper cartoon strip *Our Boarding House,* created by Gene Ahern in 1921.

20. Noting the prevalence of chatter around the time that Stein composed *Tender Buttons,* Richard Bridgman asserts that reading her "is rather like listening to an interminable tape recording made secretly in a household" (quoted in Schmitz 173).

21. Orr's endeavor corresponds to the "minoration" that Deleuze detects in Keaton's burlesque, the latter's dream of taking "the biggest machine in the world and making it work with the tiniest elements, thus converting it for the use of each one of us, making it the property of everyone" (*Cinema 1* 176–77).

22. On the persistence into the 1980s of the "neomodernist aspirations" the Stooges helped initiate, see Reynolds: "The entire postpunk period looks like an attempt to replay virtually every major modernist theme and technique via the medium of pop music" (2).

23. Ron Asheton (the group's guitar player) recalls going to visit Larry Fine at a rest home. "For me, it was my honor to hang out with one of my idols. I always liked Moe the best. I always fancied myself as Moe when I was a kid pretending to be Stooges, but a chance to be with Larry—it was wonderful." McNeil and McCain 441–42. Incidentally, the Three Stooges appear as a trio of nightclub musicians in the short film *Disorder in the Court* (1936).

24. These quotes are taken from *The Stooges: TV Eye* and "The Wild Side," volume 4 of *Rock and Roll*); see also Palmer (272).

25. John Sinclair, manager of the MC5, praised one of their 1967 shows as "a beautiful demonstration of the principles of high-energy performance: as the performer puts

out more the energy level of the audience is raised and they give back more energy to the performers, who are moved onto a higher energy level which is transmitted to the audience and sent back, etc. until everything is totally frenzied" (quoted in Bowe, *MC5*). Like the Stooges, the Michigan-based MC5 released their first album on Elektra.

26. See also Miriam Hansen ("Benjamin and Cinema" 317).

27. This is from Bardamu's description in *Journey to the End of the Night* of his co-workers during his brief stint at Ford's plant (Céline 195). "You give in to the noise," he remarks. "At the machines you let yourself go" (194).

28. Throughout "Art as Device," Shklovsky contests Herbert Spencer's notion (in *Philosophy of Style*) that art contributes to the tendency to "economize [. . .] energies."

29. A list of other musically inclined slapstick modernists would start with Bob Dylan. In a 1961 interview he stated, "If I'm on stage, my idol [, . . .] the one that's running through my head all the time, is Charlie Chaplin" (Wilentz 304). Dylan titled his 2006 album *Modern Times*. Other pertinent figures would include Frank Zappa; Captain Beefheart; Jonathan Richman and the Modern Lovers ("When Harpo Played his Harp"); the Ramones; David Byrne (the Harold Lloyd of the CBGB scene, who after leaving the Talking Heads used sentences from Kerouac's "Origins of the Beat Generation" as the lyrics of "It Goes Back"); Devo; the Beastie Boys, who once planned to star in a feature-length motion picture titled "Scared Stupid," modeled on Abbot and Costello's films; De La Soul; and the Minutemen, who pretend to be the Three Stooges in the video for their version of the war protest song "Ack Ack Ack." Also, in the Beatles' *Hard Day's Night* (1964) Richard Lester pays tribute to the Keystone tradition in the closing sequence, in which Ringo gets lost, and in his earlier short film, *The Running Jumping & Standing Still Film* (1959). See also the experimental comedy troupe Firesign Theatre, one of whose late 1960s recordings mingles a recitation of *Ulysses* with a W. C. Fields impersonation.

30. See also Cooper.

31. From Adorno's *The Philosophy of Modern Music* (1941); quoted in Shapiro (132).

Works Cited

Adorno, Theodor W. *Aesthetic Theory*. Minneapolis: U of Minnesota P, 1997.

———. "Chaplin Times Two." *The Essential Chaplin: Perspectives on the Life and Art of the Great Comedian*. Chicago: Ivan R. Dee, 2006. 267–72.

———. "On Jazz." *Discourse* 12.1 (1989–1990): 45–69.

Adorno, Theodor W., and Max Horkheimer. *The Dialectic of Enlightenment*. Trans. John Cummings. New York: Continuum, 1944.

Agee, James. "Comedy's Greatest Era." *Agee on Film: Reviews and Comments*. Boston: Beacon, 1958. 2–19.

———. *Let Us Now Praise Famous Men*. Boston: Houghton Mifflin, 1941.

———. *The Tramp's New World*. Wranovics, 159–238.

All Night Long. Dir. Harry Edwards.1924. All Day Entertainment, 2007. DVD.

Anderson, Nels, and Eduard C. Lindeman. *Urban Sociology*. New York: Alfred A. Knopf, 1928.

Appel, Alfred, Jr. *Nabokov's Dark Cinema*. New York: Oxford UP, 1974.

Artaud, Antonin. *The Theater and Its Double*. Trans. Mary Caroline Richards. New York: Grove Press, 1958.

Aumont, Jacques. *Montage Eisenstein*. Trans. Lee Hildreth, Constance Penley, and Andrew Ross. Bloomington: Indiana UP, 1987.

Axelrod, Jeremiah. *Inventing Autopia: Dreams and Visions of the Modern Metropolis in Jazz Age Los Angeles*. Berkeley: U of California P, 2009.

Baker, Elliott. *A Fine Madness*. New York: Signet, 1964.

Baldwin, Neil. *All Gentleness: William Carlos Williams the Doctor-Poet*. New York: Atheneum, 1984.

Balint, Michael. *Thrills and Regressions*. New York: International Universities Press, 1959.

Bangs, Lester. "Iggy Pop: Blowtorch in Bondage." *Psychotic Reactions*, 205–208.

———. "Of Pop and Pies and Fun: A Program for Mass Liberation in the Form of a Stooges Review; or, Who's the Fool?" *Psychotic Reactions*, 31–52.

———. *Psychotic Reactions and Carburetor Dung.* London: Serpent's Tail, 1996.

Banta, Martha. *Taylored Lives: Narrative Productions in the Age of Taylor, Veblen, and Ford.* Chicago: U of Chicago P, 1993.

Barker, Jennifer M. *The Tactile Eye: Touch and the Cinematic Experience.* Berkeley: U of California P, 2009.

Barth, John. *The Floating Opera and The End of the Road.* New York: Anchor Books, 1997.

———. *Lost in the Funhouse: Fiction for Print, Tape, Live Voice.* New York: Anchor Books, 1988.

Bataille, Georges. *The Accursed Share: An Essay on General Economy. Vol. 1. Consumption.* Trans. Robert Hurley. New York: Zone, 1991.

———. "The Notion of Expenditure." 1933. *Visions of Excess: Selected Writings, 1927–1939.* Trans. Allan Stoekl, with Carl R. Lovitt and Donald M. Leslie Jr. Minneapolis: U of Minnesota P, 1991.

———. "Sacrifice." *October* 36 (Spring 1986): 61–74.

Bean, Jennifer. "The Art of Imitation: The Originality of Charlie Chaplin and Other Moving-Image Myths." Paulus and King, 236–61.

Beckman, Karen. *Crash: Cinema and the Politics of Speed and Stasis.* Durham, NC: Duke UP, 2010.

Beller, Jonathan. *The Cinematic Mode of Production: Attention Economy and the Society of the Spectacle.* Lebanon, NH: UP of New England, 2006.

Benjamin, Walter. *The Arcades Project.* Trans. Howard Eiland and Kevin McLaughlin. Cambridge, MA: Belknap Press of Harvard University, 1999.

———. "Central Park." *Selected Writings 4*: 161–99.

———. "Chaplin in Retrospect." *Selected Writings 2*: 222–24.

———. *The Correspondence of Walter Benjamin, 1910–1940.* Chicago: U of Chicago P, 1994.

———. "A Different Utopian Will." *Selected Writings 3*: 134–36.

———. "The Formula in Which the Dialectical Structure of Film Finds Expression." *Selected Writings 3*: 94–95.

———. "Old Toys." 1928. *Selected Writings 2*: 98–102.

———. *One-Way Street. Selected Writings 1*: 444–88.

———. "On Some Motifs in Baudelaire." 1939. *Selected Writings 4*: 313–55.

———. "Outline of the Psychophysical Problem." *Selected Writings 1*: 393–401.

———. "The Paris of the Second Empire in Baudelaire." *Selected Writings 4*: 3–92.

———. "Program for a Proletarian Children's Theatre." *Selected Writings 2*: 201–206.

———. "Reply to Oscar A. H. Schmitz." *Selected Writings 2*: 16–19.

———. *Selected Writings.* Vol. 1, *1913–1926.* Cambridge, MA: Belknap Press of Harvard University, 1996.

———. *Selected Writings.* Vol. 2, *1927–1934.* Cambridge, MA: Belknap Press of Harvard University, 1999.

———. *Selected Writings.* Vol. 3, *1935–1938.* Cambridge, MA: Belknap Press of Harvard University, 2002.

———. *Selected Writings.* Vol. 4, *1938–1940.* Cambridge, MA: Belknap Press of Harvard University, 2003.

———. "Surrealism: The Last Snapshot of the European Intelligentsia." 1929. *Selected Writings 2*: 207–21.

———. "Toys and Play." 1928. *Selected Writings 2*: 117–21.

———. "The Work of Art in the Age of Its Technological Reproducibility" (1st Version). Trans. Michael Jennings. *Grey Room* 39 (Spring 2010): 11–37.

———. "The Work of Art in the Age of Its Technological Reproducibility (2nd Version; 1936)." *Selected Writings 3*: 101–133.

Bilton, Alan. *Silent Film Comedy and American Culture.* New York: Palgrave Macmillan, 2013.

Blackmur, R. P. "New Thresholds, New Anatomies: Notes on a Text of Hart Crane." *Form and Value in Modern Poetry.* New York: Anchor Books, 1967. 269–85.

Blair, Walter, and Hamlin Hill. *American Humor: From Poor Richard's Almanac to Doonesbury.* New York: Oxford UP, 1978.

Boone, April. "William Carlos Williams's *The Great American Novel*: Flamboyance and the Beginning of Art." *William Carlos Williams Review* 26.1 (2006): 1–25.

Bordwell, David. *The Cinema of Eisenstein.* Cambridge, MA: Harvard UP, 1993.

Bornstein, George. "Pound and the Making of Modernism." *The Cambridge Companion to Ezra Pound.* New York: Cambridge UP, 1999. 22–42.

Bottoms, Stephen. Introduction to *The Cambridge Companion to Edward Albee.* New York: Cambridge UP, 2005. 1–15.

Bowe, Brian J. Liner notes to *MC5 Kick Out the Jams.* Wienerworld, Ltd., 2005. DVD.

Bowser, Eileen. "Mack Sennett vs. Henry Ford." Paulus and King, 107–113.

Brakhage, Stan. *Film at Wit's End.* New York: McPherson and Company, 1989.

Brautigan, Richard. *Trout Fishing in America.* Boston: Houghton Mifflin, 1989.

Breton, Andre. "Lightning Rod." *Anthology of Black Humor.* San Francisco: City Lights, 1997. xiii-xix.

Brewster, Arthur Judson, and Herbert Hall Palmer. *Introduction to Advertising.* Chicago: A. W. Shaw, 1924.

Brunette, Peter. "The Three Stooges and the (Anti-)Narrative of Violence: De(con)structive Comedy." *Comedy/Cinema/Theory.* Ed. Peter Horton. Berkeley: U of California P, 1991. 174–87.

Buchloh, Benjamin H. D. "Figures of Authority, Ciphers of Regression: Notes on the Return of Representation in European Painting." *Art after Modernism: Rethinking Representation.* New York: New Museum of Contemporary Art, 1984. 107–36.

Buck-Morss, Susan. "Aesthetics and Anaesthetics: Walter Benjamin's Artwork Essay Reconsidered." *October* 62 (Fall 1992): 3–41.

———. *The Dialectics of Seeing: Walter Benjamin and the Arcades Project.* Cambridge: MIT Press, 1991.

Burch, Noel. *Life to Those Shadows*. Trans. Ben Brewster. Berkeley: U of California P, 1990.

Burke, Kenneth. "On Catharsis, or Resolution." *Kenyon Review* 21.3 (1959): 337–75.

Burroughs, William. *Naked Lunch*. New York: Grove Press, 2001.

Caillois, Roger. *Man, Play, and Games*. Trans. Meyer Barash. New York: Free Press of Glencoe, 1961.

Carr, Virginia. *Dos Passos: A Life*. Evanston, IL: Northwestern UP, 2004.

Céline, Louis-Ferdinand. *Conversations with Professor Y*. Trans. Stanford Luce. 1955. Normal, IL: Dalkey Archive Press, 2006.

———. *Death on the Installment Plan*. Trans. Ralph Manheim. 1936. New York: New Directions, 1966.

———. *Guignol's Band*. Trans. Bernard Frechtman and Jack T. Nile. 1944. New York: New Directions, 1954.

———. *Journey to the End of the Night*. Trans. Ralph Manheim. 1932. New York: New Directions, 2006.

Chamberlain, Kathleen. "The Three Stooges and the *Commedia dell' Arte*." *The Film Comedy Reader*. Ed. Gregg Rickman. New York: Limelight Editions, 2001. 53–59.

Charney, Leo, and Vanessa R. Schwartz, eds. *Cinema and the Invention of Modern Life*. Berkeley: University of California Press, 1995.

The Chaser. Dir. Harry Langdon. 1928. Kino International, 2008. DVD.

Christgau, Robert. "The New York Dolls." *Stranded: Rock and Roll for a Desert Island*. New York: Da Capo, 2007. 132–47.

Cine-Eye (Kino Eye). Dir. Dziga Vertov. 1924. Flicker Alley, 2015. Blu-Ray.

Clifford, James. *The Predicament of Culture: Twentieth-Century Ethnography, Literature, and Art*. Cambridge, MA: Harvard UP, 1988.

Coffman, Stanley K. *Imagism: A Chapter for the History of Modern Poetry*. New York: Octagon Books, 1972.

———. Cohen, Joshua. Introduction to *The Little Town Where Time Stood Still*. By Bohumil Hrabal. New York: New York Review Books, 2015. xii–xxii.

Cohen, Keith. *Film and Fiction: The Dynamics of Exchange*. New Haven, CT: Yale UP, 1979.

Cooper, Harry. "On *Über Jazz:* Replaying Adorno with the Grain." *October* 75 (Winter 1996): 99–133.

Coover, Robert. *A Night at the Movies; or, You Must Remember This*. 1987. Normal, IL: Dalkey Archive Press, 1997.

———. *The Public Burning*. New York: Viking Press, 1977.

Corso, Gregory. "Clown." *Mindfield: New and Selected Poems*. New York: Thunder's Mouth, 1989. 76–84.

Crane, Hart. "Chaplinesque." *Complete Poems*, 11.

———. *The Complete Poems and Selected Letters and Prose of Hart Crane*. New York: Anchor, 1966.

———. "Modern Poetry." *Complete Poems*, 260–63.

Crary, Jonathan. *Suspensions of Perception: Attention, Spectacle, and Modern Culture.* Cambridge: MIT Press, 1999.

———, ed., with Sanford Kwinter. *Incorporations*. New York: Zone, 1992.

Cummings, E. E. "The Adult, the Artist, and the Circus." *Another E. E. Cummings.* Ed. Richard Kostelanetz. New York: Liveright, 1998. 252–256.

———. "Coney Island." *Another E. E. Cummings*, 257–60.

Dahlberg, Edward. "Ariel in Caliban." *Samuel Beckett's Wake and Other Collected Prose.* Elmwood, IL: Dalkey Archive Press, 1989. 3–8.

———. *Bottom Dogs*. 1929. New York: Simon and Schuster, 1976.

———. *From Flushing to Calvary*. New York: Harcourt Brace, 1932.

Dale, Alan. *Slapstick Is a Man in Trouble: Slapstick in American Movies.* Minneapolis: U of Minnesota P, 2000.

Dao, James. "Simulators Prepare Soldiers for Explosions of War." *New York Times*, January 22, 2010. www.nytimes.com/2010/01/23/us/23simulator.html.

Dardis, Tom. *Harold Lloyd: The Man on the Clock.* New York: Viking, 1983.

Deleuze, Gilles. *Cinema 1: The Movement Image.* Trans. Hugh Tomlinson and Barbara Habberjam. Minneapolis: U of Minnesota P, 1986.

———. *Cinema 2: The Time Image.* Trans. Hugh Tomlinson and Robert Galeta. Minneapolis: U of Minnesota P, 1989.

———. "He Stuttered." *Essays: Critical and Clinical.* Trans. Daniel W. Smith and Michael A. Greco. Minneapolis: U of Minnesota P, 1997. 107–114.

———. *The Logic of Sense.* Trans. Mark Lester. New York: Columbia UP, 1990.

Deleuze, Gilles, and Félix Guattari. *Kafka: Toward a Minor Literature.* Trans. Dana Polan. Minneapolis: U of Minnesota P, 1986.

———. *A Thousand Plateaus.* Trans. Brian Massumi. Minneapolis: U of Minnesota, 1987.

Dettmar, Kevin J., and Stephen Watt, eds. *Marketing Modernism: Self-Promotion, Canonization, and Rereading.* Ann Arbor: U of Michigan P, 1996.

Dick, Bruce, and Amritjit Singh, eds. *Conversations with Ishmael Reed.* Jackson: UP of Mississippi, 1995.

Dickstein, Morris. *Gates of Eden: American Culture in the Sixties.* New York: Basic Books, 1977.

———. "Sea Change: Céline and the Problem of Cultural Transmission." Kaplan and Roussin, *Céline, USA*, 205–24.

Dixon, Bryony. "The Good Thieves: On the Origins of Situation Comedy in the British Music Hall." Paulus and King, 21–36.

Dogs of War. Dir. Robert F. McGowan. Prod. and story by Hal Roach. 1923. Kino Video, 1998. VHS.

Dos Passos, John. "Did the New Playwright's Theatre Fail?" *Major Nonfictional Prose*, 118–20.

———. Introduction to *Three Soldiers*. *Major Nonfictional Prose*, 146–48.

———. "Is the 'Realistic' Theatre Obsolete? Many Theatrical Conventions Have Been Shattered by Lawson's *Processional*." 1925. *Major Nonfictional Prose*, 75–78.

———. *Manhattan Transfer*. 1925. Boston: Houghton Mifflin, 2000.

———. *The Major Nonfictional Prose*. Detroit: Wayne State UP, 1988.

———. "Mr. Dos Passos on *Him*." *Major Nonfictional Prose*, 110–11.

———. *U.S.A.* 1937. New York: Library of America, 1996.

Dow, William. "John Dos Passos, Blaise Cendrars, and the 'Other' Modernism." *Twentieth-Century Literature* (Fall 1996): 396–415.

Dr. Jack. Dir. Fred Newmeyer. 1922. New Line Home Video, 2005. DVD.

Duffy, Enda. *The Speed Handbook: Velocity, Pleasure, Modernism*. Durham, NC: Duke UP, 2009.

Durgnat, Raymond. *The Crazy Mirror: Hollywood Comedy and the American Image*. New York: Horizon Press, 1970.

Eisenstein, Sergei. "Bolsheviks Do Laugh (Thoughts on Soviet Comedy)." *Selected Works 3*: 68–72.

———. "Charlie: The Kid." *Selected Works 3*: 243–67.

———. "A Course in Treatment." *Film Form: Essays in Film Theory*. New York: Harcourt, 1969. 84–107.

———. "*Happiness*." *Selected Works 3*: 52–55.

———. "The Montage of Attractions." 1923. Taylor, 29–34.

———. "The Montage of Film Attractions." 1924. Taylor, 35–52.

———. "The Problem of the Materialist Approach to Form." 1925. Taylor, 53–59.

———. *Selected Works*. Vol. 3, *Writings, 1934–47*. Trans. William Powell. London: British Film Institute, 1996.

Eliot, T. S. "Dramatis Personae." *Criterion* (1923): 305–306.

Ellison, Ralph. *Invisible Man*. New York: Vintage, 1952.

Epstein, Jean. "Magnification." 1921. *French Film Theory and Criticism*. Vol. 1, *1907–1939*. Ed. Richard Abel. Princeton, NJ: Princeton UP, 1988. 235–40.

Esslin, Martin. *The Theatre of the Absurd*. New York: Vintage, 2004.

Ferlinghetti, Lawrence. "Constantly Risking Absurdity." *A Coney Island of the Mind*. New York: New Directions, 1958. 30.

Fielding, Raymond. "Hale's Tours: Ultrarealism in the Pre-1910 Motion Picture." *Film before Griffith*. Ed. John L. Fell. Berkeley: U of California P, 1983. 116–30.

Fitzgerald, Robert. "Everything That Rises Must Converge: "The Teilhardian Dimension." *Notre Dame English Journal* 2.2 (1967): 36–50.

Flaig, Paul. "Brecht, Chaplin, and the Comic Inheritance of Marxism." *Brecht/Marxism/Ethics: The Brecht Yearbook 35*. Ed. Dorothy Ostmeier and Freidemann Weidauer. Storrs, CT: International Brecht Society. 39–58.

Flink, James J. "Henry Ford and the Triumph of the Automobile." *Technology in America: A History of Individuals and Ideas*. Ed. Carroll W. Pursell Jr. Cambridge: MIT Press, 1981. 177–89.

Ford, Henry (in collaboration with Samuel Crowther). *My Life and Work*. New York: Garden City Publishing, 1922.

Ford, Hugh. *Published in Paris: A Literary Chronicle of Paris in the 1920s and 1930s.* New York: Macmillan, 1975.

Foster, Gretchen. "John Dos Passos' Use of Film Technique in *Manhattan Transfer* & *The 42nd Parallel.*" *Film Literature Quarterly* 14.3 (1986): 186–94.

Foster, Hal. *Compulsive Beauty.* Cambridge: MIT Press, 1993.

———. "Survey." *Pop.* Ed. Mark Francis. London: Phaidon, 2005. 15–41.

Frohock, W. M. "The Edge of Laughter: Some Modern Fiction and the Grotesque." *Veins of Humor.* Ed. Harry Levin. Cambridge, MA: Harvard UP, 1972. 243–54.

Gaddis, William. *J. R.* New York: Alfred A. Knopf, 1975.

———. *The Recognitions.* 1955. New York: Penguin, 1993.

Gaudreault, André. *Film and Attraction: From Kinetography to Cinema.* Trans. Timothy Bernard. Urbana: U of Illinois P, 2011.

Gibson, James J., and Lawrence E. Crooks. "A Theoretical Field-Analysis of Automobile-Driving." *American Journal of Psychology* 51.3 (1938): 453–71.

Giedion, Siegfried. *Mechanization Takes Command: A Contribution to Anonymous History.* New York: Oxford UP, 1948.

Gilbreth, Frank B. *Motion Study: A Method for Increasing the Efficiency of the Workman.* 1909; 1911. London: Routledge, 1993.

Ginsberg, Allen. *The Fall of America: Poems of These States, 1965–1971.* San Francisco: City Lights, 2001.

———. "Notes Written on Finally Recording *Howl.*" 1959. *Deliberate Prose: Selected Essays, 1952–1995.* New York: Perennial, 2000. 229–32.

———. "Today." *Allen Ginsberg: Collected Poems, 1947–1980.* New York: Harper Perennial, 1984. 345–47.

———. *Writers at Work: The Paris Interviews.* 3rd series. New York: Viking Press, 1967. 279–320.

Ginsberg, Allen, and Peter Orlovsky. "Collaboration: Letter to Charlie Chaplin." *Beat Down to Your Soul.* Ed. Ann Charters. New York: Penguin, 2001. 440–41.

Gitelman, Lisa. *Scripts, Grooves, and Writing: Representing Technology in the Edison Era.* Stanford, CA: Stanford UP, 1999.

Goddard, Michael. *Gombrowicz, Polish Modernism, and the Subversion of Form.* West Lafayette, IN: Purdue UP, 2010.

Go! Go! Go! Dir. Marie Menken. 1964. *Treasures IV: American Avant-Garde Film, 1947–1986.* Image Entertainment, 2009.

The Gold Rush. Dir. Charles Chaplin. 1925. Criterion Collection, 2012. DVD.

Goldstein, Laurence. *The American Poet at the Movies: A Critical History.* Ann Arbor: U of Michigan P, 1994.

Gombrowicz, Witold. *Ferdydurke.* Trans. Danuta Borchardt. New Haven, CT: Yale UP, 2000.

Gordon, Mel. *The Grand Guignol: Theatre of Fear and Terror.* Rev. ed. New York: Da Capo, 1997.

Gordon, Rae Beth. *Why the French Love Jerry Lewis: From Cabaret to Early Cinema.* Stanford, CA: Stanford UP, 2001.

Guilbert, Rita. *Seven Voices: Seven Latin American Writers Talk to Rita Guilbert.* Trans. Frances Partridge. New York: Alfred A. Knopf, 1973.

Gunning, Tom." An Aesthetic of Astonishment: Early Film and the (In)credulous Spectator." *Film Theory and Criticism.* Ed. Leo Braudy and Marshall Cohen. 6th ed. New York: Oxford UP, 2004. 862–76.

———. "The Cinema of Attractions: Early Film, Its Spectator, and the Avant-Garde." *Early Cinema: Space, Frame, Narrative.* Ed. Thomas Elsaesser. London: BFI, 1990. 56–62.

———. "Mechanisms of Laughter: The Devices of Slapstick." Paulus and King, 137–51.

———. "Modernity and Cinema: A Culture of Shocks and Flows." *Cinema and Modernity.* Ed. Murray Pomerance. New Brunswick, NJ: Rutgers UP, 2006. 297–315.

Hansen, Mark. *Embodying Technesis: Technology beyond Writing.* Ann Arbor: U of Michigan P, 2000.

Hansen, Miriam Bratu. "America, Paris, the Alps: Kracauer (and Benjamin) on Cinema and Modernity." Charney and Schwartz, 362–402.

———. *Babel and Babylon: Spectatorship in American Silent Film.* Cambridge, MA: Harvard UP, 1991.

———. "Benjamin and Cinema: Not a One-Way Street." *Critical Inquiry* 25.2 (1999): 306–343.

———. *Cinema and Experience.* Berkeley: U of California P, 2012.

———. "The Mass Production of the Senses: Classical Cinema as Vernacular Modernism." *Modernism/modernity* 6.2 (1999): 59–77.

———. "Of Mice and Ducks: Benjamin and Adorno on Disney." *South Atlantic Quarterly* 92.1 (1993): 27–61.

———. "Room-for-Play: Benjamin's Gamble with Cinema." *October* 109 (Summer 2004): 3–46.

———. "White Skin, Black Hair: Kracauer's Theory of Film, Marseille 1940." *Critical Inquiry* 19.3 (1993): 437–69.

Harris, Stefanie. *Mediating Modernity: German Literature and the "New" Media, 1895–1930.* University Park: Penn State UP, 2009.

Heller, Joseph. *Catch-22: A Novel.* 1961. New York: Simon & Schuster, 1989.

———. "An Impolite Interview with Joseph Heller." Kiley and McDonald, 273–93.

———. "Reeling in *Catch-22.*" *Catch as Catch Can.* New York: Simon & Schuster, 2003. 313–15.

High and Dizzy. Dir. Hal Roach. 1920. New Line Home Video, 2005. DVD.

Hitchcock, Alfred. "Why 'Thrillers' Thrive." 1936. *Hitchcock on Hitchcock: Selected Writings and Interviews.* Berkeley: U of California P, 1995. 109–12.

Hobbs, Stuart D. *The End of the American Avant Garde.* New York: New York UP, 1997.

Hoffman, Frederick J. *The Twenties: American Writing in the Postwar Decade*. Rev. ed. New York: Collier Books, 1962.

Hook, Andrew, ed. *Dos Passos: A Collection of Critical Essays*. Englewood Cliffs, NJ: Prentice Hall, 1974.

Hounshell, David. A. *From the American System to Mass Production, 1800–1932*. Baltimore: Johns Hopkins UP, 1984.

Hughes, Langston. *Simply Heavenly: A Comedy with Music*. New York: Dramatists Play Services, 1959.

Huyssen, Andreas. "Mass Culture as Woman: Modernism's Other." *After the Great Divide: Modernism, Mass Culture, and Postmodernism*. Bloomington: U of Indiana P, 1986. 44–64.

Ibarguen, Raoul R."Céline, Miller, and the American Canon." Kaplan and Roussin, *Céline, USA*, 489–505.

Isenstadt, Sandy. "Auto-Specularity: Driving through the Night." *Modernism/modernity* 18.2 (2011): 213–31.

Jacobs, Steven. "Slapstick Skyscrapers: An Architecture of Attractions." Paulus and King, 152–68.

James, David. "Mapping Modernist Continuities." *The Legacies of Modernism: Historicizing Postwar and Contemporary Fiction*. New York: Cambridge UP, 2012. 1–20.

James, David E. *Allegories of Cinema: American Film in the Sixties*. Princeton, NJ: Princeton UP, 1989.

———. *The Most Typical Avant-Garde: History and Geography of Minor Cinemas in Los Angeles*. Berkeley: U of California P, 2005.

Jameson, Fredric. "Céline and Innocence." *The Modernist Papers*. New York: Verso, 2007. 45–51.

———. "The Existence of Italy." *Signatures of the Visible*. New York: Routledge, 1992. 155–230.

———. *Postmodernism; or, The Cultural Logic of Late Capitalism*. Durham, NC: Duke UP, 1992.

Jarraway, David. R. "The Novelty of Revolution/The Revolution of Novelty: Williams' First Fiction." *William Carlos Williams Review* 18.1 (1992): 21–33.

Jayamanne, Laleen. "A Slapstick Time: Mimetic Convulsion, Convulsive Knowing." *Toward Cinema and Its Double: Cross-Cultural Mimesis*. Bloomington: Indiana UP, 2001. 181–205.

Jenkins, Bruce. "Explosion in a Film Factory: The Cinema of Bruce Conner." *2000 BC: The Bruce Conner Story Part II*. Minneapolis: Walker Art Center, 2000. 185–223.

Jenkins, Henry. *What Made Pistachio Nuts? Early Sound Comedy and the Vaudeville Aesthetic*. New York: Columbia UP, 1992.

Jenkins, Henry, and Kristine Burnovska Karnick, eds. *Classical Hollywood Comedy*. New York: Routledge, 1995.

Jones, Leroi. Introduction to *The Moderns: An Anthology of New World Writing.* New York: Corinth Books, 1963. ix–xvi.

Joyce, James. *Ulysses.* 1922. New York: Random House, 1986.

Kane, Daniel. *We Saw the Light: Conversations between New American Cinema and Poetry.* Iowa City: U of Iowa P, 2010.

Kaplan, Alice Yeager. *Reproductions of Banality: Fascism, Literature, and French Intellectual Life.* Minneapolis: U of Minnesota P, 1986.

Kaplan, Alice, and Philippe Roussin. "Céline's Modernity." *Céline, USA*, 421–44.

———, eds. *Céline, USA: The South Atlantic Quarterly* 93.2 (1994).

Kenner, Hugh. *The Counterfeiters: An Historical Comedy.* 1968. Normal, IL: Dalkey Archive Press, 2005.

Kern, Stephen. *The Culture of Time and Space, 1880–1918.* Cambridge, MA: Harvard UP, 1983.

Kerouac, Jack. *Dharma Bums.* New York: Penguin, 1976.

———. "Essentials of Spontaneous Prose." *The Portable Beat Reader.* Ed. Ann Charters. New York: Penguin, 1992. 57–58.

———. *Jack Kerouac and Allen Ginsberg: The Letters.* New York: Penguin, 2011.

———. [Jean-Louis]. "Jazz of the Beat Generation." *New World Writing,* 7th Mentor ed. New York: New American Library of World Literature, 1955. 7–16.

———. *Mexico City Blues.* New York: Viking, 1959.

———. "On Céline." *Good Blonde and Others.* San Francisco: Grey Fox Press, 1993. 90–91.

———. *On the Road.* 1957. New York: Penguin, 1985.

———. "The Origin of the Beat Generation." *Marginal Manners: The Variants of Bohemia.* Elmsford, NY: Row, Peterson, 1962. 144–51.

———. *Selected Letters, 1940–1956.* New York: Viking, 1995.

———. *Visions of Cody.* New York: Penguin, 1972.

———. *Windblown World.* New York: Viking, 2004.

Kerr, Walter. *The Silent Clowns.* New York: Da Capo, 1975.

The Kid. Dir. Charles Chaplin. 1921. Warner Home Video, 2005. DVD.

Kiley, Frederick, and Walter McDonald, eds. *A* "Catch-22" *Casebook.* New York: Thomas Y. Crowell, 1973.

King, Rob. *The Fun Factory: The Keystone Film Company and the Emergence of Mass Culture.* Berkeley: U of California P, 2009.

———. "'Uproarious Inventions': The Keystone Film Company, Modernity, and the Art of the Motor." Paulus and King, 114–36.

Kittler, Friedrich A. *Discourse Networks, 1800/1900.* Trans. Michael Metteer, with Chris Cullens. Stanford, CA: Stanford UP, 1990.

———. "From Poetry to Prose: Sciences of Movement in the Nineteenth Century." *ReMembering the Body.* Ed. Gabriele Brandstetter and Hortensia Völckers. Vienna: Hatje Cantz, 2000. 260–71.

———. *Gramophone, Film, Typewriter*. Trans. Geoffrey Winthrop-Young and Michael Wutz. Stanford, CA: Stanford UP, 1999.

———. *Optical Media*. Trans. Anthony Enns. Malden, MA: Polity Press, 2010.

Klein, Scott M. "Modern Times against Western Man: Wyndham Lewis, Charlie Chaplin, and Cinema." *Wyndham Lewis and the Cultures of Modernity*. Ed. Andrzej Gasiorek, Alice Reeve-Tucker, and Nathan Waddell. Burlington, VT: Ashgate, 2011. 127–44.

Knapp, James. F. *Literary Modernism and the Transformation of Work*. Evanston, IL: Northwestern UP, 1988.

Kostelanetz, Richard. "The American Short Story Today." *12 from the Sixties*. New York: Dell, 1967.

Král, Peter. "Larry Semon's Message." 1969. *The Shadow and Its Shadow: Surrealist Writings on Cinema*. London: BFI, 1978. 109–114.

Kristeva, Julia. *The Powers of Horror: An Essay on Abjection*. Trans. Leon S. Roudiez. New York: Columbia UP, 1982.

Lacan, Jacques. "The Mirror-Stage." *Ecrits*. Trans. Bruce Fink. New York: W. W. Norton, 2007. 75–81.

Lacoue-Labarthe, Philippe. "The Caesura of the Speculative." *Typography*, 208–35.

———. "Diderot: Paradox and Mimesis." *Typography*, 248–66.

———. *Typography: Mimesis, Philosophy, Politics*. Trans. Christopher Fynsk. Stanford, CA: Stanford UP, 1989.

Lahue, Kalton C. *The World of Laughter: The Motion Picture Comedy Short, 1910–1930*. Norman: U of Oklahoma P, 1966.

Lawrence, D. H. Review of *Manhattan Transfer*. *The Portable D. H. Lawrence*. Ed. Diana Trilling. New York: Viking Press, 1981. 637–45.

Lear, Jonathan. "Katharsis." *Essays on Aristotle's* Poetics. Ed. Amelie Oksenberg Rorty. Princeton, NJ: Princeton UP, 1992. 314–40.

Lears, Jackson. *Fables of Abundance: A Cultural History of Advertising in America*. New York: Harper Collins, 1994.

Lears, T. J. Jackson. *No Place of Grace: Antimodernism and the Transformation of American Culture, 1880–1920*. Chicago: U of Chicago P, 1994.

Lenoir, Tim. "All but War Is Simulation: The Military-Entertainment Complex." *Configurations* 8 (2000): 289–335.

Lentricchia, Frank. *Modernist Quartet*. New York: Cambridge UP, 1994.

Leslie, Esther. *Hollywood Flatlands: Animation, Critical Theory, and the Avant-Garde*. New York: Verso, 2002.

Levenson, Michael H. *A Genealogy of Modernism: A Study of English Literary Doctrine, 1908–1922*. New York: Cambridge UP, 1984.

Lewis, R.W.B. *The Poetry of Hart Crane: A Critical Study*. Princeton, NJ: Princeton UP, 1967.

Lewis, Wyndham. *Time and Western Man*. London: Chatto and Windus, 1927.

Liu, Alan. *The Laws of Cool: Knowledge Work and the Culture of Information. Chicago:* U of Chicago P.

Lizzies of the Field. Dir. Del Lord. 1924. Alpha Video, 2011. DVD.

Louvish, Simon. *Keystone: The Life and Clowns of Mack Sennett.* New York: Farrar, Straus, and Giroux, 2003.

Lowry, E. D. "The Lively Art of *Manhattan Transfer.*" *PMLA* 84.6 (1969): 1628–38.

Loy, Mina. *The Lost Lunar Baedeker Poems.* Ed. Roger Conover. New York: Noonday Press, 1996.

Lukacs, Georg. "Narrate or Describe?" 1936. *Writer and Critic.* New York: Grosset and Dunlap, 1971. 110–48.

Macherey, Pierre. "A Rhetoric of Abysses: Céline's Metro." *The Object of Literature.* Trans. David Macey. New York: Cambridge UP, 1995. 132–43.

Marchand, Roland. *Advertising the American Dream: Making Way for Modernity, 1920–1940.* Berkeley: U of California P, 1985.

Marcus, Laura. *The Tenth Muse: Writing about Cinema in the Modernist Period.* New York: Oxford UP, 2007.

Mariani, Paul. *William Carlos Williams: A New World Naked.* New York: W. W. Norton, 1990.

Martin, Ronald E. *American Literature and the Destruction of Knowledge.* Durham, NC: Duke UP, 1991.

Mast, Gerald. *The Comic Mind: Comedy and the Movies.* 2nd ed. Chicago: U of Chicago P, 1979.

McCabe, Susan. *Cinematic Modernism: Modernist Poetry and Film.* New York: Cambridge UP, 2005.

McCall, Tom. "'The Dynamite of a Tenth of a Second': Benjamin's Revolutionary Messianism in Silent Film Comedy." *Benjamin's Ghosts: Interventions in Contemporary Literary and Cultural Theory.* Ed. Gerhard Richter. Stanford, CA: Stanford UP, 2002. 74–94.

McCarthy, Mary. Review of *Naked Lunch. The Olympia Reader.* Ed. Maurice Girodias. New York: Quality Paperback Club, 1965, 457–61.

McDonald, Peter D. "Modernist Publishing: 'Nomads and Mapmakers.'" *A Concise Companion to Modernism.* Malden, MA: Blackwell, 2003. 221–42.

McLuhan, Marshall. "John Dos Passos: Technique vs. Sensibility." Hook, 148–61.

———. *Understanding Media: The Extensions of Man.* New York: Signet, 1964.

McNeil, Legs, and Gillian McCain. *Please Kill Me: The Uncensored Oral History of Punk.* New York: Penguin, 1996.

Meade, Marion. *Buster Keaton: Cut to the Chase.* New York: Da Capo Press, 1997.

Miles, Barry. *Jack Kerouac: King of the Beats.* London: Virgin, 1998.

Miller, Henry. "The Golden Age." 1939. *The Cosmological Eye.* New York: New Directions, 1961. 47–62.

———. *Tropic of Cancer.* 1932. New York: Grove Press, 1961.

Miller, J. Hillis. *The Linguistic Moment.* Princeton, NJ: Princeton UP, 1985.

Miller, Tyrus. *Late Modernism: Politics, Fiction, and the Arts between the World Wars.* Berkeley: U of California P, 1999.

Moore, Robin. "'To the Center of Things': Geographies of the Anarchist City Novel." *John Dos Passos: Biography and Critical Essays.* Newcastle upon Tyne, UK: Cambridge UP, 2010. 130–42.

Moretti, Franco. *Modern Epic: The World System from Goethe to Garcia Marquez.* New York: Verso, 1996.

Munsterberg, Hugo. *Psychology and Industrial Efficiency.* Boston: Houghton Mifflin, 1913.

Musser, Charles. "Moving toward Fictional Narratives." *The Silent Cinema Reader.* Ed. Lee Grieveson and Peter Kramer. New York: Routledge, 2004. 87–102.

———. "Work, Ideology, and Chaplin's Tramp." *Radical History Review* 41 (April 1988): 36–66.

Nabokov, Vladimir. *Pnin.* New York: Vintage, 1957.

Nägele, Ranier. "The Poetic Ground Laid Bare (Benjamin Reading Baudelaire)." *Walter Benjamin: Theoretical Questions.* Stanford, CA: Stanford UP, 1996. 118–38.

Naremore, James. "Hitchcock and Humor." *An Invention without a Future.* Berkeley: U of California P, 2014. 124–38.

Nead, Lynda. "Velocities of the Image c. 1900." *Art History* 27.5 (2004): 745–69.

Never Weaken. Dir. Fred Newmeyer. 1921. New Line Home Video, 2005. DVD.

Nieland, Justus. *Feeling Modern: The Eccentricities of Public Life.* Urbana: U of Illinois P, 2008.

North, Michael. *Camera Works: Photography and the Twentieth-Century Word.* New York: Oxford UP, 2005.

———. *Machine-Age Comedy.* New York: Oxford UP, 2009.

———. *Reading 1922: A Return to the Scene of the Modern.* New York: Oxford UP, 1999.

O'Connor, Flannery. *The Habit of Being.* New York: Farrar, Straus, and Giroux, 1979.

Odier, Daniel. "Journey through Time and Space." *The Job: Interviews with William S. Burroughs.* New York: Penguin, 1989. 25–56.

Ostrovsky, Erika. *Céline and His Vision.* New York: New York UP, 1967.

Palmer, Robert. "Walk on the Wild Side." *Blues and Chaos.* New York: Scribner, 2009. 271–82.

Paraskeva, Anthony. "Wyndham Lewis vs. Charlie Chaplin." *Forum for Modern Language Studies* 43.3 (2007): 223–34.

Parvulescu, Anca. *Laughter: Notes on a Passion.* Cambridge: MIT Press, 2010.

Paulus, Tom and Rob King, eds. *Slapstick Comedy.* New York: Routledge, 2010.

Pay Day. Dir. Charles Chaplin. 1922. Image Entertainment, 2004. DVD.

Perloff, Marjorie. *The Poetics of Indeterminacy: Rimbaud to Cage.* Evanston, IL: Northwestern UP, 1981.

Peterson, Sidney. "Note on Comedy in Experimental Film." 1963. *Film Culture Reader.* Ed. P. Adams Sitney. New York: Praeger, 1970. 398–403.

Picking Peaches. Dir. Erle C. Kenton. 1924. *Harry Langdon: Lost and Found Collection*. Facets, 2007. DVD.

Plantinga, Carl. *Moving Viewers: American Film and the Spectator's Experience*. Berkeley: U of California P, 2009.

Pollack, Andrew. "Trying to Improve Training, Army Turns to Hollywood." *New York Times,* August 18, 1999. A-17.

Pound, Ezra. "A Few Don'ts by an Imagiste." *Poetry* I (March 1913): 6.

———. "Hugh Selwyn Mauberley." *Personae: The Shorter Poems*. New York: New Directions, 1990. 183–202.

———. "The Serious Artist." 1913. *Literary Essays of Ezra Pound*. New York: New Directions, 1968. 41–57.

Pynchon, Thomas. *Crying of Lot 49*. Philadelphia: Lippincott, 1966.

———. *Gravity's Rainbow*. New York: Penguin, 1973.

———. *V.: A Novel*. Philadelphia: Lippincott, 1963.

Rabinovitz, Lauren. "From Hale's Tours to Star Tours: Virtual Voyages and the Delirium of the Hyper-Real." *Virtual Voyages: Cinema and Travel*. Ed. Jeffrey Ruoff. Durham, NC: Duke UP, 2006. 42–60.

Rainey, Lawrence. *Institutions of Modernism: Literary Elites and Public Culture*. New Haven, CT: Yale UP, 1998.

Raitt, Suzanne. "The Rhetoric of Efficiency in Early Modernism." *Modernism/modernity* 13.1 (2006): 835–51.

Rancière, Jacques. "Eisenstein's Madness." 1991. *Film Fables*. Trans. Emiliano Battista. New York: Berg, 2006. 23–32.

Rees, A. L. "Moving Spaces." Wollen and Kerr, 83–94.

Reynolds, Simon. *Rip It Up and Start Again: Postpunk, 1978–1984*. New York: Penguin, 2005.

Rheingold, Howard. *Virtual Reality*. New York: Summit Books, 1991.

Riblet, Doug. "The Keystone Film Company and the Historiography of Early Slapstick." Jenkins and Karnick, 168–99.

Richards, I. A. *Principles of Literary Criticism*. New York: Harvest, 1925.

Robinson, David. *The Great Funnies: A History of Film Comedy*. New York: E. P. Dutton, 1969.

Rolfe, Edwin. "The Melancholy Comus." *Collected Poems*. Urbana: U of Illinois P, 1993. 173–75.

Ross, Kristin. *Fast Cars, Clean Bodies: Decolonization and the Reordering of French Culture*. Cambridge: MIT Press, 1995.

Roth, Philip. *Our Gang: Starring Tricky and His Friends*. New York: Random House, 1971.

Sargeant, Jack. *Naked Lens: Beat Cinema. London:* Creation Books, 1997.

Safety Last. Dir. Sam Taylor and Fred C. Newmeyer. 1923. New Line Home Video, 2005. DVD.

Saturday Afternoon. Dir. Harry Edwards. 1926. Image Entertainment, 1998. DVD.

Schivelbusch, Wolfgang. *The Railway Journey: The Industrialization of Time and Space in the Nineteenth Century.* New York: Berg, 1986.

Schleier, Merrill. *Skyscraper Cinema: Architecture and Gender in American Film.* Minneapolis: U of Minnesota P, 2009.

Schmitz, Neil. *Of Huck and Alice: Humorous Writing in American Literature.* Minneapolis: U of Minnesota P, 1983.

Schwartz, Hillel. "Torque: The New Kinaesthetic of the Twentieth Century." Crary, *Incorporations*, 70–126.

Seltzer, Mark. *Bodies and Machines*. New York: Routledge, 1992.

Shail, Andrew. *The Cinema and the Origins of Literary Modernism*. New York: Routledge, 2012.

Shapiro, Peter. "Automating the Beat: The Robotics of Rhythm." *Undercurrents: The Hidden Wiring of Modern Music.* Ed. Rob Young. New York: Continuum, 2002. 131–40.

Shklovsky, Viktor. "Art as Device." *Theory of Prose.* Trans. Benjamin Sher. Elmwood Park, IL: Dalkey Archive Press, 1990. 1–14.

Shloss, Carol. *In Visible Light: Photography and the American Writer, 1840–1940.* New York: Oxford UP, 1987.

Sigal, Clancy. *Going Away.* Boston: Houghton Mifflin, 1962.

Singer, Ben. "Modernity, Hyperstimulus, and the Rise of Popular Sensationalism." Charney and Schwartz, 72–99.

Sitney, P. Adams. "The Poet as Film Viewer—Hart Crane's 'Chaplinesque.'" *Motion Picture* 1 (1986): 7, 17.

———. "The Sentiment of Doing Nothing: Gertrude Stein's Autobiographies." *Modernist Montage: The Obscurity of Vision in Cinema and Literature.* New York: Columbia UP, 1990. 146–63.

———. *Visionary Film: The American Avant-Garde, 1943–2000.* 3rd. ed. New York: Oxford UP, 2002.

Slade, Joseph W. *Thomas Pynchon.* New York: Warner, 1974.

Smile Please. Dr. Roy Del Ruth. 1924. *Harry Langdon: Comedy Classics 2.* Alpha Home Entertainment, 2012. DVD.

Smith, Terry. *Making the Modern: Industry, Art, and Design in America. Chicago:* U of Chicago P, 1993.

Soldier Man. Dir. Harry Edwards. 1926. All Day Entertainment, 2007. DVD.

Solomon, William. "Slapstick Modernism: Charley Bowers and Industrial Modernity." *Modernist Cultures* 2.2 (2006): 170–88. E-journal.

Sontag, Susan. "Going to the Theatre, etc." *Against Interpretation and Other Essays.* New York: Farrar, Straus, and Giroux, 1966. 140–62.

Speedy. Dir. Ted Wilde. 1928. New Line Home Video, 2005. DVD.

Spindler, Michael. "John Dos Passos and the Visual Arts." *Journal of American Studies* 15.3 (1981): 402–405.

Stallabrass, Julian. "Just Gaming." *Gargantua: Manufactured Mass Culture.* New York: Verso, 1996. 84–112.

Stein, Gertrude. *Lectures in America.* Boston: Beacon Press, 1935.

Steinman, Lisa. *Made in America: Science, Technology, and American Modernist Poets.* New Haven, CT: Yale UP, 1987.

Sterritt, David. "Kerouac, Artaud, and the Three Stooges." *Mosaic: A Journal for the Interdisciplinary Study of Literature* 31.4 (1998): 83–98.

Stevens, Wallace. "From the Journal of Crispin." *Collected Poetry and Prose.* New York: Library of America, 1997. 985–95.

Stewart, Garrett. *Between Film and Screen: Modernism's Photo Synthesis.* Chicago: U of Chicago P, 1999.

———. "Keaton through the Looking Glass." *Georgia Review* 33.2 (1979): 348–67.

———. "Modern Hard Times: Chaplin and the Cinema of Self-Reflection." *Critical Inquiry* 3.2 (1976): 294–314.

Stewart, Susan. *Poetry and the Fate of the Senses.* Chicago: U of Chicago P, 2002.

The Stooges: TV Eye. Anonymous Film Archives #42. n.d.

Stratton, Matthew. *The Politics of Irony in American Modernism.* New York: Fordham UP, 2014.

Strauven, Wanda, ed. *The Cinema of Attractions Reloaded.* Amsterdam: Amsterdam UP, 2006.

Strike. Dir. Sergei Eisenstein. 1925. Image Entertainment, 2000. DVD.

Stromberg, Peter G. *Caught in Play: How Entertainment Works on You.* Stanford, CA: Stanford UP, 2009.

The Strong Man. Dir. Frank Capra. 1926. Kino Video, 2010. DVD.

Suarez, Juan A. *Pop Modernism: Noise and the Reinvention of the Everyday.* Urbana: U of Illinois P, 2007.

Super-Hooper-Dyne Lizzies. Dir. Del Lord. 1925. Image Entertainment, 2002, DVD.

Tanner, Tony. *City of Words: American Fiction, 1950–1970.* New York: Harper & Row, 1971.

Tate, James. "An O'Connor Remembrance." *Flannery O'Connor Bulletin* 17 (1988): 65–68.

Taylor, Richard, ed. *Eisenstein Reader.* London: British Film Institute, 1998.

Thompson, Hunter S. *Fear and Loathing in Las Vegas: A Savage Journey to the Heart of the American Dream.* New York: Random House, 1971.

Three's a Crowd. Dir. Harry Langdon. 1927. Kino International, 2008. DVD.

Tichi, Cecilia. *Shifting Gears: Technology, Literature, Culture in Modernist Literature.* Chapel Hill: U of North Carolina P, 1987.

Trahair, Lisa. *The Comedy of Philosophy: Sense and Nonsense in Early Cinematic Slapstick.* Albany: SUNY Press, 2007.

Tramp, Tramp, Tramp. Dir. Frank Capra. 1926. *Harry Langdon: The Forgotten Clown.* Kino Video, 2003. DVD.

Tratner, Michael. *Deficits and Desires: Economics and Sexuality in Twentieth-Century Literature*. Stanford, CA: Stanford UP, 2001.

———. *Modernism and Mass Politics: Joyce, Woolf, Eliot, Yeats*. Stanford, CA: Stanford UP, 1995.

Tretyakov, Sergei. "Art in the Revolution and the Revolution in Art (Aesthetic Production and Consumption). *October* 118 (Fall 2006): 11–18.

———. "Our Cinema." 1928. *October* 118 (Fall 2006): 27–44.

———. "The Theatre of Attractions." 1924. *October* 118 (Fall 2006): 19–26.

Trotter, David. *Cinema and Modernism*. Oxford: Blackwell, 2007.

Tyler, Parker. "Kafka's and Chaplin's Amerika." *Sewanee Review* 58.2 (1950): 299–311.

Urish, Ben. "The Case for Harry Langdon: How and Why Frank Capra Was Wrong." *Journal of Popular Culture* 41.1 (2008): 141–57.

Väliaho, Pasi. *Mapping the Moving Image: Gesture, Thought, and Cinema Circa 1900*. Amsterdam: Amsterdam UP, 2010.

VanDerBeek, Stan. "Culture: Intercom and Expanded Cinema." *Film Culture* 40 (1966): 15–18.

———. "A Statement" (1964). Liner notes to *Visibles*. Paris: Re-Voir Video, 2000. 4.

Virilio, Paul. "Dromoscopy; or, The Ecstasy of Enormities." Trans. Edward R. O'Neil. *Wide Angle* 20.3 (1983): 11–22.

———. *War and Cinema: The Logistics of Perception*. Trans. Patrick Camiller. New York: Verso, 1989.

Virno, Paulo. *Multitude: Between Innovation and Negation*. New York: Semiotext(e), 2008.

Vonnegut, Kurt. *Slapstick: Lonesome No More*. New York: Dell, 1976.

Vorkapich, Slavko. "The Psychological Basis of Effective Cinematography." *Bulletin of the Academy of Motion Picture Arts and Sciences* (September 1934): 8–10.

Ward, Richard Lewis. *A History of Hal Roach Studios*. Carbondale: Southern Illinois UP, 2005.

Weber, Brom, ed. *Letters of Hart Crane, 1916–1932*. Berkeley: U of California P, 1952.

Weitzman, Erica. *Irony's Antics: Walser, Kafka, Roth, and the German Comic Tradition*. Evanston, IL: Northwestern UP, 2015.

Welty, Eudora. *One Writer's Beginnings*. Cambridge, MA: Harvard UP, 1984.

West, Rebecca. "Imagisme." *New Freewoman* 1.5 (August 15, 1913): 86–87.

White, Eric B. "Continental Conjecture: Ephemera, Imitation, and America's (Late) Modernist Canons in the Three Mountains Press and Robert McAlmon's Contact Editions." *European Journal of American Culture* 32.3 (2013): 285–306.

Why Worry? Dir. Fred Newmeyer and Sam Taylor. 1923. New Line Home Video, 2005. DVD.

Wicke, Jennifer. *Advertising Fictions: Literature, Advertisement, and Social Reading*. New York: Columbia UP, 1988.

"The Wild Side." *Rock and Roll*. Vol. 4. WGBH and BBC, 1995. VHS.

Wilentz, Sean. *Bob Dylan in America.* New York: Doubleday, 2010.
Williams, Raymond. "Advertising: The Magic System." *Problems in Materialism and Culture.* London: Great Britain, 1980. 170–95.
Williams, William Carlos. *The Autobiography of William Carlos Williams.* New York: New Directions, 1967).
———. *The Descent of Winter. Imaginations*, 234–65.
———. *The Embodiment of Knowledge.* New York: New Directions, 1974.
———. "For a New Magazine." *Blues* 1 (March 1929): 30–31.
———. "George Antheil and His Cantilene Critics." *Selected Essays.* New York: New Directions, 1954. 57–61.
———. *The Great American Novel.* 1923. *Imaginations*, 155–227.
———. *Imaginations.* New York: New Directions, 1971.
———. *A Novelette.* 1932. *Imaginations*, 272–306.
———. *Paterson.* New York: New Directions, 1992.
———. Prologue to *Kora in Hell: Improvisations. Imaginations,* 6–28.
Wimsatt, W. K., Jr., and Monroe C. Beardsley. "The Affective Fallacy." *20th Century Literary Criticism.* Ed. David Lodge. London: Longman, 1972. 345–58.
Winokur, Mark. *American Laughter: Immigrants, Ethnicity, and 1930s Hollywood Film Comedy.* New York: St. Martin's, 1996.
Witemeyer, Hugh. "Plagiarism in *The Great American Novel*: The Ethics of Collage." *William Carlos Williams Review* 23.1 (1997): 1–13.
Wolfe, Thomas. *You Can't Go Home Again.* 1940. New York: Dell, 1960.
Wollen, Peter. "Introduction: Cars and Culture." Wollen and Kerr, 10–20.
———. "Modern Times: Cinema/Americanism/The Robot." *Raiding the Icebox: Reflections on Twentieth-Century Culture.* New York: Verso, 1993. 35–71.
———. *Signs and Meaning in the Cinema.* London: British Film Institute, 1972.
Wollen, Peter, and Joe Kerr, eds. *Autopia: Cars and Culture.* London: Reaktion, 2000.
Wranovics, John. *Chaplin and Agee: The Untold Story of the Tramp, the Writer, and the Lost Screenplay.* New York: Palgrave Macmillan, 2005.
Zach, Natan. "Imagism and Vorticism." *Modernism: A Guide to European Literature, 1890–1930.* Ed. Malcolm Bradbury and James McFarlane. New York: Penguin, 1976. 228–42.
Žižek, Slavoj. "'In His Bold Gaze My Ruin Is Writ Large.'" *Everything You Always Wanted to Know about Lacan (But Were Afraid to Ask Hitchcock).* New York: Verso, 1992. 211–72.
Zukofsky, Louis. "Modern Times." *Prepositions: The Collected Critical Essays of Louis Zukofsky.* London: Rapp and Carroll, 1967. 51–58.

Index

WILLIAM SOLOMON is an associate professor of English at the University at Buffalo.

The University of Illinois Press
is a founding member of the
Association of American University Presses.

University of Illinois Press
1325 South Oak Street
Champaign, IL 61820-6903
www.press.uillinois.edu